Independence or Death!

ENDLEAVES: THE HUMAITA CAMPAIGN
(*From*: George Thompson, *The War in Paraguay*, London, 1869.)

Other Latin American Titles

ARE WE GOOD NEIGHBORS? by Donald Marquand Dozer
DIFFERENTIAL FERTILITY IN BRAZIL by J. V. D. Saunders
THE EMERGENCE OF THE REPUBLIC OF BOLIVIA
 by Charles W. Arnade
THE EXISTENTIALISM OF MIGUEL DE UNAMUNO
 by José Huertas-Jourda
FERTILE LANDS OF FRIENDSHIP edited by Daniel E. Alleger
FIDEL CASTRO'S PROGRAMS FROM REFORMISM TO "MARXISM-
 LENINISM" by Loree Wilkerson
FROM COMMUNITY TO METROPOLIS by Richard M. Morse
THE "FUERO MILITAR" IN NEW SPAIN by Lyle N. McAlister
GRINGO LAWYER by Thomas W. Palmer
INDUSTRIAL RELATIONS AND SOCIAL CHANGE IN LATIN AMERICA
 by W. H. Form and A. A. Blum
HIGH JUNGLES AND LOW by Archie Carr
JOSE MARTI by Richard B. Gray
LAND REFORM AND DEMOCRACY by Clarence Senior
LATIN AMERICAN POPULATION STUDIES by T. Lynn Smith
MAKING AN INTER-AMERICAN MIND by Harry Bernstein
MAN AND LAND IN PERU by Thomas R. Ford
MIRANDA by Joseph J. Thorning
NATIONALISM IN LATIN AMERICA, PAST AND PRESENT
 by Arthur Whitaker
PEASANT SOCIETY IN THE COLOMBIAN ANDES by Orlando Fals-Borda
PUERTO RICAN POLITICS AND THE NEW DEAL by Thomas Mathews
THE RAIN FORESTS OF GOLFO DULCE by Paul H. Allen
SANTA CRUZ OF THE ETLA HILLS by Helen Miller Bailey
SEA POWER AND CHILEAN INDEPENDENCE by Donald E. Worcester
SEARCH FOR A LATIN AMERICAN POLICY by T. W. Palmer, Jr.
THE SIEGE OF ST. AUGUSTINE IN 1702 by Charles W. Arnade
SIXTY-FIVE VALIANTS by Alice Houston Luiggi
THE UNITED STATES AND INTER-AMERICAN RELATIONS
 by George Wythe
WOMAN SUFFRAGE IN MEXICO by Ward M. Morton
A WORKING BIBLIOGRAPHY OF BRAZILIAN LITERATURE
 by José Manuel Topete

PARAGUAY'S VIA DOLOROSA—THE ARMY'S RETREAT IN AUGUST, 1869

COURTESY, MINISTRY OF THE INTERIOR OF THE GOVERNMENT OF PARAGUAY

CHARLES J. KOLINSKI

Independence or Death!
THE STORY OF THE PARAGUAYAN WAR

University of Florida Press
Gainesville / 1965

To the nameless dead of Paraguay, Brazil, Argentina, and Uruguay, whose heroic struggles in the Paraguayan War shall remain as a monument to the best traditions of mankind's courage and devotion to honor.

A University of Florida Press Book

Copyright © 1965, by the Board of
Commissioners of State Institutions of Florida
All Rights Reserved
Library of Congress Catalog Card No. 65-27282
printed by the e. o. painter printing co., deland, florida
bound by universal-dixie bindery, inc., jacksonville, florida

Foreword

THE PARAGUAYAN WAR was for Latin America a conflict of tragic proportions, in many ways a counterpart of our own Civil War. No other war involving only the nations of Latin America has been so bitter, hard-fought, and costly, nor has any other Western Hemisphere president died facing his nation's enemies, as did Paraguay's Francisco Solano López. The very sides that were drawn—land-locked Paraguay pitted against Argentina, Brazil, and Uruguay—made the contest appear so one-sided that no one anticipated more than a few harmless skirmishes.

When the Paraguayans resisted literally to the death, however, and when Marshal López refused to abandon his country to certain partition, the war became long and bitter beyond all expectations. López, whatever his enemies said of him, "was Paraguay." He led a doomed nation in a titanic death-struggle, a war in which no quarter was asked or given. It was a heroic struggle, and the victors were especially affected by it. The Brazilian officers developed so strong an *esprit de corps* that two decades after the war ended the loyalty to comrades-in-arms was still stronger than that to the Emperor for whom they had fought. The very survival of Paraguay, with most of her men gone, was a tribute to the determination of her women.

The story of Paraguay has usually been told by her enemies. Seldom before has it been told with objectivity or even sympathy. Dr. Kolinski has accomplished a memorable feat in his account of the war; no one who reads this volume can escape sharing the feeling of cornered desperation of the Paraguayans or the loyalty and pride of the Allied soldiers and officers, whether *Voluntários da Pátria* from Brazil or *porteño* volunteers from Buenos Aires.

This book is especially appropriate in the same decade as the centennial of the American Civil War. It commemorates Latin America's major conflict, and it reminds us forcibly that not all the history of the Americas occurred north of the Tropic of Cancer.

DONALD E. WORCESTER

Preface

𝓕OR MANY AMERICANS speeding south, Florida-bound, along the eastern seaboard highway through Virginia's cities of Fredericksburg and Petersburg, signs denoting the location of "The Sunken Road" and "The Crater" are often interpreted as indications of local scenic curiosities. Similarly, tourists enjoying the fantastic wonders of Brazil's fabulous Rio de Janeiro, Paraguay's inland capital of Asunción, or the marvels of the Iguazú Falls, more often than not find themselves perplexed by the frequently strange-sounding names of avenues, suburbs, parks, or nearby villages, such as "Avenida Uruguaiana," "Bairro Voluntários da Pátria," "Rua Riachuelo," "Avenida Humaitá," and "Ytororó," and "Piribebuy." Few are those among the hundreds daily making the cable-car ride to the summit of Sugar Loaf at Rio, for example, who give more than a passing glance at the statue below them marked "Retirada da Laguna."

Yet in both cases these strange, even curious, names refer to events and places which are burned deeply into North American and South American history. Because of the current prominence given to American Civil War centennial celebrations, "The Sunken Road" and "The Crater" are fortunately being recalled to the public mind in their proper historical status as grim, memorable way points in the Union Army's several campaigns to crush the Confederates of Robert E. Lee. It is doubtful if similar centennial celebrations will occur to cast light upon the odd, often tongue-twisting, place names in Brazil and Paraguay; they could well remain obscure in meaning to most tourists with the exception of the occasional person who has explored Latin America's past or to the one who may have pursued military history as a hobby.

That South America experienced a war concurrent with our Civil War, which was equally as significant for its tragedy, its heroics, and its impact, may well be unknown to most Americans. Few indeed are those of us who have learned that while Grant was steadily clamping a vise around Lee's positions at Petersburg in November, 1864, the capture of a riverboat named the "Marquês de Olinda" by a Paraguayan gunboat in far-off Paraguay had ignited a war which was just as tragic and equally as important for its effects. To many school-age Brazilians and Paraguayans of today the names "Ytororó," "Curupaity," "Tuyuty," and "Avay"—famed battles of that long-ago war—ring with as much patriotic fervor as do "Shiloh," "Antietam," "Chickamauga," and "Gettysburg" to our own youngsters, let alone our centennial buffs.

The purpose of this work then is to portray as accurately as possible South America's most costly and bloody war—known as the Paraguayan or Triple Alliance War—which commenced precisely 100 years ago. It is hoped that the novitiate to Latin American studies, the reader interested in the history of distant places, and the scholar, will all discover in these pages something of the timeless spirit of sacrifice and lasting traditions which have stemmed from this fascinating event and which are yet a factor in the relationships of the diverse peoples of Brazil and La Plata.

My original interest in the story of Paraguay's epic defense in the war with her neighbors developed from pre-World War II undergraduate studies at The George Washington University under Dr. A. Curtis Wilgus. Subsequently, an all too brief official tour of duty at Asunción during 1959 afforded the edifying opportunity to develop a close friendship with Dr. D. Edgar Ynsfrán, Minister of the Interior of the Government of Paraguay, and an amateur historian deeply interested in his nation's exciting past. In Dr. Ynsfrán's company, it was my lasting pleasure to have been a member of the first motorized expedition to have successfully traversed practically the same route through the dense jungle area of Paraguay's Alto Paraná region followed in the army's last retreat to Cerro Corá in 1870. I must likewise record my gratitude for the stimulation provided by Dr. Ynsfrán and the expedition's members who, during many enjoyable hours of campside chatting aided by the incomparable *tereré*, or cold yerba maté, suggested the thesis that knowledge of their country's past might yield a better understanding of its traditions, frustrations, and hopes. Likewise, I must remember my many Brazilian friends, including Dr. J. Freitas Marcondes in particular, who urged that an account in English of Brazil's determined effort in the 1860's might serve to illustrate the tough fiber of national pride and loyalty lying beneath the accepted exterior impression of a calm people in a land of the future.

Finally, it would have been entirely impossible to complete

this work without the unflagging willingness and determination of Peggy to accept the austere existence of a graduate student's wife, and the persistent encouragement on the part of my graduate committee at the University of Florida. To each I must render this humble tribute: Chairman Dr. Donald E. Worcester: For his steadfast faith that the task could and would be accomplished, and for his stamina in fighting it through to the last battle. Dr. Irving R. Wershow: For his deep belief that language proficiency is a key to a new world of adventure in literature. Dr. Lyle N. McAlister: For his constant reminders that history must be accurate and documented. Dr. Raymond E. Crist: For his boundless enthusiasm for South America's lands and peoples. Dr. Pedro Villa Fernández: For his lessons that a true understanding of Spanish America requires knowledge of the Soul of Spain. Dr. A. Curtis Wilgus: For his unswerving twenty-year confidence in a student.

C.J.K.

Contents

Foreword by Donald E. Worcester		v
Introduction		xiii
I.	Prologue	1
II.	The Setting—La Plata, 1864	4
III.	Dramatis Personae	17
IV.	Arms and Armies	36
V.	A Sound of Guns	69
VI.	Viva la República del Paraguay!	81
VII.	Viva Dom Pedro Segundo!	96
VIII.	War of Positions	114
IX.	War of Maneuvers	149
X.	Campaign in the Cordillera	171
XI.	Cerro Corá	181
XII.	Epilogue	192
Notes		201
Appendix		217
Bibliography		225
Index		231

Introduction

*F*EW OF THE WORLD's great international wars have been so extensively treated in literature yet so little understood for their characteristics and impact as South America's Paraguayan War. Known also as the War of the Triple Alliance, this conflict occurring between 1864 and 1870 is held to have been the bloodiest and most costly in the history of Latin America. The dead of both sides totaled at least 350,000—a figure more than twice the population of Buenos Aires in 1864, and about equal both to the population of Uruguay and to the estimated population of Rio de Janeiro in that year.

Involving the republics of Argentina and Uruguay in alliance with Imperial Brazil against landlocked Paraguay, the war marked the culmination of a major period of change in the southern half of South America. It also heralded a new era of development which has persisted well into the twentieth century. Though it concerned the two largest nations of South America as well as two of the smallest, its course was neither closely followed by the world nor appreciated for its significance. While its outbreak and progress were of deep concern to the other South American nations, the Paraguayan War evoked relatively minor official or public interest in the United States and Europe.

Its place in history coincided with other important events including the final stages of the American Civil War; the Austro-Prussian attack on Denmark; Maximilian's ill-fated, French-backed, monarchical venture in Mexico; the bellicose emergence of Prussia within the European power scheme; and Spain's abortive efforts to regain lost prestige in Latin America through the reacquisition of Santo Domingo and the Chincha Islands episode with Peru. The Paraguayan War also occurred during the interlude between the Crimean and Franco-Prussian Wars.

Perhaps the most compelling factor for the relatively unimportant contemporary role assigned to the Paraguayan War stemmed from geographical aspects. Paraguay in 1864 was still largely an unknown, tiny republic in the middle of the South American continent, and noted mainly in the literary world for the inspiration which its fantastic dictator, Dr. José Gaspar Rodríguez de Francia, had imparted to Thomas Carlyle. Though both Imperial Brazil and the Argentine Confederation were somewhat more widely known due to the gradual development of European economic interests in the Río de la Plata zone and the diplomatic questions of the Rosas era, they too were still regarded generally as far-off regions of the mysterious South American continent.

Deeply absorbed with the abrupt appearance of Prussia as a major power, and largely unaware of La Plata developments because of the lack of rapid communication facilities and the almost total absence of established news services, the peoples of Europe remained far more engrossed in such events as the Battle of Sadowa than the Battle of Curupaity. The august *Illustrated London News* in 1866, for example, devoted only occasional space to information from its River Plate correspondent, while its pages presented sketches of every conceivable aspect of the Austro-Prussian War.

Likewise in the United States, the conflict in Paraguay received scant attention in its early stages. In 1864 and 1865, the final sledge hammer blows against the Confederacy directed by Grant and Sherman, together with the subsequent impact of Lincoln's assassination, made headlines which relegated River Plate affairs to an extremely minor role in dispatches. Such events were soon to give way to bulletins describing Maximilian's Mexican venture and the persistent refusal of a Mexican Indian named Benito Juárez to acknowledge defeat. Though the United States had recognized the government of Paraguay and had been forced to adopt an extremely belligerent attitude in the dispatch of the Bowlin mission in 1858 to resolve the Rhode Island Company question, relations with Paraguay had by no means become significant in the growth of United States Latin American policy.

Only in its later stages did the Paraguayan War attain the status of a newsworthy event. By the late 1860's the world had gradually become aware of a persistent conflict among several of South America's most important nations which was producing strange and absorbing news reports. A British House of Commons document had made public the terms of a secret treaty between Argentina, Brazil, and Uruguay, which seemed aimed at the partition of Paraguay; British and French manufacturers and exporters were enjoying a mounting volume of South American orders for war supplies; Brazilian and Argentine diplomats busied themselves with propaganda efforts regarding the conduct of the war; a fiery Argentine named Juan Bautista Alberdi wrote strong essays critical of River Plate affairs; and above all, a series of exciting adventure accounts by foreigners who had been residing in the war's theater commenced to circulate in Europe's capitals.

British subjects George F. Masterman and George Thompson hastily wrote memoirs of their Paraguayan experiences, which, upon publication, found an immediate and receptive market. Such accounts appeared simultaneously with the vivid and ably prepared reports of Captain Richard F. Burton, a British consular official whose earlier descriptions of his adventures in the highlands of Brazil had enhanced his reputation for appealing, well-written travel literature. Captain Burton, awake to the generally prevailing ignorance in Britain regarding both the geography and history of the River Plate and Paraná River areas, set about to inform his reading public of what he considered to be the true state of affairs in the war zone.

In the United States, news of the prolonged conflict in the River Plate region suggested to the Secretary of State, William H. Seward, the possibility of extending the good offices of the United States to bring about an amicable end to the war. Reports of such official interest in the war were soon followed by energetic publicity efforts on behalf of his country by the serious-minded new Argentine minister, Domingo Faustino Sarmiento, and by a rash of fascinating reports emanating from Charles Ames Washburn, former American minister to Paraguay. Ex-minister Washburn, the brother of a former Secretary of State, waxed loud and at length on his troubles with the Paraguayan government and with certain United States naval officers. His newsworthy complaints were accompanied by sensational descriptions of conditions in Paraguay, both of his authorship and of that of a former unofficial assistant named Porter Bliss. Washburn's revelations were shortly contrasted with the reports of his successor, General Martin T. MacMahon, a popular Civil War hero, who lent his pen in defense of Paraguay in the form of articles published in *Harper's New Monthly Magazine*. The upshot was the calling of a special House of Representatives inquiry into relationships with Paraguay, and thus, the generation of more public interest in the River Plate area.

On March 1, 1870, the Paraguayan War came to an abrupt end

with the death of Paraguay's Marshal President, Francisco Solano López, in a final skirmish with Brazilian troops. Its news value abroad swiftly diminished, to be rekindled briefly in subsequent negotiations over territorial boundary claims in which President Rutherford B. Hayes figured prominently as arbiter. With the end of the war, however, returning veterans of the allied armies and historians of the several participating nations soon turned to the record of the war as a field for literary exploitation. The subsequent vast production of memoirs, essays, and histories by Brazilian, Argentine, and Paraguayan authors sought to present and to justify each nation's participation in the most favorable light possible. The extremes of partisanship reflected in such efforts generated controversies regarding the war's personalities and episodes which are still active today. The heights of emotion attained in such writings, comparable to and perhaps even exceeding levels exhibited in writings of the American Civil War, have rendered the task of the impartial historian a most difficult one.

Though numerous histories of the war have appeared in the countries involved, the partisanship reflected in them, coupled with research difficulties and language considerations, have tended to handicap severely the preparation of an objective history, particularly in English. The principal effort in this field, and a monumental if not definitive one, prepared by British historian Pelham Horton Box, was confined to the subject of the origins of the war. This work was later translated into Spanish by Paraguayan historian Pablo M. Ynsfrán, now professor of history at the University of Texas.[1]*

The Paraguayan War of 1864-70 has thus remained largely an enigma for the English-speaking historian. Though its outlines and place in the history of Latin American are known, an impartial and accurate account in English of its characteristics, major episodes, principal personalities, and of its impact upon the political, social, and economic institutions of the participating nations is still lacking. The purpose of this study, therefore, is to present an account of this tragic war and its effects on the three main participants, Paraguay, Brazil, and Argentina.

*Notes begin on page 201.

Chapter 1

PROLOGUE

August 12, 1869. At 6:30 A.M., Piribebuy, an interior village of normally about 4,000 people and the third capital of Paraguay, awoke slowly in the winter chill to the sudden roar of enemy cannon. The village, a grouping of whitewashed brick or stone houses with red tile or thatched roofing, laid out in regular colonial pattern around a large square featuring a church built in 1767, lay on the slope of a small plateau bordering a steep arroyo. Its population swollen to almost 10,000 since the army's retreat from Lomas Valentinas and Asunción in December, Piribebuy now held the government of Paraguay's treasury and state archives.[1] To the northwest, near the dirt road to Asunción, the bulk of the Marshal President's army held positions along the Azcurra escarpment overlooking the wide valley reaching to Lake Ypacaraí. In sharp contrast to the old colonial village, a newly dug trench in the deep, red Paraguayan earth traced a semicircle along the village perimeter facing east, south, and west.

The unexpected blast of cannon fire that erupted along the edge of the forest from the south came from the rifled La Hitte field guns of Emilio Mallet's famed Brazilian artillery regiment. They were the opening shots of the Conde d'Eu's Cordillera campaign to end the war, now in its fifth year.

As the La Hitte gun crews found their range, the barrage pounded across the defenders' trench and crashed through the village, blasting the cottages and igniting the thatched roofing. Two hours later, at 8:30 A.M., the pounding of the guns ceased and the white-kepied veterans of General João Manoel Mena Barreto moved to the attack. Leaning forward in the face of the sharp rifle fire of 1,500 Paraguayan defenders, Brazil's infantry and cavalry slowly drew closer to the trenches. A last bayonet assault, and the trench was reached.

A final cry: "Independencia o Muerte! Viva la República del Paraguay!"

And the answer: "Viva Dom Pedro Segundo! Viva o Império do Brasil!"

Fighting at this point raged fiercely, the defenders being a mixed force of old men, convalescent wounded, young boys, and even women. Lacking artillery support and reduced to the use of stones, dirt, and bottles and broken glass as weapons, the defenders proved no match for Brazil's infantry. Resistance slowly ceased, and the attackers charged into the village. Of the last shots fired by the defenders, two struck General Mena Barreto in the stomach, wounding him mortally.

Enraged at the loss of their commander, the Brazilian infantry went beserk. In what was perhaps the war's most savage moment, infantrymen and cavalry swept down upon the helpless crowd of refugees and their baggage carts seeking to escape by the Caacupé road, and a massacre ensued. Behind them the Paraguayan field hospital suddenly caught fire, dooming the 300 wounded men within. Paraguayan survivors later alleged that the uncontrollable troops caught Paraguayan Colonel Pablo Caballero and several of his staff, swiftly disarmed them, and cut their throats.

As order gradually returned, the victors searched the village and discovered both Paraguay's state archives and treasury, the former destined to become the private collection of the Visconde do Rio Branco. A young aide to the Conde d'Eu, Captain Alfredo d'Escragnolle Taunay, soon to become one of Brazil's greatest authors, located the former residence of Elisa Alicia Lynch, in which the piano of Solano López' famed Irish consort still remained. Taunay, undaunted by the presence of a shell-blasted, decapitated Paraguayan soldier, sought to dispel war's effects through a long-postponed practice session, and the sound of piano music added a bizarre note to the silence that fell over the field of carnage.

A brother officer soon called Taunay to the *quintal*, the backyard of the residence, where the wine cellar had been discovered and a victory celebration was in progress. Taunay was to note in his memoirs that "unfortunately, the quantity of champagne was quite small." He also searched among the abandoned belongings of Francisco Solano López and Elisa Lynch which were lying about, and discovered the handsomely bound second volume of an edition of *Don Quijote*. To his regret, he was unable to locate the first volume.[2] The soldiers, meanwhile, had become excited at the discovery of many silver coins in the house. These coins were *colunares* because they bore the arms of Castile and Aragon engraved between two columns.[3] Elsewhere among the victors were Adjutant Lieutenant Manoel do Nascimento Vargas, who was to become the father of one of Brazil's most famous presidents, and young Sublieutenant Dionísio Cerqueira, later to be the author of one of the most engaging and informative memoirs of the war.[4]

When the sporadic gunfire at Piribebuy had died down, organized Paraguayan resistance, which had been grimly maintained for five years against her giant neighbors, was virtually at an end. The war that Argentina's Bartolomé Mitre had predicted in 1865 would last for three months was in its final stages, though few Argentine troops were present to witness the somber triumph. Only one task remained to be accomplished, for though Paraguay was prostrate, a dying nation, Emperor Dom Pedro II of Brazil would not recall his forces as long as Francisco Solano López remained alive on Paraguayan soil.

The superhuman defense of the Paraguayans is almost unequalled in the history of warfare. That a tiny, landlocked country would resist the two large nations in whose shadow she lived at first glance seems incredible. That the Paraguayans, with few means at their disposal, should be able to maintain this bitter, unequal struggle in the face of overwhelming odds for five discouraging years is equally difficult to comprehend. The story of this defense, and the reasons for it, are the subjects of the chapters to follow.

Chapter 2

THE SETTING — LA PLATA, 1864

South America's La Plata region in 1864 exhibited striking contrasts among its component nations. Embracing Argentina, Uruguay, and Paraguay, the area reflected a number of dissimilarities from country to country which had both geographical and sociopolitical factors as their bases.

Though all three countries bordered on the Plata estuary or its principal tributary, the Paraná-Paraguay river system, the immense distances involved in the latter system formed a geographic factor representing a barrier to unification or homogeneity. While the area had been united under the colonial viceroyalty system of the late eighteenth century, the achievement of independence in the early 1800's had brought with it the abandonment of the viceroyalty delineation and a return to the regional pattern of the earlier colonial period. All three nations spoke Spanish as their official language and might therefore have been considered of the same family. Since independence, however, geographical and sociopolitical factors had tended to cement regional differences which had in turn promoted the growth of nationalism.

Argentina

By 1864 the development of Argentina reflected clearly the dichotomy of two contrasting regions which has persisted to the present: the port city and the interior.

Buenos Aires in 1864 was a seaport with a population of about 150,000, which stood on the threshold of an era of enormous progress. Though still colonial in appearance, it had recovered from the vexing international questions of the Rosas period and was rapidly becoming the trade entrepôt and center of civilization for La Plata. The era of greatest commercial expansion, railway construction, and massive immigration was yet to come. Buenos Aires, nevertheless, had firmly achieved its position as the capital city of the United Provinces and as the center of progress in La Plata.

In contrast, the interior provinces reflected but little development since the collapse of the Spanish colonial regime. Still unrecovered fully from the devastating effects of the Rosas era with its constant *montoneras* or caudillo-led revolutionary movements, the interior provinces exhibited slight economic or social progress. Though there were signs of a growing river export trade from Corrientes south through Paraná and Rosario to Buenos Aires, and though plans were underway for the construction of a railway west from Rosario, the gaucho and the estancia were still the major features of provincial economy. Immigration, principally from Germany, was only a trickle in the early 1860's; yet a few colonies of immigrants such as that of La Esperanza in the Santa Fé area had been established. Marauding bands of Indians, a menace not to be considered lightly, were still a problem south of Buenos Aires along the Río Negro as well as in the provinces west of the Paraná.

The river port of Paraná, once the capital of the Confederation, was still a small city with unpaved streets, one-story houses, and only a minimum of the contemporary social refinements such as theaters and hotels. Farther upstream near the Paraguayan border, Corrientes was a sleepy river port of about 10,000 served only occasionally by river vessels which frequently took eight days to make the upstream passage from Buenos Aires. Visitors to Corrientes at mid-century found it an unattractive, hot place inhabited mainly by Indians and mestizos, all of whom had to converse in Guaraní rather than Spanish.[1]

Perhaps the most optimistic sign to be observed in the Argentine in 1864 concerned the political situation. By the mid-1860's there was evidence that the long struggle between Federalists and Unitarians had ended, and that a trend had set in toward unification of the several provinces into a national whole. Three dates were of significance in this development which covered the preceding twelve years. First, on February 3, 1852, an allied army composed of a Brazilian expeditionary force, a Uruguayan unit, and a provincial army, under command of General Justo José de Urquiza, had defeated Juan Manuel de Rosas and his Buenos Aires forces at Monte Caseros, thus forcing his immediate flight into exile in England. Subsequently, a federal pact had been agreed upon at San Nicolás de Arroyo, and the provinces became united under the new constitution of 1853. The ensuing peace was short-lived, however, for the old antagonisms between Buenos Aires and the provinces again appeared with the former's refusal to accept the new political organization, including the selection of the city of Paraná as the capital. In a renewal of civil strife, Justo José de Urquiza led his provincial army against the forces of Buenos Aires and won a victory over Bartolomé Mitre at the Battle of Cepeda, October 23, 1859. In the agreement reached at San José de Flores, for which the services of Paraguayan arbiter Francisco Solano López were largely responsible, Buenos Aires was again incorporated within the new political structure. Once more peace proved to be short-lived. In a renewed campaign to achieve its ascendancy in Argentine affairs, Buenos Aires refused to accept provincial domination in the form of the government at Paraná, and civil war again broke out. On this occasion, in an inconclusive action at the Battle of Pavón, September 17, 1861, the Entre Ríos gaucho forces of General Urquiza retreated in disorder, leaving Bartolomé Mitre and his Buenos Aires forces the victors. General Urquiza, discouraged and perhaps disillusioned by his lack of success in the political field, retired to his San José estate in Entre Ríos province, seemingly content with his reputation as the "Tigre de Montiel" and "Vencedor de Monte Caseros."

By 1864, therefore, the bitter, bloody, factional struggles which had marked recent Argentine history had subsided. Buenos Aires had achieved prominence with its liberal *unitarios* exemplified by Bartolomé Mitre and the theorists and *pensadores* of the "Asociación de Mayo." Though the principles of liberal republicanism had prevailed in the national political scene, conditions in the Argentina of the 1860's could not be classed as entirely satisfactory. The national population, estimated at about 1.5 million, reflected the exhaustion and cost of years of civil warfare. While the provinces nominally accepted the leadership of Buenos Aires, future events were to show that the old animosities were still latent. The period of *autonomistas* and *mitristas* had yet to come to a close.

Paraguay

Far up the Paraná River, nearly 1,000 miles from Buenos Aires, the Paraguay of 1864 exhibited some remarkable signs of casting aside its former role as a hermit nation. Semitropical by virtue of its latitude as compared to the temperate lower Paraná zone, Paraguay could nearly lay claim to the status of an Arcadia. Endowed by nature with both excellent climate and fertile soil, the landlocked little nation had enjoyed relative peace and tranquillity since declaration of its independence in 1811. Its peoples, almost wholly a mestizo race in which the basic Guaraní Indian stock was predominant, were of a docile yet virile nature, subsisting entirely on an agricultural economy.

Paraguay's population in 1864 has been variously estimated from 450,000 to 1.3 million, with the former probably being more correct.[2] The first national census, taken in 1840, showed the total to have been 220,000. This population occupied the third of the present national territory which lies east of the Paraguay River—a region of forested, rolling hills extending to the Paraná plateau along the Upper Paraná River. Westward of the Paraguay River the remaining two-thirds of Paraguay comprised the semiarid Chaco region, an almost impenetrable area of thick, scrub forest inhabited by savage, uncivilized Indian tribes.

The factor of geographic location has consistently played an important role in Paraguay's history. Though it was the site of Spain's first permanent settlement in southern South America, the absence of precious minerals and the difficulties and delays involved in navigation of the winding, sluggish, and often shallow Paraná-Paraguay river system contributed to the eventual decline of the colony to the position of a relatively unimportant outpost off the main Buenos Aires–Upper Peru–Lima trade route.

This trend toward obscurity was given added impetus after independence with the rise to power of Dr. José Gaspar Rodríguez de Francia. Famed in history as Paraguay's "El Supremo," Dr. Francia converted his country into an "Inland Japan." Administering a total autocracy in which all controls were centered in his hands, El Supremo concluded that strict isolation from her neighbors was best for Paraguay's future. The most plausible reasons which have been advanced to explain this policy are Dr. Francia's suspicions regarding Argentine designs for the re-inclusion of the "Province of Paraguay" within the Argentine Confederation, the punitive actions of Dictator Rosas in denying recognition of Paraguay and of blockading the Paraná River against transit by Paraguayan shipping, and his anxiety over the possible infiltration of the newly developing liberal theories of government at Buenos Aires.

Following El Supremo's death in 1840, control of Paraguay eventually passed into the hands of Carlos Antonio López. An enormously fat individual with a pear-shaped appearance, who preferred to be known as "El Ciudadano" (The Citizen), President López proved a less saturnine ruler than El Supremo. His administration, from 1844 to 1862, was marked by a relaxation of the previous isolation policy and a corresponding increase in Paraguay's relations with the outside world. He sought recognition for his country and encouraged development of foreign trade. In political matters, however, he departed but slightly from Dr. Francia's totalitarian policies. Likewise, he seems to have inherited El Supremo's apprehension over political developments in Argentina. The following police regulation, issued early in his administration, reflects his concern with Argentine conditions.

It is absolutely prohibited to speak of the parties and of the civil war which, sad to say, is breaking up the neighboring provinces, and insults and threats to the refugees of either party will not be permitted. Those who wish to live in this republic must understand that they have to keep profound silence concerning the occurrences and parties on the other side, in Corrientes, and the Commissary of Police will advise all foreigners and refugees that we wish here to know nothing of their disastrous hatreds and rancours, and those who do not like it may retire at once from the country.[3]

On the death of Carlos Antonio López in 1862, the presidency of Paraguay passed to his eldest son, Francisco Solano López, upon due election by Paraguay's Congress. The new president possessed character traits contrasting strongly with those of his father. Impulsive, ambitious, and equipped with an iron will, Francisco Solano reflected little of the cautious conservatism of his father. Attracted to military life and made aware of contemporary innovations in industry and transport through an extended European visit, he embarked upon a plan to transform the colonial appearance of Paraguay and to secure for his country a position of respect in La Plata.

By 1864 the order and progress which had characterized the administrations of the two López, father and son, had produced developments in Paraguay which were in visible contrast with conditions in neighboring countries. Under the direction of engineers and technicians imported from Europe, La Plata's first railway had been built, linking Asunción with the military camp southeast at Cerro León; a telegraph line was under construction from Asunción south to the river fortress of Humaitá; a new railway station, a government palace, and a theater were being erected; a renovated arsenal and shipyard had been equipped to produce war materials and river vessels; efforts were being made to encourage the development of a cotton textile industry; and the government had undertaken a program of scholarships for selected students to study abroad. Such material progress had been accompanied in the cultural field by the introduction of dramatical performances in the theater, by the encouragement to arts and letters provided by a Spanish professor brought to Paraguay, and by the sudden and deep change in social customs among the upper class wrought by the appearance and activities in Asunción of the new president's Irish-born consort, Elisa Alicia Lynch.

The contrast in political conditions between Paraguay and neighboring Argentina was equally apparent. Because his childhood had been under the regime of Dr. Francia, and also due to the training of his father, El Ciudadano, Francisco Solano López showed no signs of departure from the autocratic totalitarian form of government for the Republic of Paraguay. The single-party system allowed for no effective opposition, and the power of the president was supreme. Government, commerce, church matters, social customs—all were subject to direction and supervision by the president. Unquestioning loyalty to the government was expected of all, and a police force which included plain-clothes men undertook to root out dissident elements. Those who had the misfortune to run afoul of the government's directives, or who for personal reasons opposed the López family, found it expedient to seek exile abroad, usually at Buenos Aires.

Asunción, in 1864 a river port of about 20,000, reflected the vitality and determination of Paraguay's new president, who was sponsoring a large-scale program to transform his capital city and its dormant, old colonial atmosphere. While foreign visitors remarked upon this intense activity, they also did not fail to note

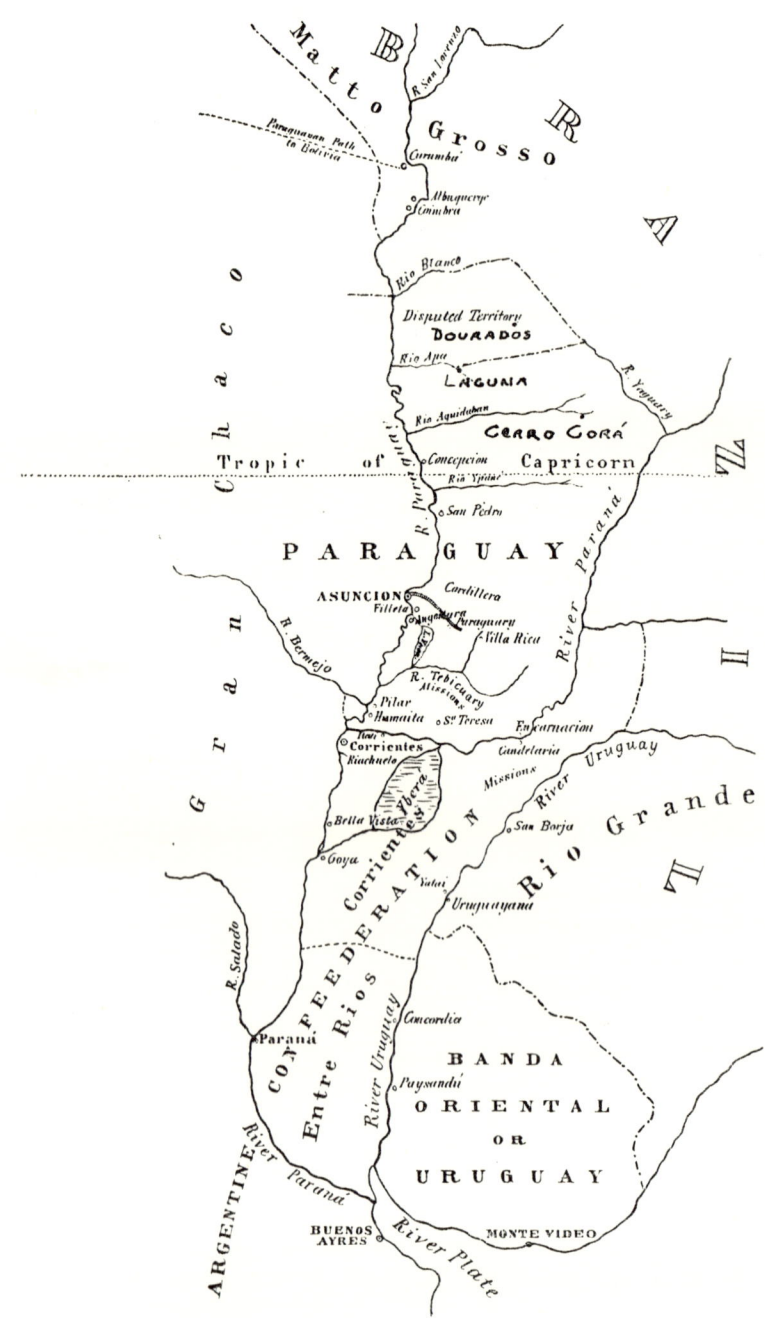

THE THEATER OF THE PARAGUAYAN WAR
(*From* Charles A. Wilburn, *The History of Paraguay*, 2 vols.; Boston, 1870)

the strict regulations which curbed their movements, as well as the surprising number of soldiers in the streets who seemed to comprise nearly the whole of the male population.[4]

Paraguay's entrance into the Plata international scene under the leadership of its dynamic new president generated increased focus upon problems of foreign relations. Under the guidance of Carlos Antonio López, Paraguay had pursued a conservative yet wily policy which had successfully kept it from becoming deeply embroiled in questions with other countries. Though such incidents as the Rhode Island Company dispute and "Water Witch" affairs with the United States in the mid-1850's, the Nuevo Bordeus colony tiff with France, and the Canstat affair with Britain, had erupted into serious and thorny problems, El Ciudadano's native ability and conservatism had aided the resolution of each incident without prejudice to Paraguay. With the developing policies of the new president, Paraguay's attitude in foreign relationships assumed a far more nationalistic and aggressive aspect.

By 1864, therefore, the earlier question with European countries and the United States had been successfully resolved. Several other serious clouds, however, still loomed darkly on the international scene. These were concerned primarily with neighboring Argentina and Brazil. To the south, Argentina had finally recognized Paraguayan independence and had opened the Plata estuary and the Paraná for transit by Paraguayan-flag shipping. Two delicate matters remained to be solved. Both concerned frontier boundaries. The old Misiones or Candelaria region lying east of the Paraná, between the Upper Paraná River and the Uruguay River, was claimed by both nations. Though considered by Argentina to be a portion of Corrientes Province, Paraguay believed it still had a valid claim to the old Jesuit mission region. West of the Paraguay River, the two nations had similarly not been able to agree on national frontiers in the Chaco area. Paraguay's claim to the Bermejo River as the frontier, slightly north of the Paraná-Paraguay confluence, was not recognized by Argentina, which held hopes for demarcation of the frontier at the Pilocomayo River, across from Asunción, or perhaps even farther north.

The problem of unresolved frontier limits was equally as critical to the north. Paraguay, concerned with Brazilian development of Mato Grosso since the early 1800's, held that its national territory extended northward to the left bank of the Blanco River.

In a counterclaim, Brazil persisted in its rights to the territory extending southward from the Blanco to the right bank of the Apa River. In addition to this border question, Paraguay had continually resisted Brazil's demands for navigation rights on the Paraguay River in order to maintain her river communications to Mato Grosso. In this matter Brazil's demands varied sharply with imperial policy toward the Amazon River, which in 1864 still remained closed to foreign navigation.

These several questions had been treated during the 1850's in negotiations between Paraguay and her neighbors. No final agreements had been reached, however, and all were still lacking solution. Following a strong naval demonstration in early 1855, Brazil had managed to obtain rights for the transit of the Paraguay River by her vessels en route to Mato Grosso. Such movement was viewed with concern by Paraguay which, under its new president, commenced construction of a modernized defensive fortress at Humaitá, 15 miles above the confluence of the Paraguay and Paraná rivers.

To recapitulate, Paraguay in 1864 exhibited a newly kindled spirit of nationalism characterized by an intelligent program for internal development and a foreign policy aimed at recognition of Paraguay as a sovereign nation possessing full juridical status within the Plata region. Its government, now exemplified by the person of Francisco Solano López, represented a bulwark of nineteenth-century authoritarianism against the spreading theories of democratic liberalism. Possessing a standing army of approximately 50,000 men and a sizable naval force, Paraguay was now an effective instrument for the support of the ambitious policies and objectives of its new president.[5]

Uruguay

Frequently referred to as the "Cockpit of La Plata," little Uruguay in 1864 was a powder keg to which a slow fuse had already been ignited. With a population of perhaps 400,000, similar in racial strain and manner of living to that of the neighboring Argentine province of Entre Ríos, Uruguay was caught up in the throes of the perennial desperate effort to retain her status as an independent buffer state between Argentina and Brazil. Montevideo was comparable to Buenos Aires for the persistence of its colonial atmosphere.

The problem for Uruguay in 1864 was how to resist mounting pressure from Brazil regarding border troubles while at the same time overcoming a rising internal revolt alleged to have Argentine support. The Uruguayan Blanco government, in power for its last time until 1958, was shortly to discover that a solution to this dilemma was completely and thoroughly impossible. To the north, prominent citizens in Brazil's Rio Grande do Sul province were increasing their demands upon the Imperial Brazilian Government for measures to secure redress from Uruguay over border incidents and alleged mistreatment of Brazilian subjects residing within Uruguay. A diplomatic mission under the able guidance of Counsellor José Antônio Saraiva had met with little success in Montevideo, and the fleet under Admiral Joaquim Marques Lisboa, the Barão de Tamandaré, had sailed to the Uruguayan port city to support the negotiations with solid force if necessary. In a later comment upon Brazil's demands against Uruguay, American minister in Asunción Charles Ames Washburn concluded that the reparations specified by Brazil equalled about $43 per each Uruguayan on the basis of the small nation's population in 1864.[6]

Internally, Uruguay was torn by vicious civil strife which may have stemmed from a political debt to Argentina. General Venancio Flores, an Uruguayan gaucho caudillo and head of his country's Colorado party, had aided Bartolomé Mitre in his victory over General Urquiza at Pavón, in September, 1861. Subsequently in exile at Buenos Aires through a turn in political fortunes, Venancio Flores schemed against the Blanco government at Montevideo. Reportedly with the unofficial support of Mitre, and aided by Argentine supplies and financial assistance, Flores crossed the Uruguay River and raised the standard of revolt.[7] His movement gained momentum, and by 1864 the Blanco government was near collapse. The powder keg was about to explode.

Brazil

Conditions in Imperial Brazil in 1864 exhibited perhaps even greater contrasts than those observable in La Plata. Geographically, the nation had approached closely the extent of its present limits. The tide of expansion, however, was not over. *Sertanejos*, or backwoodsmen, in the distant recesses of Mato Grosso and Amazonia, were still erecting crude crosses to be held as evidence of effective possession of land under Brazil's *uti possidetis* policy conception. The vast Brazilian empire, commonly referred to as a sleeping giant, was divided roughly into four distinct areas: the Northeast, with its old slaveholding sugar *fazenda* system centered on Recife and Bahía; the central coastal area in which Rio de Janeiro figured as the heart of the empire; the extreme South, represented by Rio Grande do Sul province—a continuation of the rolling hill and prairie lands of North Uruguay; and the western backlands, an area of jungles, low mountains, plateaus, and extensive river basins, stretching to and including the westernmost province of Mato Grosso.

These dissimilar regions and the diverse peoples which inhabited them were held together within a relatively loose framework of empire by the central government at Rio de Janeiro. This framework was delicate indeed. In 1864 the railway was still a novelty in Brazil, the first short line connecting Rio de Janeiro and the Serra de Petrópolis area having been constructed in 1854. The most feasible and dependable form of transport continued to be coastwise shipping. Communications with and in the interior consisted of post carriage or mule pack trains over rough roads and trails. Travel to interior points customarily involved weeks and even months in time. Outside of Rio de Janeiro, Bahía, Pôrto Alegre, and infant São Paulo, newspapers were a rarity. For all purposes, Rio de Janeiro, or the "Côrte" as the capital zone was then called, was the hub of both government and civilization. Sugar, slavery, and the wealthy *fazendeiro* were still the dominant features of Brazil's economy, although the land was about to experience the spectacular rise of coffee as king as well as the era of heavy European immigration. The nation's population in 1864 was estimated at about 9 million, including almost 2 million Negro slaves.

At the pinnacle of this continental-sized empire stood a lone man—Dom Pedro II. He was to be known more popularly at a later time as "The Magnanimous." A dignified, scholarly man, imbued with a deep desire to administer to his people's wishes rather than to the objectives of any political party, Dom Pedro de Alcântara had succeeded in molding a united, constitutional monarchy which had become the most powerful nation in Latin America. The task had not been an easy one. In the thirty years prior to the outbreak of the Paraguayan War, Brazil's empire had experienced a number of crises including several provincial revolts, the ten-year Farroupo Rebellion of 1835-45, the "Guerra Grande" in which Brazilian expeditionary forces had been instrumental in forcing Argentina's Dictator Juan Manuel de Rosas into exile in 1852, and finally the "Questão Ingleza," or English Question, of 1862-65.

Though all of these episodes with the exception of the last had become history by 1864, there were still several difficult questions facing the Imperial Government along the national frontiers. As indicated earlier, negotiations with Paraguay regarding the delimitation of frontier boundaries had not been successful, and Brazil's claims to its lower Mato Grosso area thus lacked a definitive status. In addition, the Imperial Government viewed the need to maintain transit rights along the Paraguay River to Mato Grosso as of primary importance in its foreign policy due to the almost total impossibility of maintaining overland communications with the interior province.

To the south, the Peace of Poncho Verde, signed March 1, 1845, had spelled both the end of the long Farroupo Revolt and its Piratini Republic and the amalgamation of Rio Grande do Sul and its peoples within the imperial structure. This development, due principally to the military and diplomatic skills of one of the empire's greatest figures—Luís Alves de Lima e Silva, later to become Duque de Caxias—augured well for the future. With the advent of the 1860's, however, the Imperial Government found itself plagued with a rising volume of protests from Liberal Riograndense ranchers over border incidents involving Uruguayans. In addition, Uruguay paid scant heed to complaints regarding unjust treatment of Brazilians resident within the former Cisplatine province. The pressure of these circumstances eventually persuaded a leading Rio Grande landowner and Liberal politician, General Antônio de Sousa Netto, to present an exposition to the government in the name of the Brazilians resident in Uruguay. In effect, General Souza Netto made it clear that unless punitive action was forthcoming, Rio Grande do Sul would take it upon itself to obtain redress from the Uruguayan Blancos.[8]

Dom Pedro II thus found himself faced with a serious quandry: were the complaints of Rio Grande do Sul justifiable? Did they warrant intervention by Brazil? Would there be a reaction on the part of Argentina and Paraguay? Since Argentina had given evidence of supporting Venancio Flores, little danger might be expected from Buenos Aires. Paraguay was another matter. The new government in Asunción had made no move, however, and perhaps a swift show of force could rectify matters in Uruguay without engendering further complications. Besides, the pressure on the part of the Rio Grande do Sul Liberals constituted a factor not to be dismissed lightly, especially in view of the events of the earlier Farroupo period. Reluctantly, Dom Pedro II acceded to the demands for official Brazilian representations against the Blanco government at Montevideo. The stage for the tragic Paraguayan War had been set.

Chapter 3

DRAMATIS PERSONAE

PERHAPS THE MOST UNUSUAL and most fascinating aspect of the Paraguayan War is represented by the extremes between the leading personalities of the contending nations. When viewed from the standpoint of the personal characteristics of the chief executives of the Plata nations and Brazil as well as their goals, ambitions, and outlook regarding the future of their countries, the tendency is encouraged to appraise the Paraguayan War as a struggle between two completely differing modes of existence. On the one hand, Paraguay appears as a nation dominated entirely by the ambitions and will power of a single individual obsessed with the desire for recognition and stature for his hitherto insignificant and largely unknown country. On the other, Brazil stands forth as an empire bent upon retaining its position of supremacy, and represented by a thoughtful, peace-loving monarch who could yet place his nation's honor above all other considerations. Others of the war's personalities paled before the contrasts between the two prime contestants: Francisco Solano López and Dom Pedro de Alcântara.

Francisco Solano López

Born July 24, 1826, Paraguay's president was 38 years old on the outbreak of the war.[1] The eldest of a family of five children, he had received possibly the best in education that his country had to offer: the principles of a liberal education provided by a Spanish teacher residing in Asunción and a measure of training in Latin by a local priest and theologist. Early adjusted to positions of command through the preference shown him by his father, the president, he soon became accustomed to assuming initiative and to accepting responsibility. Smitten by the attractions of military life through his early appointment as chief of his nation's army, Francisco Solano López was assigned at the age of 18 to head the 4,000-man Paraguayan contingent sent to assist General José María Paz, an opponent of Rosas and regarded by many as La Plata's leading military tactician.

Though Paraguay's military participation in Argentine affairs was both short and unspectacular, young Solano López acquired a strong liking for military life which had a profound influence on his future career. In discussing his Argentine experiences with a visiting Chilean observer during the campaign, he is alleged to have compared himself favorably with General Paz and to have inferred that military service held no secrets for him.[2]

In 1853, President Carlos Antonio López decided to send his eldest son on a special mission to Europe to convey Paraguay's gratitude for recognition, and of seeking technicians and equipment, including naval vessels. In terms of results the decision was among the most fruitful of those made during Carlos Antonio's period of office. In descriptions of this trip it has been the customary practice of commentators to confine themselves solely to accounts of Solano López' reaction to the lures of the social life of Paris and London and to his association with Elisa Alicia Lynch, who became his mistress. Though such activities undoubtedly consumed a part of the young Paraguayan's time, perhaps a substantial part, the record also shows that he was by no means blind to the more solid benefits which could accrue from his European visit. The Hero of Corrientes and Envoy of the Republic of Paraguay made visits to major industrial installations in Britain; contracted for the purchase of new ships suitable for river naval operations; undertook to engage the services of J. and A. Blyth and Company, London, as Paraguay's purchasing and supply agent; and hired for employment in Paraguay a number of British technicians who were later to perform invaluable wartime services for him. In France he attended military reviews and took notes of equipment and military organization procedures.[3]

Returning to Paraguay late in 1854, Francisco Solano López exhibited new polish and evidence of culture which contrasted favorably with his previous habits and customs. Aided materially by his most striking European acquisition, Elisa Lynch, he embarked upon a program to renovate Paraguay. While General López administered plans for material changes and the expansion of the army, his Irish consort sought to transform Asunción's social atmosphere by introducing new feminine styles, stimulating an interest in music and drama, and organizing tea parties, costume balls, and literary evenings. Presumably because of her earlier, unhappy marriage to French Doctor Jean Louis Armand de Quatrefages and her inability to obtain a divorce, her association with Francisco Solano López was never legitimized. She bore him five children and remained loyal to him to his last moments. Though much maligned in historical accounts for alleged cruelty to prisoners, and accused of having exerted a perverse influence on López, Mrs. Lynch, as she was commonly known, was a cultured and beautiful woman who reflected unswerving devotion to and deep affection for Francisco López. Similarly, she developed a sincere affection for Paraguay and its humble peoples which she retained throughout the remaining pathetic years of her life.[4]

Born in Ireland in 1835, Elisa Lynch was 29 years old at the outbreak of the Paraguayan War. As a result of his visits with her at Asunción in 1856, Argentine journalist Hector F. Varela concluded that Mrs. Lynch was a mixture of grace, beauty, and distinction. Struck with her superior beauty, Varela nevertheless commented that her physical aspects might also be surpassed by her talent and high education.[5] Though he never met Mrs. Lynch, Captain Richard F. Burton wrote that an English officer whom she "had impressed most favorably" described her as "somewhat resembling Her Imperial Majesty of France." The officer's wartime description of her also noted that she was tall, "belle-femme," handsome, with grey-blue eyes—once blue, and "hair *chatâin-clair* somewhat sprinkled with grey."[6] In 1869, Minister MacMahon found Elisa Lynch to be a clever and cultured woman who had not forgotten that she was Irish.[7]

In 1859, upon the outbreak of renewed hostilities between Buenos Aires and the government supported by General Urquiza, President Carlos Antonio López offered the services of Paraguay as a mediator and sent his eldest son to encourage the rival parties to reach an amicable agreement. Though too late to prevent the Battle of Cepeda, General Francisco Solano López negotiated a truce between Urquiza and Mitre and showed clear signs of skill as a mediator by engineering the Pact of San José de Flores. In tribute to his success, which has generally been glossed over or conveniently forgotten, Paraguay's arbiter was praised both by the government and people of Buenos Aires as well as by General Urquiza. On November 13, 1859, Carlos Tejedor, representative of the government of Buenos Aires, addressed Francisco Solano López in these terms:

> The diplomatic action of Paraguay in bringing together the members of the same family and allaying difficulties which until now had appeared insuperable, has contributed strongly to the solution, by peaceful means, of questions which could never have been resolved honorably for all through recourse to arms.
>
> It is a pleasure to inform Your Excellency that the Government of Buenos Aires shall conserve the pleasant impressions inspired in it by the distinguished person of the representative of Paraguay as a complement of the noble and successful mission which he has performed.[8]

The Vice President of the Argentine Confederation, in an official decree of November 20, declared General Urquiza to be "The founder of the National Union of the Argentine Republic," and offered a "vote of gratitude to the Supreme Government of the Republic of Paraguay and to His Excellency Brigadier General and Minister Mediator D. Francisco Solano López, who with noble and generous effort, has employed his good and paternal offices to promote the union of the dissident parties of the Argentine Republic."[9] The highlight, of course, was the universal acclaim accorded Francisco López by the people of Buenos Aires, who as a token of esteem presented him with an album bearing the following dedication:

> The people of Buenos Aires dedicate this token of gratitude and respect to His Excellency Brigadier General D. Francisco Solano López, Minister Plenipotentiary of the Republic of Paraguay, to whose friendly interposition is due the saving of the blood of their sons, the fortunate peace in which they now find themselves, and the long-sought union of the Argentine family.
>
> Our best wishes shall always accompany the illustrious mediator and His Excellency President Carlos Antonio López, and the Republic which they represent. Our gratitude for their valued assistance shall be eternal.[10]

Among the signatures to this dedication was that of Bartolomé Mitre. Less than six years later the dedication had been completely forgotten amidst the ugly cries of war to the death against the "monster" López.

Not the least of the tributes which were showered on General López for his mediation efforts was that of Justo José de Urquiza. The Entrerriano gaucho chieftain issued a manifesto paying high tribute to "the illustrious mediator of Paraguay," and stating further, "no demonstration of gratitude will be too much to honor his friendship."[11] Subsequently, from his San José palace near Concepción del Uruguay, the gaucho chieftain wrote Francisco Solano López on December 27 presenting him with the sword he had worn at the Battle of Cepeda. Urquiza wrote:

I wish to present Your Excellency with a token of the appreciation which I entertain for your virtues and I can find no more suitable object than the sword I wore at Cepeda. I present it to you as a modest token of friendship. Please accept it. I shall always look forward with pleasure to the occasion on which I can prove my friendship and gratitude to the Government of Paraguay and to you.[12]

Francisco Solano López replied to the general on January 26, 1860, from Humaitá, in the following terms:

Your Excellency's wishes for my personal prosperity are most cordially appreciated, and although the invaluable friendship of Your Excellency is the greatest token which you could offer me, it is my deep pleasure to accept the generous gift of the sword which you wielded at Cepeda with much glory. When the occasion shall require that I unsheath it, I shall do my utmost to render it the honor it deserves.[13]

Indeed, fateful words on the part of two of La Plata's greatest figures. History has so far not recorded any reference regarding the ultimate resting place of the sword of Cepeda after López' death at Cerro Corá.

Francisco Solano López presumably met General Urquiza during the 1858 Bowlin Mission negotiations at Asunción, the success of which has been attributed in large measure to the good offices of General Urquiza. The sword of Cepeda, if it did not cement this friendship, was at least evidence of an esteem or understanding between the two men which was to have important repercussions in the future Paraguayan War.

By 1864 the Hero of Corrientes, Arbiter of La Plata, and now

President of Paraguay, was well on the way toward achievement of both his personal ambitions and his program for Paraguay's material progress. Though his administration closely followed those of his predecessors in its political aspects, rumors at least on one occasion held that a change in its character might have been contemplated. According to these rumors, President López was alleged to have entered into secret diplomatic negotiations related to his possible marriage with Princess Isabel, the daughter of Dom Pedro of Brazil.[14] The story, if it had basis, died swiftly with the marriage of Isabel to the Conde d'Eu in October, 1864. Purported proof of the existence of such a scheme was exhibited at Buenos Aires, where a confiscated Paraguayan cargo yielded a set of "imperial-type" furniture and the model of a crown allegedly sent for the inspection of "Francisco I of Paraguay." Observer Captain Richard F. Burton was later informed that the furniture had been sold at auction.[15] Paraguayan historians have claimed the crown model to have involved simply an order designed for the embellishment of the "Virgin de Asunción."[16] The empire rumor subsequently helped generate the belief that López' prime objective was that of forming an empire composed of all the Plata nations.

Both Carlos Antonio and Francisco Solano López were continuously suspicious of the intentions and policies of Imperial Brazil. Carlos Antonio, on his death, reportedly counselled his eldest son to beware of Brazil and to settle any problems with the empire through peaceful means, not warfare. Likewise, Carlos Antonio may not have been particularly convinced by his eldest son's early tendency to expand the relatively small Paraguayan army inherited from Dr. Francia's era. Young Francisco Solano, however, keenly attracted by the military life which he had experienced during the earlier Corrientes campaign in 1845-46, and possessing positive personality traits contrasting with his father's conservatism, became convinced that Paraguay's best defense lay in an offensive capacity which would command respect. The early development of these beliefs on his part is clearly seen in the following transcript of remarks attributed to him during a conversation with Buenos Aires journalist Hector Varela at Asunción in December, 1857:

> I will never be able to return to Europe because my destiny is completely linked with that of my people. My worthy father is

old and suffers from a chronic malady which, because of his advanced age, will cause his death. His wish and that of my countrymen is that I should succeed him. On the day that happens, I will do that which he has not wished to do in spite of my counsel. I know that Brazil and you Argentines covet Paraguay. We have here sufficient means to resist both, but I do not believe in waiting for you to make the attack. It will be I who shall make it. In other words, on the first pretext which they give me, I will declare war on the Brazilian empire and on the Plata republics who, if they continue to live in distrust of each other, will have to unite in order to fight me.[12]

PORTRAIT

A brief personal portrait of Francisco Solano López in 1864 shows him to have been about five and one-half feet in height, and generally inclined toward a stocky build in which sturdy, well-padded shoulders were prominent.[13] In facial characteristics he reflected his mestizo origin though presumably not to the extent suggested by British pharmacist George F. Masterman, who believed he had the traits of the nearly extinct and fierce Guaycurú Indian tribe. Both hair and full beard were black, the latter being cut in the style which, according to Captain Burton, was popularly known at the time as the "Newgate Frill." A broad forehead but somewhat close-set eyes were additional characteristics. His eyes, in particular, seem to have attracted the attention of those who knew him. In repose they were said to be kindly and intelligent; in anger they were said to undergo a radical change—bulging, staring, emotion-packed, and capable of instilling fear in all in his presence. His teeth were the only reported physical defect he had. Though they were in bad condition, he reportedly paid them scant attention, with the result that in later life they became blackened and unsightly. They were said to have caused him much pain on occasion, to the extent that he acquired the habit of rinsing his mouth with brandy to alleviate the discomfort.

In later years during the war, Francisco Solano had a tendency to put on excess weight, a condition doubtlessly abetted by an enormous appetite. Several observers held that he was both a gourmand and a gourmet. Large dinners were a ceremony to him, and he delighted in having his favorite officers as his guests along with Mrs. Lynch and his sons. Minister Washburn, in a commendable display of diplomatic writing ability, described a dinner with the Marshal at Cerro León in the following terms:

The dinner is worthy of description, if for nothing else for the number of courses. Everything was cooked in Paraguayan fashion. Soups, stews, forced meats, asado, vermicelli in a pottage with eggs, rice in the same way, and a variety of dishes I have never seen elsewhere than in Paraguay, were brought on, one after another, till it seemed that the dinner would not end until somebody died of repletion. To the credit of the President's stomach, it must be admitted that no dish was dishonored by his neglect. He partook of all with apparently a keen, if not a discriminating relish (See Note 18).

Paraguay's president also seems to have been irregular in his habits regarding alcoholic beverages. In some accounts he is portrayed as a heavy drinker who maintained a huge wine cellar in his train whether at Asunción, Cerro León, or on active campaign. Another characteristic distinguishing Francisco López was his inveterate custom of smoking large, hand-rolled, black Paraguayan cigars, a product still in ubiquitous use at Asunción. Seldom observed in repose without one, he is reported to have acquired the habit of smoking them close to the butt after the fashion of Ulysses S. Grant, whose likeness on campaign he may have seen in papers describing the progress of the American Civil War.

Generally fastidious in his dress, especially in his later years, President López was described by Hector Variela as having the appearance of a fashionably clothed gentleman of striking aspect.[19] A good conversationalist, excellent at oratory particularly among his troops, and a charming host when it suited him, he was equally fluent in Spanish and French as well as in his native Guaraní. In addition, he understood Portuguese and had a slight, though working, knowledge of English. With Mrs. Lynch he always spoke in French. With his troops he used Guaraní, as that was the only language which the vast majority of his men could understand.

A man of many moods, his mercurial disposition was difficult for those near him to gauge. At times he was angry, sullen, introspective, and perhaps pessimistic. At other times he was jocular, optimistic, and an excellent comrade. Endowed with an alert sense of suspicion, probably an inheritance from his father and from his youth during the era of El Supremo, he was inclined rather to credit than to discredit any tales brought to him regarding his subordinates and even his own family. As a result of his suspicious nature, he never had any close friends. Perhaps the only person for whom he felt warm personal regard other than Mrs. Lynch was General José Diáz Barboza Vera, one-time Asunción chief of police and the most renowned of Paraguay's generals.

Intense industry, enormous will power, iron determination, and an almost superhuman tenacity were other major features of his personality. Inclined to place supreme faith in his own decisions, López found it extremely difficult to change his mind even in the face of overwhelming evidence and to admit that an earlier policy decision may have been erroneous. Like El Supremo and El Ciudadano, he preferred to perform all major tasks personally. While he had competent administrative assistants who occasionally drafted correspondence at his precise instructions, he frequently composed his own personal and diplomatic correspondence. It was not unusual to observe him hard at work preparing dispatches beyond midnight on the eve of the departure of a river steamer for Buenos Aires.

The personal portrait of Francisco Solano López is by no means without its warm, human aspects.[20] There is much evidence that he held a strong regard for Mrs. Lynch, his children by her, his mother, and for his troops. Always warmly affectionate in his treatment of his children by Mrs. Lynch, he was usually cool toward his other children with the exception of Emiliano, the son of Juana Pessoa of Villa del Pilar. For his nation, however, he reserved his greatest love. Paraguay to Francisco Solano López was something more than his personal domain. Like his troops he was a Paraguayan, and like them he was to give his life for his country.

Dom Pedro II Of Brazil

Dom Pedro de Alcântara João Carlos Leopoldo Salvador Bebiano Francisco Xavier de Paula Leocádio Miguel Gabriel Rafael Gonzaga, Second Emperor of Brazil, was born on December 2, 1825. He was destined to die in exile at Paris almost exactly 66 years later, on December 5, 1891.

The Imperial Prince as of August 2, 1826, under the reign of his father Dom Pedro I, the young Dom Pedro was subsequently acclaimed Constitutional Emperor and Perpetual Defender of Brazil on April 7, 1831. On July 23, 1840, he assumed full power as emperor, and brought the Regency to a close. He was then 14 years old.

The ensuing half century, until the proclamation of the republic in 1889, is known as the Golden Age of Brazil. Under the leadership of Dom Pedro II and through the generally successful operation of the government's parliamentary system, inaugurated in 1837, Imperial Brazil developed from a thin band of loosely connected provinces along the extended coast line into a powerful nation welded by a constantly growing sense of unity and nationalism. Credit for this most successful and longest experiment in constitutional monarchy in Latin America must clearly be given to Dom Pedro II. A studious intellectual, far more attracted by literary and scientific developments than by the grinding, daily political chores of a chief of state, he provided an example for his peoples which has since caused him to be regarded as the First Brazilian. As one historian suggests, "In Brazil Dom Pedro II personified the national dignity; his spirit of abnegation and the shadow of his immense stature extended themselves over the nation like a paladin."[21]

In personality characteristics Dom Pedro II reflected well-defined contrasts when compared with his father. Though a Braganza, the young emperor was less headstrong and impulsive than his father, exhibited a far more patient and understanding relationship with his advisers and with cabinet members, and above all, possessed a preference for intellectual matters and the material progress of his country rather than for the attractions of life's frivolities and lures. During a discussion of political trends within the empire, Dom Pedro II is said to have stated, "If my countrymen should decide to choose another form of government, it will not be I who shall oppose them; the selection of my new profession, if that event occurs, has already been made—I shall become a teacher."[22]

Curiously enough, the lives of both Brazil's emperors reflected the effect of their relationships with women of high social standing. The comparison of this aspect of the lives of the two emperors, however, presents further contrasts. While the relations between Dom Pedro I and the Marquesa de Santos assumed a flagrant character which became offensive to imperial court society, those of his son with the Condessa de Barral were both discreet and wholly platonic.²³ Married by proxy on April 20, 1842, to the Princess Teresa Cristina Maria de Bourbon, daughter of King Francis I of the Two Sicilies, the young Dom Pedro was shocked almost to the point of losing his reason to discover on his bride's arrival at Rio de Janeiro that she was older than he, that she was a brunette instead of the hoped-for blonde, that she was of visibly much shorter height in comparison to his imposing figure, and that she was lame. Though the marriage was eventually consummated and proved an enduring one—it lasted 46 years—the empress could never provide her husband with either strong emotional fascination or a mental stimulation based on equality of intellect.

These voids in the life of Dom Pedro II were filled by Luisa Margarida Portugal de Barros, Condessa de Barral. Born at Salvador in 1816, the condessa was nine years older than Dom Pedro. Her father was minister to the court of Charles X of France, senator of the empire, and later Visconde de Pedra Branca. Luisa Margarida was married to French nobleman Eugene de Barral in 1837. In 1848 the couple returned to Bahía. The condessa's relationship with Dom Pedro began in 1856 with her acceptance, at the court's request, of the position as private tutor and companion to the two young imperial princesses. Her position terminated in 1864 with the marriage of the princesses, and the Barrals returned to France. Following her husband's death in 1868, the condessa returned to Brazil in 1874 and remained there until 1876. She died in France on January 14, 1891, at the age of 75, about eleven months before her great friend's death on December 5, 1891.²⁴

Schooled carefully to the need for maintenance of constant devotion to the requirements of dignity and moral integrity demanded of an emperor, Dom Pedro II apparently was never able to allow his sincere affection for the condessa to transform itself from pure friendship to perhaps more earthy levels. The condessa, for her part, appreciated these circumstances. She exercised a carefully controlled discretion in her relationship with the emperor which never once occasioned either scandal or court gossip.²⁵

The Condessa de Barral, though considerably older than Dom Pedro, was a cultured, intelligent, and beautiful woman who became the emperor's confidential correspondent and counsellor. In a remarkable series of 256 letters which have only recently come to light through disposition of the condessa's heirs, Dom Pedro wrote most intimately of his daily life, his hopes, ambitions, and achievements; of his happiness and his sorrow; and of events and trends of his era. The subjects of his letters were vast in scope: literature, art, science, music, the theater, travel, and the social, political, and administrative life of Imperial Brazil.[26] While the condessa replied faithfully to her emperor's letters, her correspondence, unfortunately, did not survive for history's appraisal. As was his custom, Dom Pedro burned his private correspondence shortly after its receipt.[27]

His letters to the condessa immediately prior to the outbreak of the Paraguayan War and during its early stages show Dom Pedro to have been a deeply sensitive man, devoted to intellectual pursuits, who possessed a keen sense of duty to his nation. Above all, he wanted to be a Brazilian, a benign, fatherly adviser in the management of his country's destiny. He preferred not to become identified with any political faction and abhorred talk of the formation of an "imperial" party. His sincere objective, as reflected in his letters, was that of protecting and upholding the national honor of Brazil.

Dom Pedro's relations with the Condessa de Barral also provide an absorbing contrast to those between Francisco Solano López and Elisa Alicia Lynch. Both women were the object of profound affection on the part of their admirers. The young General López, however, had few qualms concerning his union with Mrs. Lynch in the light of the reaction of Asunción's society. Emotional and determined, he was unwilling to observe or even to consider the restraints which governed Dom Pedro de Alcântara. As in the case of the condessa, there is little written record of Mrs. Lynch's private relations with Francisco Solano López. Her letters to him were infrequent, of course, because she normally resided with him in Paraguay. Her sole contribution to the record of her era was a brief *Exposición y protesta* refuting the accusations against her, published in Buenos Aires after the war.[28]

By 1864 the 39-year-old Dom Pedro II was commencing his twenty-fourth year as Brazil's emperor. Though his reign had been relatively stable he had had to face numerous crises including one international war. Among the internal problems which had occurred since the late regency period were the regional revolts known as the Sabinada, the Abrilada, the Balaida, and the Sorocaba. The most serious internal revolt was the ten-year Farroupo

Rebellion of Rio Grande do Sul. Fortunately, with the inestimable and constantly successful and competent aid of Luís Alves de Lima e Silva, future Duque de Caxias, this movement had been terminated in a spirit of fairness and union which was to prove significant in the 1860's.

Among Brazil's international troubles there had been two of major concern: the war against Rosas and the Questão de Christie or Questão Ingleza. The former had been swiftly resolved in 1852 with the success of an allied army including Brazil's expeditionary force, at the Battle of Monte Caseros. The second matter, involving both the intransigent actions of British minister William Dougal Christie in an affair stemming from the detention for public misconduct at Rio of three British naval officers in late 1862, and the overall slavery question, had caused Dom Pedro intense worry and anxiety. This episode is held as the point at which he visibly commenced to grow old—a physical transformation which was soon to become even more apparent with the advent of his most difficult period of trial, the Paraguayan War.[29]

Imperial Brazil's relations with Paraguay, never on a fully satisfactory basis, had become increasingly more important to the empire's foreign policy. The crux of the matter was the maintenance of river communications with interior Mato Grosso. Paraguay's reluctance to grant transit rights along the Paraguay River had, during the period 1852-56, caused Mato Grosso to become "virtually amputated from the trunk of the nation," in the words of one historian.[30] Of the two provisional conventions signed with Paraguay in 1858, one had provided for the periodic free transit of Brazilian vessels to Mato Grosso. By the early 1860's, however, Dom Pedro was receiving complaints that the agreement was not being honored fully. Surgeon-officer Francisco Pinheiro Guimarães aboard the naval vessel "Paraguaçu," for example, wrote his father at the imperial court that Paraguayans at Asunción had refused to raise their flag in a recognition salute of the "Paraguaçu," that the ship's officers were not permitted to conduct hydrographic observations, that the officers were closely watched during their shore excursions, and that President López was rumored to have approved a price scale for naval supplies to Brazilian-flag vessels which was four times the normal selling rate. Deeply incensed at such treatment, Pinheiro Guimarães closed his letter with the following remarks:

Shall it be, my father, that our government will tolerate the affronts we have suffered at Asunción? Will the government not experience a reaction of patriotism and convey orders to our sailors and soldiers to sweep away this worthless "gauchada estúpida" which exists only by virtue of our scanty kindness?[31]

Caustic comments such as these were echoed in 1864 by pleas from officials in Mato Grosso pointing out the need to provide the province with more adequate defenses. To the south, the Liberals of Rio Grande do Sul were growing more vociferous in their complaints regarding Uruguayan border incidents. Though peace-loving and not a military man at heart, Dom Pedro found himself slowly being drawn into a vortex from which there seemed to be no escape. As news reports acquired grim aspects, he was later to write to his friend the condessa that the war had proven to be a strong electric shock to Brazilian nationalism.[32]

Mitre and Flores

The remaining chief executives in office in 1865, Bartolomé Mitre and Venancio Flores, never quite attained the wartime importance of Paraguay's Francisco Solano López and Brazil's Dom Pedro II. Each was the president of his respective nation at the commencement of the war. Neither survived the full period of the conflict in this capacity. Flores was assassinated at Montevideo on February 19, 1868, and on October 12, 1868, Mitre transferred the presidency of Argentina to Domingo Faustino Sarmiento.

BARTOLOMÉ MITRE

In 1864 Bartolomé Mitre had attained the apex of his political career. Born on June 26, 1821, at Buenos Aires, and thus a true *porteño*, he had by the outbreak of the Paraguayan War distinguished himself in the fields of literature, history, journalism, military science, diplomacy, politics, and statesmanship. Other members of his generation, which was perhaps the greatest which Argentina has produced, included Juan B. Alberdi, Domingo F. Sarmiento, and Justo José de Urquiza.

The first important episode in the career of Bartolomé Mitre as a major figure in Argentine public affairs concerned his services as an 18 year old artillery lieutenant serving in December, 1839, with the Uruguayan Colorado forces of General Rivera. As a member of the *unitarios* exiled in Uruguay during the era of Juan Manuel de Rosas, Mitre acquired knowledge of military affairs during the long siege of Montevideo. He participated in the Battle of Arroyo Grande in December, 1842, and had reached the rank of lieutenant colonel by the time he was 25. He is said to have become acquainted with Garibaldi at Montevideo and undoubtedly knew two young Argentine authors both destined to become famous—Esteban Echeverría and José Marmol.[33]

Following an extended period of further exile in Bolivia, Peru, and Chile, during which he participated in military events in Bolivia and commenced his first efforts in the fields of journalism and literature in Chile, he returned to his native Argentina in order to take part in the final 1852 campaign against Rosas. Justo José de Urquiza appointed him to the command of an artillery battery. Following the Battle of Monte Caseros he returned to Buenos Aires and soon rose to the leadership of the new liberal group stemming from the former *unitario* faction of the Rosas era.

During the period 1858-59 Mitre published his *Historia de Belgrano*, a detailed biographic account of the famous Argentine patriot and an outstanding early contribution to the field of Argentine historical writings. Concurrently with this literary effort, Governor Mitre found himself again faced with the necessity of returning to his earlier role, that of a soldier. With the outbreak of civil strife between Buenos Aires and the other provinces over the question of political supremacy and the new political organization for Argentina, Bartolomé Mitre found himself an adversary of his former commander from Entre Ríos, General Urquiza. Though soundly defeated at Cepeda in October, 1859, Mitre reorganized his forces during the peace interval afforded by the Pact of San José de Flores, negotiated by Francisco Solano López. In renewed fighting in 1861, the Mitre-led army of Buenos Aires finally achieved a narrow victory over General Urquiza at Pavón. Urquiza, never an admirer of Mitre, was later to refer to his adversary's military ability as that of a "general de papel" (paper general).[34]

On October 12, 1862, Bartolomé Mitre assumed office as the first constitutional president of the entire Argentine nation. As a new type of citizen-soldier in Argentina, he had managed to form a union of the loosely federated provinces which was to become the basis of modern Argentina. Described as a peace-loving, political visionary, he sought to eradicate the vestiges of caudillismo in his country and to substitute in its place the principles of democratic government. The task which he faced in 1862 was not easy. While relative peace prevailed throughout the provinces, there were many provincial leaders, including the famous General Urquiza, who viewed the ascendancy of Buenos Aires with apprehension if not hostility. Moreover, there remained not only the constant plague of Indian border raids but also the problems of foreign relationships. In Uruguay a former colleague, Venancio Flores, had raised a revolt and was counting upon support from Buenos Aires. In faraway Paraguay the former arbiter of San José de Flores and new president was showing unmistakable signs of seeking greater prestige for himself and for his nation in La Plata affairs.

In Buenos Aires President Mitre could legitimately contemplate with pride the early accomplishments of his administration. In addition to the establishment of a strong political organization, he had found time to effect some material improvements directed toward modernization of the colonial city. Argentina's first railway had been laid in 1857, and was now in operation over a ten-kilometer line from Buenos Aires to suburban Chivilcoy. A plan for the construction of a municipal tramway system contemplated the inauguration of services in 1865. Similarly, plans were about complete for the construction of the Central Argentine Railway to link the upriver port of Rosario with inland Córdoba. In addition to these projects, Bartolomé Mitre was able in 1862 to assist José María Gutiérrez in founding the newspaper *La Nación Argentina*, shortly to become the official news organ during his presidency.

Fortunately for the historian an excellent contemporary portrait of President Mitre has been preserved. The following description of him appeared in *The Buenos Aires Standard* of December 13, 1866:

> General Mitre is a man of talent, a good politician, and one of the finest generals from Mexico to Cape Horn. He is negligent of dress, but of strict morals, and full of a sense of justice, whilst partaking of the character of a stoic, and brave beyond a parallel. Like Numa of old, he is very reserved, but affable to all who ap-

proach him. The Grecians would have banished him like Aristides, and he would have accepted his fate without a murmur. He has a childish faith in his lucky star, and sustains reverses with the utmost serenity. His countenance has neither movement nor expression, but resembles that of a statue, whilst the mind within is untiring and enterprising. He is sparing of words and flattery, but his heart is in the right place, and he never forgets a kindness or service done him. Upright and honest, he is little suited for the present age of deceit, treachery, swindling, falsehood, and other vices that are a passport to high positions. He is, no doubt, destined one day to become a prey to the wolves that surround him. He is passionately attached to his family, his studies, his country, and the cause of human freedom. With sword and pen, in the tented field and as a journalist, he has ever warmly espoused the cause of liberty, and progress, with all the faith of an apostle. During his administration of the last six years, the Argentine people have enjoyed the freest exercise of their rights. He is a good ruler, but would make a bad dictator.[35]

When this pen portrait was written, Mitre's lucky star was about to experience a sudden descent.

VENANCIO FLORES

General Venancio Flores is often regarded in history as the last of Uruguay's most famous gaucho caudillo leaders. A product of the Artigas, Rivera, Oribe era, he sought to achieve complete victory over his nation's Blanco party and, as leader of the Colorado party, to make himself Uruguay's president. Early in 1865 he attained this goal with the assistance of armed support from Brazil as well as less-formal support from President Mitre at Buenos Aires.[36] After a brief but violent intervention into Uruguayan affairs, Brazil's Imperial Government recognized Provisional President Venancio Flores in the peace negotiations at Villa de Unión on February 20, 1865.

The new provisional president's activities were almost immediately to be wholly concerned with the Paraguayan War. A true gaucho chieftain possessing a bare minimum of what might have then been called military training, Venancio Flores personally led his nation's contingent against Paraguay. His informal dress and relations with his men caused him to be known affectionately among his troops as "el cabo viejo" (the old corporal).[37] He is still remembered among Uruguay's foremost national heroes.[38]

None of the contemporary British observers during the war left a description of General Flores. American minister Washburn, however, included a brief portrait of him in his memoirs. Though obviously biased, the details presented by Washburn are nevertheless of historical interest:

The leader of the small band of gauchos that in 1863 invaded the Banda Oriental with the avowed object of overthrowing the established government was one Venancio Flores. He had been long known as a leader of gauchos, or caudillo. He was of mixed blood, the Indian predominating over the Spanish. Inferior in natural parts to Artigas, he was nevertheless distinguished for all the bad qualities of that famous freebooter. Of iron frame and tireless activity, the wild life of the gaucho was, in his opinion, the perfection of human happiness. Crafty, cruel, and ignorant, all his tastes and instincts found free indulgence as a leader of banditti. The luxuries and comforts of civilized life were things which he could not appreciate.[39]

In late 1866 disturbed political conditions at Montevideo forced Venancio Flores to leave the war front. As the culmination of alleged plotting stemming from a temporary combination of Blanco party leaders and conservatives aimed at the expulsion of the victorious Colorados, Flores was brutally assassinated on February 19. The circumstances of his funeral were somewhat unusual. According to Captain Richard F. Burton, the embalming estimate of 100 pounds sterling presented by a regular practitioner was thought exorbitant, and the corpse, now becoming decomposed, was given to an Italian taxidermist specializing in the mounting of birds. This artist was reported to have performed his work by sewing the collar of a uniform around the neck of the corpse, the face having still retained a reasonable semblance of conservation.[40]

General Urquiza

Though events were to preclude the active participation of Justo José de Urquiza in the Paraguayan War, a survey of the prominent figures of the period would be incomplete without appropriate reference to him. Histories of La Plata may never arrive at a definitely persuasive conclusion regarding the relative merits of Urquiza and Mitre. Both men are held to have sought order and liberty for Argentina; Urquiza believed order to be more important than liberty, while Mitre was prepared to sacrifice order for liberty. While final judgment is still wanting, supporters of Mitre believe his role to have been of greater significance, particularly when account is taken of literary efforts in addition to military and political skills.[41]

Following his defeat at Pavón, General Urquiza retired from active participation in Argentine politics. His previous domination of the Argentine scene, however, together with the adulation he continued to enjoy on the part of his loyal Enterriano gauchos, still made him a prominent figure in La Plata. His latent hostility toward Buenos Aires and Mitre, moreover, and his seemingly excellent relationship with the new president of Paraguay were factors of definite importance to the formulation of the policies to be adopted by the new constitutional government at Buenos Aires. A cornerstone of Mitre's diplomacy in early 1865 was the effort to convince Urquiza of the need to maintain Argentine solidarity at all costs. Mitre's success in this effort stands among his most striking achievements, but it is equally a reflection of Urquiza's intelligence and dedication.

Early in the war years, Her Britanic Majesty's consul at Rosario, Thomas J. Hutchinson, visited Urquiza at his San José palace. Consul Hutchinson's portrait of the "Vencedor de Monte Caseros" proved memorable:

General Urquiza, although a man of 65 years, is still hale and hearty, as well as most active in habits, and equally temperate in living. He never smokes, nor drinks any kind of spiritous liquor. The portrait in his general's uniform, one of which is published with Baron du Graty's work on the Argentine Confederation, bears no more resemblance to him than I to Hercules. His nose is slightly aquiline, and his face has a combined expression of vigour, energy, and decision. This is marked most characteristically about his mouth. The eyes, although gray, and therefore deficient in semblance of vivacity, seem as if they had the faculty of reading the thoughts of anyone with whom he is conversing, although he seldom keeps them for more than a second in any fixed position of regard. His hair is black, with no tinge of the white of old age; but it is becoming thin on the top of his head, and he keeps it arranged in such an artistic style as to conceal the small patch of baldness. He is in appearance the very beau ideal of an English gentleman farmer, as he walks about, dressed in summer-time with a suit of white jean, and a black hat that is allowed to incline rather jauntily to the back of his head.[42]

Chapter 4

ARMS AND ARMIES

ONE OF THE MOST hotly debated issues of the Paraguayan War has revolved around the status of military preparedness of the participating nations at the time of the war's outbreak. On the one hand, several historians and commentators have supported the view that Paraguay in 1864 was a miniature Prussia possessing a gigantic army trained to perfection and equipped with the ultimate in the world's firearms.[1] Representatives of this school have likened the Paraguay of Francisco Solano López to the Prussia of Kaiser Wilhelm II in 1914 and have not hesitated to compare the war's early events with the German invasion and treatment of Belgium. A few historians, on the other hand, perhaps more devoted to the precepts of research, have given minute attention to the problem particularly from the standpoint of the military histories of the countries involved, and have arrived at a different conclusion.[2]

Paraguay

During the era of Dr. Francia the maintenance of a strong army was not essential for the support of the government nor for the support of the nation's foreign policy. Still largely isolated from the outside world both by geography and by the deliberate policies sponsored by El Supremo, Paraguay had little need of a large military establishment. The standing army during these times was thus small. From the few travelers' accounts available, it appears that the army was more a plaything subject to the whims of El Supremo than a defensive force. It was Dr. Francia's custom, for example, to dole out cartridges carefully before any exercise and to count the remainder upon the return of the troops to their barracks. He also took a personal hand in their training.[3]

With Paraguay's population wholly subservient to his will, Dr. Francia had no great need for an army to protect his domestic policies. Since he had sealed the nation's borders against foreign trade and had issued severe instructions against the entry or departure of foreigners, there was scant reason for the maintenance of either an offensive or defensive force. In addition, the chaotic conditions prevailing in the neighboring Argentine provinces were such as to diminish any fears of further Argentine attempts to conquer Paraguay. The lesson inflicted upon the new Argentina of 1810-11 had been a sound one. General Belgrano, backed by insufficient troop strength, had been soundly defeated by Paraguayan irregulars at the Battle of Tacuarí. Unless Argentina could organize a larger army, hopes for the forcible reincorporation of Paraguay within the Argentine Confederation were meager.

Since the administration of El Ciudadano was largely a copy of that of El Supremo, there was slight need for Carlos Antonio López to alter Paraguay's military establishment. Although the previous isolationist policy was relaxed, Paraguay's domestic political situation and the relative strength of the neighboring Argentine provinces remained unchanged. The new element which appeared at this time was the attitude toward military affairs shown by the president's eldest son, Francisco Solano.

Through his Corrientes experiences in aid of General Paz and as a result of his new interest in military affairs, Francisco Solano López became convinced that a sound defensive force would best promote his nation's interests in the light of possible future delicate border delimitation problems with both Brazil and Argentina. In a display of astute foresight, President Carlos Antonio López requested Brazil's Imperial Government in 1851 for the assignment of instructors to train Paraguay's army. In particular, he is reported to have desired specially trained officers with previous experience in the Plata wars. In a decision which appears almost incredible in the light of subsequent events, Minister Dr. Manoel Felizardo de Souza e Melo approved the request and chose Captain Hermenegildo de Albuquerque Portocarrero and Lieutenant João Carlos de Vilagran Cabrita for the mission.[4] The former, destined to become the hero of the defense of Fort Coimbra at the opening of the Paraguayan War, presented President López with a battery of field artillery. The latter, one of the best artillery instructors and engineer officers in Brazil's army, was assigned the task of preparing specifications for the expansion and improvement of the Humaitá fortifications. Lieutenant Vilagran Cabrita remained in Paraguay until November, 1852. He was also to become one of Brazil's early war heroes.

Located about 15 miles above the confluence of the Paraná and Paraguay rivers at the site of a former Indian fortress, Humaitá was destined to achieve fame as the Sebastopol of America. Its name became known just as widely throughout Latin America as Vicksburg was known in the United States. Humaitá, an Indian word, is best translated as "the stone is now black."

Projects for the development of Paraguay's military establishment received a new and sudden thrust as the result of the 1853-54 European mission of Francisco Solano Lopez. While abroad, he negotiated contracts for two new steamers capable of adaptation to river naval warfare and made an apparently close inspection of the latest type of weapons in use among Europe's armies. According to Prussian Army Major Max von Versen, Francisco Solano was among the first observers outside of Europe who recognized the advantages of the newly developed needle rifle, forerunner of the breach-loading, bolt-action, Mauser repeating rifle adapted for center-fire cartridges.[5] Unable to obtain a contract for this type of rifle, López sought to procure weapons of the Minié type—a single-shot muzzle-loader, rifled for greater range and flatter trajectory. This model was similar to the Springfields and Enfields used by Union and Confederate troops in the American Civil War.

In this effort he was only partially successful. He managed to receive a shipment of Wittons rifles with which to equip his personal escort battalion, but his efforts to obtain Minié rifles failed.[6] He was also unable to obtain any significant park of modern artillery. At the start of the war, Paraguayan artillery was so varied in type and caliber and contained so many outmoded guns that observer Richard Burton believed López had acquired all the old smoothbores which had previously decorated Montevideo street corners as trash receptacles.[7]

From a military standpoint, by far the most important result of his European mission was Francisco López' success in obtaining the services of J. and A. Blyth, Limehouse, London, as Paraguay's general agents. Through the efforts of the Blyth firm he obtained under contract the services of competent stonemasons, sawmill operators, medical advisers, and mechanical engineers. Among those Englishmen who agreed to service in faraway Paraguay and whose names are indelibly linked with that nation's military history were William Whytehead, Lieutenant Colonel George E. Thompson, Alonzo Taylor, George F. Masterman, Dr. William Stewart, and John Watts. Their careers were marked by epochs of zenith and eclipse. Yet the value of their services to the Marshal President and especially to the people of Paraguay is clearly evident. While his later treatment of several of them cannot escape condemnation, the foresight of Francisco Solano López in providing for their employment must likewise be acknowledged.

Among these men, the figure of Colonel George Thompson stands out in particular relief. A former British Army officer with no previous military engineering training or experience, he accepted an appointment as an officer in Paraguay's army, first as a topographic engineer and later as a regular army commander. He remained steadfast to the cause of Francisco López to the last, and only surrendered his poorly equipped, exhausted Paraguayan army detachment at the last moment at Angostura when he had first assured himself that his defensive position was utterly hopeless.[8]

Much credit must also be given to William Whytehead, first director of the Arsenal at Asunción. A man who threw himself with all his energy into his task, Whytehead developed a staff of British and local Paraguayan assistants capable of casting 150-pounder Whitworth field and siege guns—a feat which has been overlooked in histories of the war. At least three of these heavy guns figured prominently in the defense of Humaitá, Angostura, and Asunción—they were called "El cristiano," "El criollo," and "El General Díaz."[9]

George F. Masterman, in his account of his Paraguayan experiences, stated that the untimely death of Whytehead in the first year of the war represented a heavy blow to the Paraguayan cause. In his opinion, the course of the war might well have been different had Francisco López been able to continue to count upon his services and advice.[10]

Another British technician who gave Paraguay's president loyal and competent service was Dr. William Stewart. A young British Army medical technician who had arrived in Paraguay penniless as a survivor of an early abortive colonization project, Dr. Stewart found favor with President López and rose in category to become chief surgeon of the Paraguayan army. Stewart remained loyal to the López cause almost to the end. Captured during the Lomas Valentinas campaign, he decided to turn against his former employer for reasons which, on the surface at least, involved his distaste for the excesses of the conspiracy period. Stewart's reputation was later to acquire some tarnish for his action during a postwar legal suit with Mrs. Lynch over the disposition of monies she claimed she had given him for safekeeping.[11]

A review of Paraguay's military strength as of early 1864 reflects the vast expansion and improvement which had occurred during the preceding ten years. Several of the achievements were no less than remarkable.[12] With the aid of his British technicians, General López had succeeded in renovating Paraguay's arsenal to the point that it could now construct naval vessels of up to 280 feet in length, as well as cannon and ammunition. An iron foundry at Ibicuí, to the east of Asunción, was expanded for the production of raw materials for the arsenal, and efforts had been made to seek local sources for sulphur needed for the production of gunpowder. Large military camps were in existence, the principal one being at Cerro León at the terminus of the newly constructed railroad. On becoming president, Francisco López frequently spent half his time at this base. British physicians assigned to the army were amazed at the rigid discipline of the training program and privately expressed worries that it was too severe.[13] Mindful of the benefits of education, Paraguay's new president also devised training programs which made every sergeant a tutor responsible for the elementary education of members of his platoon.[14]

ARMY ORGANIZATION AND CHARACTERISTICS

In late 1864 the Paraguayan army was variously estimated in size from 50,000 to 100,000 men, with the former probably being more correct on the basis of the national population.[15] While it had received some military training, it could scarcely be classed as it has by many writers as the most modern military power in South America. Lacking competent military professionals with the exception of a few foreign advisers, it was mainly armed with outmoded muskets and the dregs of discarded European artillery. None of the army ranks wore shoes, and supplies in the later war years were either poor; locally made substitutes, or captured material.[16]

The army was organized on the old Spanish system and obeyed the Spanish ordinances. It was composed of 48 battalions, each with a complement of approximately 1,000 officers and men. The famous 40th Battalion, for example, recruited from the population of Asunción and trained by former chief of police José Díaz, was 1,050 strong at the war's outbreak.[17] The total infantry force in 1864 could therefore be closely estimated at about 50,000. With the addition of about 5,000 cavalry and artillerymen, and an estimated 2,000 officers and men of the navy, Paraguay's original overall military strength was approximately 57,000. Captain Burton estimated that Paraguay's effective manpower, covering the age bracket 12 to 60 years, was 150,000 on the basis of a 450,000 population. His pen-portrait of the typical Paraguayan soldier is worthy of quotation:[18]

The figure is somewhat short and stout, but well put together, with neat, shapely, and remarkably small extremities. The brachycephalic head is covered with a long straight curtain of blue-black hair, whilst the beard and mustachios are rare, except in case of mixed breeds. The face is full, flat, and circular; the cheekbones are high, and laterally salient; the forehead is low, remarkably contrasting with the broad, long, heavy, and highly developed chin; and the eyes are often oblique, being raised at the exterior canthi, with light or dark-brown pupils, well-marked eyebrows, and long, full, and curling lashes.

Burton added that this man's arm was better than his head, and that, significantly, he despised pain.[18]

The reservoir of manpower referred only to the population which was considered as "hispanicized," or the racial stock which stemmed from the blending since colonial times of the Spanish and Guaraní-speaking Indian races. Pure Indians were a rarity in the army. In 1864, as in modern days, the surviving Indian tribes were confined to the Chaco or to sparsely settled areas in the heavily forested regions of extreme eastern and northern Paraguay. Likewise, the small Negro population immediately to the north of Asunción apparently contributed few conscripts to the army. Colonel Thompson reported that to his knowledge only one Negro soldier was commissioned from the ranks. This man, however, was a specialist in the grim technique of dispatching unwary allied scouts and sentries; on one occasion he returned from a foray with a sack of severed heads.[19]

Paraguayan soldiers in 1864 wore uniforms which consisted of a white shirt and drawers, white cotton or wool trousers, a scarlet-colored type of military blouse with black or blue facings, over which were worn white waist belts and shoulder belts holding the cartridge box. The distinguishing feature of the uniform was the hat or cap. This item was described as comparable to the undress cap of the French Imperial Guard. It had a peak, however, and was either black with red facings or red with black facings. Since none of the ranks were permitted to wear shoes, young men from prominent Asunción families were forced to go barefooted upon their enlistment. As in the case of the French army of that era, all officers were promoted from the ranks. As uniform replacement supplies became nonexistent during the war, the original uniforms of Paraguay's infantry were to give way to the use of *chiripás*, rough leather breechclouts, or any rags or other material which became available. An effort was made, however, to keep the higher ranking officers and the files of the escort battalion dressed in the traditional red blouses with blue collars and white trousers.[20]

Army pay, according to Colonel Thompson, was nominally $7 monthly for a private soldier. This pay was customarily received only every two months. A third was paid in silver, another third in paper money, and the remainder in goods which the soldiers were permitted to choose from a government store maintained for that purpose. The army received no pay once the war commenced. Marshal López, however, approved three "gratifications" during the war, each reported as being equal to about a month's pay.[21]

Discipline was carefully preserved among the ranks. Colonel Thompson considered the Paraguayan soldiers as the most respectful and obedient men imaginable. From the privates upward, all ranks and officers were taught to show immediate respect to their superiors. The common salute was that of coming to stiff attention with one's cap in hand. Superiors never returned the salute. Desertion, dereliction of duty, cowardice, even retreat in the face of overwhelming enemy forces, were acts which brought frequently severe punishment upon offenders under the terms of the old Spanish ordinances. Soldiers were expected to reflect unswerving loyalty, and a security system was devised whereby each man literally was expected to keep an eye upon his companion.[22]

Small Arms and Artillery

The character of the firearms with which the army was equipped was varied indeed. The 250 men of the government escort were armed with Turner breech-loading carbines, while the regiment of escort dragoons had muzzle-loading rifled carbines. Only three infantry battalions were equipped with Wittons rifles. An additional three or four battalions possessed percussion rifles. The remainder were armed with old flintlock Brown Besses bearing the Tower of London mark. The Conde d'Eu at the Siege of Uruguaiana, for example, observed that all the rifles and carbines carried by Paraguayan infantrymen were old flintlocks.[23] Prussian observer Max von Versen also noted many old-style German muskets bearing the marks of Potsdam, Suhl, and Danzig.[24] Infantrymen wore no sidearms except their bayonets, for which they had no scabbards.[25]

The army's artillery park consisted of from 300 to 400 cannon of all sizes and calibers. Most of them were described as old honeycombed iron guns which may have been used by ships for ballast and later sold to the government of Paraguay. In a comment regarding them which closely paralleled the opinion of Captain Burton, Colonel Thompson described the artillery as being like the guns which did duty as posts on London's Woolwich Common.[26] After the fall of Humaitá, Captain Burton noted on the earthworks two Paraguayan guns which had been cast at Seville—one was named "San Gabriel" and bore the date of 1671; the other was named "San Juan de Dios" and was dated 1684. At Uruguaiana the Conde d'Eu reported that all five of the captured Paraguayan cannon were old and inferior: one had been cast at Barcelona in 1788, another at Douai in 1790, and a third at Seville in 1679![27]

Elite Units

The most striking unit appearing in the Paraguayan army was the president's personal guard regiment. It was referred to as the "acá-carayá" (monkey-heads), since its members wore leather helmets faced with brass, on the top edge of which was sewn a black monkey's tail. Further decoration was provided by a long black horsetail which hung down behind from the helmet to the waist. Other notable units were the "acá-morotí" (white heads)—a crack cavalry regiment using white horses; and the "acá-verá" (shining heads)—the brass-capped escort regiment of Marshal López[28] Among the infantry battalions, an outstanding unit was the 40th—Asunción's Own"—recruited from among *los dandys* of the capital city. The 40th saw more fighting during the war than any other unit. Five times it was almost completely annihilated, but each time it was reorganized as much as possible with new recruits from Asunción.[29] Its losses were so heavy in the early battles as to lead some observers to believe that the flower of the Spanish race in Paraguay had been obliterated.[30]

The navy in late 1864 consisted of 17 small vessels of varying sizes, all of them designed for passenger service, with the exception of the "Anhambay" and "Tacuarí," which had been especially constructed for conversion into gunboats. It was under the command of Captain Pedro Ignacio Mesa, an officer with no previous experience in naval warfare. Similarly, the entire navy itself had never been tested under combat conditions. During 1864 and as late as October, 1865, President López maintained hopes that it might be possible to have new ironclads constructed in Europe for his navy. He was especially interested in a monitor-type ironclad equipped with two turrets and mounting heavy Krupp-made cannon, a model which, if it had been constructed, would indeed have produced a sensation in La Plata.[31] Inability to obtain financing caused these projects to be cancelled, and Brazil was subsequently able to arrange for the purchase of the ironclads.[32]

Paraguay's military strength at the outbreak of the war was concentrated at the extreme ends of an approximate 250-mile arc which faced westward. This arc ran from its eastern extremity at the major Cerro León military base along the 60 miles of single-track railway past Lake Ypacaraí to Asunción. From the capital the arc swept south about 200 miles to its other extremity at Humaitá, the anchor of the defensive system. Communications between the capital and Humaitá were maintained both by river vessel along the Paraguay River and by the newly constructed telegraph line. Thus President López, when he moved to the war's theater, was able to maintain dependable connections with the capital until the last stages of the Humaitá siege. Overland travel between the capital and the fortress was practically impossible. On the east bank of the Paraguay, the land topography assumed a flat, swampy aspect shortly below the small river port of Villeta. Though trails passed through this zone, all travel was halted during the period of heaviest rains, when the terrain became transformed into one gigantic morass. Further to the east lay the extensive, low-lying, swampy region known as Lake Ypoa. Along the west bank of the Paraguay River, stretching from the Bermejo River northward past Asunción, lay the mysterious and almost impenetrable thickets, jungles, and swamps of the Chaco's river border.

Several innovations were under study or were being improved by foreign technicians in Paraguay's army in 1864. The telegraph, in effective operation and already proving itself a tremendous asset to Paraguay's president, was being operated and maintained by an energetic and resourceful German engineer named Fischer von Truenfeldt.[33] At Asunción an American inventor named Kruger, whose origin and previous career are still obscure, was engaged in experiments with river mines and torpedoes.[34] Also probably at Asunción, another German technician almost wholly overlooked by history, had commenced experiments to develop a multiple Congréve rocket launcher, later to be a device which sobered Brazilian inspectors for its advanced design and efficiency. Captured records were to show that this man was Wilhelm Wagener, a professional armorer whose services were contracted for by Paraguay on January 5, 1864.[35] The ingenuity of these technicians, coupled with the alert and resourceful mind of Paraguay's Marshal President, were destined to cause the future allies both problems and anxiety.

The most highly effective weapon of Paraguay's army was the universal belief on the part of its soldiers that each of them was more than a match for a dozen of their adversaries. Together with this intense pride, the Paraguayan soldiers reflected a fanatic loyalty to the person of their Marshal President and, especially after the terms of the Triple Alliance Treaty became known, an intense devotion to the cause of preserving the sovereignty of their nation.[36]

EXPERIENCE AND TRADITIONS

Francisco Solano López had no reservoir of trained, professional officers from which to draw the leadership of his army. Paraguay in 1864 had no formal military school for officers such as Brazil's Escola Militar at Rio de Janeiro. Likewise, the army possessed no strong military traditions or history similar to those of Brazil's Imperial Army, which stemmed from the constant Cisplatine revolts and wars, and which included such famed battles as those of Ituzaingó in 1827 and Monte Caseros in 1852. The only military exploit which Paraguay's army could point to was the 1811 repulse of Belgrano's Argentine invasion force, an episode now long-dimmed by time.

THE GENERALS

For the defense of Paraguay and the direction of its army, no one had demonstrated either talents or experience comparable to those of President López.

In 1864, now at the prime of life at the age of 38, López faced clearly the most momentous and challenging phase of his career. An appraisal of his qualifications and ability as a soldier shows that they closely paralleled those which were characteristic of him as Paraguay's chief diplomatic agent. He had never received the benefit of formal military instruction, either in Paraguay or abroad, nor did his private studies exceed the level of his avid reading of Napoleon's life and times. His first taste of military life came with his participation in the early Corrientes campaign. Perhaps his next close contact with military affairs came during his European mission when he may have had opportunity to observe the return of French army units from the Crimea. Subsequently, in 1859, he was able to observe and to guage Argentine military capacity during and after the Battle of Cepeda.

The defects of a lack of training and experience in military affairs were, in the case of Francisco Solano López, considerably balanced by his attributes of cunning resourcefulness, stolid determination, and dedication to his cause. Among other factors which made him a formidable general were his knowledge of the terrain in Paraguay, his willingness to accept the advice of foreign technicians, particularly from Colonel Thompson, and the loyalty shown to him by his men. On balance, while he has frequently been classed as a military leader whose grievous blunders led to the extermination of his army, his record in the Paraguayan War was more than favorable when compared to the efforts of the allied commanders. At least one allied officer who was to attain prominence after the war was impressed by López' ability. In a discussion with a fellow officer, Floriano Peixoto reportedly commented, "De um homen daqueles é que nos carecemos no Brasil" (What we lack in Brazil is a man like that).[37]

With but few exceptions, Paraguay's officer corps was composed of men who had little or no native ability or capacity to grasp military strategy and tactics. They had received experience in the training of troops at the military base at Cerro León, but they had yet to face trial under enemy fire. Perhaps the only soldiers who were to develop abilities which could be compared to those of the Civil War's Stonewall Jackson, Bedford Forrest, and John B. Gordon, were generals José Díaz and Francisco Isidoro Resquín, and a group of junior officers including Bernardino Caballero and Juan C. Centurión.[38] General Díaz, for example, possessed a native genius for warfare which made him López' right hand in the early battles before Humaitá. However, he lacked both advanced education and formal training. His untimely death on February 7, 1867, from a mortal wound received during a river reconnaisance partol, represented as severe a loss to Francisco Solano López, both on personal and official grounds, as that of the death of Stonewall Jackson at Chancellorsville to General Lee.[39]

Brazil

The many historians who have expressed partiality and the few who have sought to be impartial have generally assigned Imperial Brazil a role stressing the benign, peace-loving traits of its monarch and the devotion on the part of its administrators to the settlement of disputes by peaceful means. So strong has this tendency been in historical writings that Brazil often assumes the appearance of a peaceful nation dedicated to the supremacy of the civil branch over the military. While more than sufficient grounds exist to justify such an appraisal, it would be an error closely bordering on injustice to overlook the role played by the military and the traditions which have stemmed from this role. Even a brief survey of the nineteenth century indicates that the armed forces in that period, by their devotion to their monarch and to their honor, stimulated a spirit of proud nationalism which aided materially in the development of modern Brazil.

DEVELOPMENT OF THE ARMY

Dating from the period of the Dutch expulsion from Recife, the all-black fighting battalions of the "Caçadores Henriques" had become nearly a legend in Brazilian military annals.[40] Subsequently, at the close of the colonial period, the old provincial *terços,* or thirds, of regiments were substituted by the formation of a regular army. Composed mostly of Portuguese regulars under General Lecor rather than of provincial conscripts, the army built a fighting record for itself during the Cisplatine operations against José Artigas. In the late 1820's, under Felisberto Caldeira Brant Pontes, Marquês de Barbacena, it again showed its combat ability on the field of Ituzaingó. Known in Brazil as the Battle of Passo do Rosário, this action on February 20, 1827, was held as an Argentine victory.[41]

Defeated by superior forces, Barbacena's troops retired in good order. They made a note of the setback of Passo do Rosário which the army was to redeem later at Monte Caseros against Juan Manuel de Rosas. Among the young officers under Barbacena's command there were three whose names were to figure among Brazil's greatest heroes: Manoel Marques de Souza, Manoel Luís Osório, and Emilio Luís Mallet. Mallet, a 25-year-old Frenchman, assumed command of four artillery batteries after their commanders had been wounded. Barbacena promoted him on the field of battle to the rank of captain.[42] In writing later of his defeat, Barbacena remarked bitterly on the foreign mercenaries in his army, whom he felt to have been inferior and almost physically incapacitated soldiers.[43] Emilio Mallet was definitely an exception.

Though the peace with Argentina of 1828 and the appearance of independent Uruguay tended to relegate the army to the background, the several minor revolts of the 1830-40 period and the ten-year Farroupo Rebellion provided periodic activity for the forces. The importance of the constant skirmishing and guerilla warfare in the Rio Grande do Sul from 1835 to 1845 is shown by the circumstance that nearly all of the empire's generals in the Paraguayan War received their baptism in campaign life while fighting either for or against the Farroupilhas. Prominent among them was Luís Alves de Lima e Silva, later the Duque de Caxias. As the trusted and thoroughly loyal supporter of the empire, the Barão de Caxias squelched the abortive República de Piratini; yet he negotiated a peace pact at Poncho Verde which was both just and honorable for the defeated Farroupo leaders. Caxias' wise and diplomatic action guaranteed active support for Dom Pedro by the former Farroupo generals when war broke out with Paraguay.[44]

With the conclusion of the Farroupo Rebellion, the army experienced a six-year period of inactivity. A reorganization occurred which included the release and repatriation of many of the mercenary troops and the retirement of the commissions of most foreign-born officers. The earlier law of November 24, 1830, for example, had resulted in the retirement of the Ituzaingó hero Emilio Mallet.[45]

In 1851 the call to arms against Juan Manuel de Rosas again sent the army on active campaign. On this occasion, under the command of Caxias, now Brazil's most experienced soldier, the stain of Ituzaingó was fully removed from the green and gold colors of the empire. At Monte Caseros, Caxias' lieutenant, Manoel Marques de Souza, commanded a Brazilian expeditionary force which, with Urquiza's gauchos, soundly defeated the army of Rosas.

Traditions and Experience

Brazil's Imperial Army, therefore, could in 1864 justly lay claim to a substantial record of active campaigning and battle experience. Among its files were many an officer and infantryman who had learned to greet the whistle of an enemy ball with the ringing cheer of "Viva Dom Pedro Segundo!" During many skirmishes and endless marching, the essential elements of pride and tradition had been born. Such names as that of the 2d Battalion—"Dois de Ouro," the 12th Battalion—"Trema Terra," and the 16th Battalion—"O Glorioso," had not been earned through barracks life alone.[46]

The Army in 1864

On the eve of the Paraguayan War, Imperial Brazil's population of some 9 million was served by a small standing army of 16,834 effectives, with a reserve of an estimated 200,000 members of a *Guarda Nacional* semipolice force scattered among the provinces.[47]

The regular army, divided into 22 battalions of about 800 men each, was almost wholly on station in Rio Grande do Sul and along the Uruguayan frontier. In composition, this force was heterogeneous. While the small cavalry force, organized mainly from the Portuguese and foreign settlements of Rio Grande, was of white racial stock, the bulk of the infantry was composed of mestizos, mulattoes, and Negroes from the empire's lower class and slave population segments.[48] Through inactivity and a decline in morale among the officer corps for which long delays in promotion may have been a factor, organizational efficiency had suffered and the army had become accustomed to quiet garrison-post life. Some officers had yet to learn how to mount a horse.[49]

RECRUITMENT

The racial composition of the Imperial Army, with its sharp emphasis on *gente de côr*, is believed to have reflected directly the effects of the primitive and often harsh methods of recruitment which were then in practice.[50] In the 1830's, at the commencement of the reign of Dom Pedro and during the contests with Argentina over Uruguay's status, the backbone of Brazil's army had consisted of holdover ex-Portuguese regulars and of mercenaries. The bulk of the army, however, comprised either members of the militia or "recruits" who were enlisted by the simple expedient of seizing all males of military age found in city streets after a specified curfew who could not offer satisfactory reasons why they should not be detained. Those compelled to perform military duty were required to serve 16 consecutive years. If they appeared for service voluntarily, however, the time was cut in half. Sons of upper-class families, or "filhos de gente de haveres," were called "semestreiros" (six-month men), since they were required to serve only six months during the first year and only three months a year during the following seven years.[51]

Subsequently, in 1837, a more complicated and ingenious method of recruiting came into general use. Under the terms of a government decree of October 13, 1837, officers were to be given a bonus of four milreis in currency for every "recruit" they were able to bring in. Recruits who felt little inclined to serve in the army were to be allowed to pay a tax of 400 milreis and to send a slave in their stead. This practice, according to Brazilian military historian Lieutenant Colonel Lima Figueiredo, was responsible for the fact that the composition of Brazilian infantry battalions was almost exclusively of mulattos and Negroes.[52]

Such methods of recruiting, with some variations demanded by wartime necessities, continued to be the principal means for the supply of soldiers to the army until late in the empire period. In 1874 a decree was approved which, on paper, provided for recruitment by the more humane and democratic "lottery," or draft system. The lottery method, however, never actually became wholly operative until after the republic was born.[53]

The inquisitive student is inclined to wonder how, with such a foundation, Brazil's army managed to put down the violent Farroupo revolts of the 1830's, and how it managed to win a victory against Argentina's Rosas in 1852. Perhaps the answer was Brazil's competent, well-trained professional officer corps. These men, almost exclusively of the upper wealthy white class, were usually products of the Escola Militar at Rio de Janeiro, a government military academy to which the sons of well-to-do families seem to have been much attracted. The school graduated two classes of general staff officers: those of the first class included students who had successfully passed all tests and who were certified for regular army duty; those of the second class comprised inferior students who were assigned to the reserve. In commenting upon the efficiency of these officers, Lima Figueiredo stated that some observers believed that their level of training, on a world-wide comparative basis, was exceeded only in Prussia.[54] The major complaint of the officer corps in the pre-Paraguayan War era concerned the extreme slowness of promotions, a circumstance attributed to Dom Pedro's lack of interest in the army.

ORGANIZATION

Since 1851 the national territory of the empire had been divided for military purposes into six districts. Plans for the distribution of the army within the national territory called for the assignment in each of these districts of *côrpos especiais* (special corps) and *côrpos combatentes* (combat corps), the latter composed of infantry, cavalry, and artillery units, and being divided into *côrpos moveis* (mobile corps) and *côrpos fixos* or *guarnição* (garrison corps).[55] Because of the almost constant troubles in Rio Grande do Sul and along the Uruguayan border, the army, as previously indicated, had largely been transferred to the south. In addition to the infantry battalions, the army in the 1850's possessed four regiments of cavalry, one regiment of horse artillery, and four battalions of foot artillery.[56]

In view of the lack of communications facilities except by coastwise shipping, many families accompanied the regular army to its garrison posts in Rio Grande do Sul. This social movement represented a principal factor in the establishment of many urban centers including Bagé, Alegrete, Santa Maria, Cachoeira, and Rio Pardo.[57]

Formal regulations for the organization and combat procedures of the army were adapted from European systems. As of October, 1850, infantry regulations were patterned after those developed by a Portuguese officer named Bernardo Antônio Zazalo, cavalry regulations followed those developed by British Marshal Beresford in Portugal, and artillery organization followed the procedures of the French Royal Guard.[58]

All three branches of the army were greatly expanded following the war's outbreak. In particular, the artillery was reorganized and given a more prominent role as new, more effective cannon were obtained. With the war's progress new engineering and supply units were added to the army's organization, improvements which were due largely to the initiative of the Marquês de Caxias.

Armament

With the exception of some important innovations in infantry weapons and certain artillery types, the armament used by the Imperial Army in its three foreign wars was practically the same.[59]

During the period of the 1851-52 campaigns in Uruguay and Argentina against Oribe and Rosas, Brazilian infantry still carried caliber 17 flintlocks which threw a round lead ball weighing 30 grams. The weight of the rifle was 4.600 kilograms, and its length with bayonet was 1.935 meters. The small artillery park consisted mainly of 12-pounders, smoothbored, using black powder and shooting solid round shot. Artillery fire was either of direct, plunging, or ricochet type. Maximum artillery range was about 1,500 meters.[60]

The first major innovation in firearms was the use by a company of Schleswig-Holstein mercenary sharpshooters, during the 1852 Monte Caseros campaign, of Prussian-made model 1841 Dreise needle rifles, breech-loading type.[61] Subsequently, in 1855, the Imperial Army received its first shipment of 1,200 rifles and 1,000 carbines of the Minié type, which had been ordered from Belgium. These rifles, muzzle-loaders of 16 mm. caliber, had rifled bores and used percussion caps instead of the old flintlock device. By the outbreak of the Paraguayan War, these original rifles were being supplemented by newer type Minié rifles of 14.80 mm. caliber and Enfields, both British and Belgian make, of 14.66 mm. caliber. These latter rifles were similar to those in use during the American Civil War. They were capable of a rate of fire equal to two shots per minute—a considerable improvement over the old flintlocks, and a feature outmoding the use of the old-style mass bayonet charge.

The confusion among infantrymen which obviously resulted from the employment of a variety of calibers was compounded by a decision by the Brazilian War Ministry to manufacture only 14.66 mm. ammunition. Infantrymen using 14.80 mm. rifles thus were often startled to see their fire practically trickling out the barrel of the rifle, due to decreased muzzle velocity. This defect was corrected early in the war by further modifications in ammunition and withdrawal from service of weapons which could not be adjusted to a standard caliber.[62]

As the Paraguayan War progressed, both Prussian needle rifles and American breech-loading carbines appeared among Brazilian army units. The Prussian guns, the Dreise model 1857, were used during the last years of the war, particularly in the final actions in the envelopment of the fortress of Humaitá. The 15th Regular Battalion, for example, used them at the taking of the Ciervo or Estabelecimento redoubt.[63] For some reason, possibly because of the high incidence of misfires, the model was later withdrawn in favor of the standard muzzle-loading Enfield.[64] In commenting upon this type of weapon in his letter of August 7, 1866 to the Condessa de Barral, Dom Pedro noted that he had been acquainted with them for a number of years but that he did not think they would prove valuable to Prussia in its war with Austria since, as he put it, they were both extremely heavy and required well-trained soldiers in their use and maintenance.[65]

According to military historian Lima Figueiredo, a Brazilian purchasing commission went to the United States late in the war and obtained 5,000 Roberts-type rifles and 2,000 Spencer repeating seven-shot .50 caliber carbines. The same source indicated that the commission failed to obtain a type of cartridge which would enter perfectly into the breech of these weapons, and therefore, that they were not fully satisfactory.[66] Considerable controversy developed after the war over the question whether breech-loading rifles and carbines had actually been used by the Brazilian forces. Eyewitness accounts by Captain Richard F. Burton and Brazilian Major E. A. da Cunha Mattos, as well as the existence even today of metallic cartridge cases on battlefield sites, leave no doubt regarding the use of such arms.[67]

Side arms used by the Brazilian army included triangular- and

"T"-type bayonets, lances, short swords, 14 mm. caliber cap and ball pistols, and Colt and Lefaucheaux revolvers of 10.7 and 10.8 mm. respectively.[68]

Artillery

As a result of the practical training given to officers through the efforts of Field Marshal Francisco de Paula Vasconcelos and his Commission for the Improvement of Army Equipment, established in December, 1849, as well as the presence of such artillery experts as Emilio Mallet, now reinstated to duty, the army's artillery park had been revamped by 1865. Though many old and potentially dangerous guns were still in service, artillery units had been given a number of modern La Hitte, Paixhans, and Whitworth rifled muzzle-loaders of calibers from 90 to 120 mm. The La Hitte rifled guns were of 4.6 and 12 caliber, based on weight of projectiles in kilos, and were of the type then standard in the French army. Range for these new guns varied according to caliber from 2,000 to 4,100 meters. The main pride of the reorganized artillery branch, however, were the 32-pounder Belgian-made rifled Whitworth guns, which had a maximum range of 4,389 meters.[69] They proved so efficient that Paraguayan Marshal López insisted on the capture of one late in the Humaitá defensive phase of the war so that he, too, could engage in long range target practice.

A variety of projectiles was used in artillery fire, ranging from solid spherical shot and canister to conical shells filled with black powder charges. The percentage of nonexploding shot proved high, and Paraguayan forces soon discovered that the constant heavy firing of the Brazilian artillery was a good source for replenishment of ammunition supplies.

Logistics

At the commencement of the war, the problems of logistics were serious for the Brazilian army. Concentrated in Rio Grande do Sul and Uruguay, it possessed no rail facilities for the transport of supplies and had to depend entirely on sea transport. Brazil's first railway was limited to service near Rio de Janeiro. By 1864 the total national rail network amounted only to 475 km., none of which was available for military use in the Paraguayan War. Likewise, the telegraph, which had made its Brazilian debut in 1852, had attained a total extension of only 187 km. as of 1864.

Thus, ocean transport to Montevideo and up the Uruguay River, or haulage by ox-drawn cart overland, were the only supply facilities available to the army in the war's early stages.

Fortunately for Brazil, this problem was soon resolved. With the virtual destruction of the Paraguayan fleet in the war's only major naval battle at Riachuelo, June 11, 1865, the Paraná River became available to the Imperial Army as a communications line direct to the army headquarters and supply base at the junction of the Paraná and Paraguay rivers. The Paraná, by April, 1866, had changed from a sleepy, seldom-used river to a busy artery of traffic in which the flags of all nations were to be observed. Paso la Patria and Corrientes, almost overnight, became huge Brazilian supply depots. The army's major hospital was established at the latter port. Subsequently it was moved northward as the allied invasion began to push the Paraguayan army back from its positions at Humaitá. The availability of the Paraná during most of the war was of basic importance to Brazil as a means of keeping its army fully supplied. While the river blockade gradually strangled Paraguay, the allies had the advantage of a direct supply line from Buenos Aires, Rio de Janeiro, and from both the United States and Europe.

During the four years from April, 1866, when the allies forced the crossing of the Paraná into Paraguayan territory, until March, 1870, Brazil maintained an average of about 40,000 men on campaign in Paraguay. Logistics for the supply of this force involved transport by the river of manufactured essentials and equipment from Brazil and abroad and the purchase or requisition locally of needed foodstuffs. So great was the expense involved, and so heavy was the dependence upon Argentine sources both at Buenos Aires and in Corrientes province, that Brazilian historians have suggested that during the Paraguayan War Brazil was responsible for the financial rejuvenation of Argentina. At least one has implied that Argentina may even have hoped for prolongation of the war in order to reap the maximum of financial benefit from it. "The river of gold to Buenos Aires" and "galinha de ovos de ouro" (chicken which lays golden eggs) are typical expressions found in Brazilian commentaries on this subject.[70]

Not all of the Imperial Army's local foraging for supplies was for purely logistics purposes. In late 1865 and thereafter, for example, General Osório managed to purchase about 30,000 horses from the Entre Ríos gaucho chieftain General Urquiza, an astute move which was considered to have effectively immobilized Urquiza's cavalry forces whose loyalty in the war had been of some question.[71]

Among Brazil's logistics problems the need for adequate engineering services soon became important. The Marquês de Caixas had originally organized an engineer battalion in 1851. Its services, however, were found to be in need of expansion in view of the serious obstacles to troop movements presented by the extremely swampy territory in southwestern Paraguay and the necessity for constant crossings of the Paraná and Paraguay rivers. The engineer service, therefore, was expanded to the point that it proved to be a decisive factor in the eventual Brazilian victory. Its greatest feat was the construction of an 11-km. road through the Chaco in 23-days' time, during which an estimated 6,000 palm trees had to be cut down to provide the required corduroy topping. This road enabled Caxias to outflank López in the final Lomas Valentinas campaign of late 1868.[72]

A notable lack among the technical and auxiliary services of the army proved to be the limited information concerning the geographic characteristics of Paraguay. Although Captain Portocarrero and Lieutenant Vilagran Cabrita had served on a mission to Paraguay prior to the war, no maps of the campaign area were available. Furthermore, Portocarrero was stationed in Mato Grosso at the war's outbreak, and Vilagran Cabrita was mortally wounded in one of the first general actions along the Paraná. The republic of López, therefore, was literally a land of the unknown for the Brazilian army staff planners, a circumstance which was to handicap offensive planning until the Marquês de Caixas assumed command. In contrast, the Paraguayan army benefited from the use by Marshal López of a copy of a map presented to him by Lieutenant Thomas Jefferson Page, U. S. Navy, who had prepared it on the basis of information collected during his visits to Paraguay in the 1850's.[73] Paraguay's Marshal President also utilized the efficient system of giving a name to every land feature of strategic or or tactical importance.

THE NAVY

Brazil's Imperial Navy at the outbreak of the Paraguayan War was easily the largest and most powerful naval force in Latin

America. It consisted of 45 vessels—33 steamers and 12 sailing ships. About one-third of these vessels had been constructed at the Ponta da Areia arsenal near Rio de Janeiro. Total manpower complement of this force amounted to 2,384 officers and men.[74]

The principal units of the prewar fleet according to type were: sidewheelers—the "Amazonas," "Paraense," "Recife," and "Taquarí"; propeller-type—the "Niterói" "Jequitinhonha," "Belmonte," Parnaíba," Iguatemí," "Araguarí," "Ivaí," and Ipiranga"; sailing vessels—the "Baiana; transports—the "Peperiguassu" and Iguassu." The most powerful unit was held to be the "Niterói," which, however, was equipped only with an auxiliary engine. Other major vessels were the side-wheeler "Amazonas" and the propeller-driven "Beberibe," "Jequitinhonha," and "Magé."[75]

This fleet was large and reasonably well equipped. It had one important defect, however, when viewed from the requirements which would stem from the impending war with Paraguay—it had been constructed mainly for high-seas rather than for river operations. The "Paraense" and "Recife," for example, had draughts which were disproportionately deep in relation to their artillery power and had therefore to be dispensed from active river operations. The most important fleet units which were available in 1864 for possible river operations were the gunboats of the type of the "Belmonte," "Mearim," and "Araguarí," which had been constructed in 1857-58 as a result of the empire's earlier Paraná River difficulties with the government of Carlos Antonio López.[76]

The first Brazilian ironclad to join the fleet was the "Brasil," which arrived in December, 1865. It had been purchased as a result of a popular subscription arising from the 1862 Questão de Christie with Great Britain.[77] Subsequently, as the fleet's role grew in importance with the advance to the Humaitá area, a program was undertaken for the purchase and construction of monitor-type ironclads similar to those of the Union Navy in its Mississippi operations.

Like the army, the Imperial Navy had also established a fighting tradition by 1864. During the early independence wars, under the direction of the famed Admiral Lord Cochrane, it had initiated a tradition of loyal service to the empire which grew steadily through the period of the internal revolts and Cisplatine struggles with Argentina. It had received solid battle experience in the Plata actions against the Argentine navy commanded by the resourceful Admiral William Brown. Perhaps the navy's most valuable element was its well-trained and experienced officer corps. From its earliest days, the Imperial Academia da Marinha had attracted those sons of well-to-do Brazilian families who were not inclined to enter the rival professions of politics, medicine, the army, or the priesthood. Dr. Francisco Pinheiro Guimarães, for example, later to become a prominent Rio de Janeiro surgeon and a hero among the Voluntários da Pátria officers, began his career as a navy surgeon.

At the command of Brazil's naval division assigned to the Plata stood an imposing figure—Admiral Joaquim Marques Lisboa, the Barão de Tamandaré. He was born on December 13, 1807, in the city of Rio Grande, Rio Grande do Sul. His birthday anniversary was later to be made the official "Dia do Marinheiro" (Navy Day) of Brazil's navy.[78] He is also remembered in Rio de Janeiro today by an imposing statute at Praia de Botafogo. Tamandaré, a testy seaman known for his rigorous discipline, was reported to have preferred a block of wood in place of a pillow when sleeping.[79] Impulsive in his actions during the early stages of the war, he was later criticized for alleged hesitation in attacking and attempting to pass Humaitá, and for his bitter quarrels with others of the allied high command.

Brazil's generals.—A brief focus upon Brazil's principal generals as of 1864 suggests that they were professional soldiers who indeed had acquired considerable experience through nearly a lifetime devoted to military affairs. There were four prominent men: Luís Alves de Lima e Silva, future Duque de Caxias; Manoel Luís Osório, future Marques de Herval; Manoel Marquês de Souza, future Conde de Pôrto Alegre; and General David Canabarro, former military leader of the Farroupo Rebellion.[80]

Caxias, born in Rio de Janeiro province on August 25, 1803, was 61 years old by 1864. Already acclaimed as the "pacificador" of the empire, he was destined to become immortalized as Brazil's greatest soldier. He is known today as the Patron of the Army; his birthday is commemorated as the "Dia do Soldado" (Army Day). As senator, crown counselor, provincial president, minister of state, president of the council, baron, count, viscount, and duke, Caxias was a veritable pillar of strength for the empire of Dom Pedro II. A staunch conservative and constantly loyal supporter of the emperor, Caxias was in temporary eclipse in 1864 as a result of the ascendancy of a Liberal government to power. He never suffered military defeat. Known for his ability as a strategist and organizer, his cautious yet sound planning of the final Humaitá campaign period was to spell defeat for Paraguay.

Captain Richard F. Burton drew an excellent description of Caxias on campaign in Paraguay. In 1868, the Marquês, though 65 years of age, appeared as if only 52. In features, his forehead was marked by deep traverse lines; he had stiff, gray hair; a white, bristly mustache; and his complexion though fresh and ruddy, showed a hard network of wrinkles. Burton found him tough and spare, well-knit, of moderate height, and possessing great endurance, having been known to sit his horse for twelve hours at a stretch. In the presence of visitors, he had the trick of bending his body slightly forward as though he could be seeking some sort of information.[81]

Manoel Luís Osório, considered to be second only to Caxias among Brazil's greatest soldiers, proved himself a capable tactician and noted for his aggressive fighting ability and cool courage under fire. He was a perfect complement to the strategic ability of Caxias. The most popular officer in the Brazilian army, he was also admired by both Argentine and Uruguayan officers. Osório, who was known as "O Legendário" (the Legendary), is also remembered in Brazil's army today as the Patron of the Cavalry. Born in Rio Grande do Sul in 1808, he was 56 years old at the outbreak of the Paraguayan War. He had fought at Passo do Rosário (Ituzaingó) in 1827, had risen in rank during the Farroupo era, and had commanded a Rio Grande lancer unit which captured a five-gun battery at Monte Caseros in 1852.

In his person, according to Captain Burton, Osório was a stout, portly man with "the bearing of a Rio Grande gentleman." He had gray hair and beard, his eyes were bright and young, and his handsome features reflected a "frank and kindly expression."[82]

Two postwar anecdotes are worthy of citation for their reflection of the personalities of General Osório and his emperor. During a meeting of the Council of Ministers which included Osório, Dom Pedro, never keenly attracted to military affairs, fell asleep. When Osório purposely let his sword fall with a clatter, the emperor awoke and grumbled, "O Sr. Osório tambem deixava cair sua espada nos campos do Paraguai?" (Osório, did you also let your sword drop in Paraguay?) To which Osório replied, "No

Paraguai, Magestade, o inimigo não dormia!" (In Paraguay, your Majesty, the enemy never slept!).

On another occasion Dom Pedro, always mindful of morals, was reluctant to approve the promotion of an officer rumored to be a gadabout. He is said to have commented to Osório, "Este oficial tem mão proceder. Consta-me ser por demais amigo de mulheres e andar-se metendo com as esposas de colegas" (This officer has bad habits. I am told he is attracted too greatly to women and that he has been having affairs with the wives of his colleagues). Osório quietly replied, "Se fosse por ser amigo de mulheres eu nem cabo seria. Entretanto, Magestade, sou Ministro de Guerra!" (If the question of being friendly with women had been considered, I wouldn't have even become a corporal. As it stands, however, your Majesty, I am the Minister of War!). Dom Pedro reportedly approved the officer's promotion at once.[83]

Manoel Marques de Souza achieved fame in Brazil's military history both as the "Vencedor de Monte Caseros" (Victor of Monte Caseros) and as "o Bravo de Curuzú" (the Brave One of Curuzú). Considered one of the most able corps commanders of the war, the Conde de Pôrto Alegre, like his chief Caxias, possessed a long record of military service. Born in the city of Rio Grande on June 13, 1804, he obtained parental permission to join the 1st Light Cavalry Regiment at Montevideo when he was only 13 years old. He fought both at Passo do Rosário and in the Farroupo Rebellion, during which he was imprisoned for a time by the rebel forces. Then a colonel, he was chosen by Caxias to carry the news of the peace of Poncho Verde to Dom Pedro. A general officer in 1850, he commanded Brazil's expeditionary forces at Monte Caseros against Rosas. In recognition of his services, he was promoted to the rank of field marshal and named Barão de Pôrto Alegre in March, 1852.

Pôrto Alegre retired for health reasons in 1856, but returned to active duty upon the invasion of Rio Grande do Sul by Paraguayan forces. In July, 1865, he was named commander of the army in Rio Grande do Sul. Pôrto Alegre was known among his troops for his addiction to perfection in his personal uniform. He is said to have retreated only once during his career—and then only when ordered to do so. His comment on that occasion became a tradition in Brazil's military annals: "Obedeço porque sou a isso obrigado!" (I obey because I am required to do so!).

In 1864, the defense of the northwestern frontiers of Rio

Grande do Sul—the Quarahy and Missões region—was entrusted to a small force under Brigadier General David Canabarro. Highly popular in Rio Grande do Sul, General Canabarro had achieved fame as the chieftain of the earlier Farroupo armies. Born David José Martins on August 22, 1796, he was 68 years old at the start of the Paraguayan War— possibly the oldest of Brazil's general officers on active duty. Initiated early in life to military affairs, he participated in the Uruguayan campaign of 1827, figured prominently in the Battle of Rincón de las Gallinas against Rivera, and fought against Rosas in the 1852 campaign. He changed his name to Canabarro at the outset of the Farroupo Rebellion.[84]

David Canabarro was one of the last of the great gaucho chieftains of Rio Grande do Sul. He was not destined, however, to attain further fame in the Paraguayan War. Under a cloud because of his strategic retreat in the face of superior Paraguayan forces, he was called to face a formal board of inquiry. Although his old adversary and friend, Caixas, was able to have these proceedings dismissed, and also sought to reinstate him, the blow proved heavy for the old Farroupilha leader. Embittered by the injustice he felt had been his lot, David Canabarro died on April 12, 1867.

Caxias, Osório, Pôrto Alegre, and Canabarro were by no means the only skilled, professional soldiers in positions of command in the Imperial Army of 1864. While perhaps at that time not fully at their level of experience and training, there were other officers whose names were to become bywords in Brazil's history: José Antônio Corrêa da Câmara—to become the youngest of Brazil's general officers and later the Visconde de Pelotas; Antônio Sampaio —remembered as the Patron of the Infantry; Emilio Luís Mallet— future Barão de Itapevi and Patron of the Artillery; José Joaquim de Andrade Neves—"Os Olhos das Fôrças" (eyes of the army) and future Barão do Triunfo; João Manoel Mena Barreto—a hard-riding cavalryman fated to die at Piribebuy; and Hilário Maximiano Antunes Gurjão—"O Sacrificado de Ytororó" (the martyr of Ytororó) and the most famous soldier of extreme northern Brazil.[85]

As an example of this second echelon of officers, it may be pertinent to include a brief portrait of Alexandre Gomes de Argolo. General Argolo was born in Bahía of a distinguished father. A student of tactics, he commenced the war as a major. At its end he had become a field marshal with the title of Visconde de Itaparica. In appearance, Captain Burton described him as the bird-of-rapine type." He was short, thin, small; he had a high nose, "hawk's eyes," a broad forehead, and straight hair and beard tending to gray in color. Argolo was known for his steadiness under fire and was loved by his men. He was not, however, a favorite among the Argentines. At a camp dinner, Burton reported having observed General Argolo personally feed a Brazilian private who had lost both arms in the Battle of Curupaity. Burton also noted with obvious admiration that the general had adopted a young Paraguayan boy who had been captured at the fall of Humaitá.[86]

THE YOUNG LIONS

In addition to the division, brigade, and battalion commanders, described above, who were prominent in the army in 1864, Brazil's military branch had yet another reserve upon which to draw for future leadership. This reserve comprised the students of the Escola Central and Escola Militar da Praia Vermelha at Rio de Janeiro—elite training academies frequented by the sons of many of Brazil's foremost families. Immediately prior to the war's outbreak, there were several among these students whose names were shortly to become famous. Cadet Alfredo d'Escragnolle Taunay, to become one of Brazil's greatest authors, was striving hard in early 1864 to pass his examinations in order to receive his commission as an artillery officer. A fellow student, young Floriano Peixoto, was likewise nearing the completion of his studies. Cadet Peixoto, according to Taunay, was "always mysterious and aloof," seeking to lead his life apart from the other students, and possessing an "enigmatic smile which seemed partly ironical."[87] The future Iron Marshal of Brazil was dubbed a "mitrado" (a sly-one) by his classmates for his ability to avoid scholastic duties without attracting too much attention.[88] Taunay was shortly to face the possibility that he might be assigned to an artillery unit commanded by a young captain named Manoel Deodoro da Fonseca, destined 24 years later to overthrow Dom Pedro and to become President of the Republic.

The school's director, according to Taunay, was one of the most rigid disciplinarians in the history of the institution. Comandante Polidoro da Fonseca Quintanilha Jordão, a famed corps commander in the Paraguayan War, had the custom of arriving at the school by rowboat. His approach was watched carefully by the students. If he was seen wearing white trousers the cadets could expect a rigorous day. Blue trousers worn by the commandant meant a less exacting time.[89]

SUMMING UP

Comparisons of the strengths, characteristics, training, and experience of the armies of Paraguay and Brazil as of 1864 indicate strongly that the balance was in the latter's favor. Though the empire's standing regular army was only about one-third of the size of the force which Francisco Solano López had mobilized by that year, it could look back with much pride upon a sound record of fighting experience. Moreover, Brazil's army was commanded by trained officers many of whom had become professionals by 1864. In terms of equipment that was slight difference between the two forces. Brazil, however, could count upon access to foreign sources for manufactured arms and raw supplies in the event of war, while Paraguay's sources remained subject to the maintenance of communications down the Paraná River to Buenos Aires. The advantage in superior numerical strength which might have favored Paraguay at the war's outbreak was likewise temporary in view of the overwhelmingly larger human resources upon which the empire might draw.

The one factor as yet unevaluated in 1864 concerned the *esprit de corps* of the private soldier. In this category Paraguay was to exhibit a performance scarcely equalled if not unexceeded in the record of the world's great wars.[90]

Argentina and Uruguay

With the exception of several major actions in the early war years, notably the battles of Corrales, First Tuyuty, and Curupaity, the participation of Argentine and Uruguayan armed forces in the Paraguayan War was of token proportions. The military branch of neither of the two republics was in sufficient condition to provide a sustained, heavy contribution to the cause of the Triple Alliance. After 1867 the war assumed the character of a desperate struggle to the death between only two nations—Paraguay and Brazil. In the case of both Argentina and Uruguay, the reasons for this relatively minor participation in the last stages of the war stemmed from internal political conditions.

Argentina

Argentina's armed forces in 1864 still reflected the rancor and tension of the fractricidal struggles which had kept the newly united republic in a turmoil since the end of the Rosas era in 1852. The scars of the Battle of Cepeda (1859) and of Pavón (1861) were still evident. Though the Buenos Aires of Bartolomé Mitre had temporarily won its long battle against the federalist forces of the provinces, the emotions of animosity, rivalry, loyalty to regional caudillos, and even hatred, still burned deeply in the minds of many Argentines. The Paraguayan War was about to act as a catalyzing agent in the process toward the achievement of Argentine unity. This process, however, was neither sudden in its impact nor totally embracing in its scope. It proved to be rather the major feature of an extended period of transition in La Plata's history.

Weary from constant civil warfare and severely affected by both battle losses and the devastation wrought upon their economics, the people of Argentina in 1864 were neither able nor emotionally willing to support a large army to suppress Paraguay. To many sectors of the provinces, especially those lying to the north of Buenos Aires, Francisco Solano López appeared as a local caudillo hardly different from the many heroes they had themselves championed in the *montoneras* of the 1830-60 period. Moreover, the bonds of race, language, custom, and tradition, which existed between the peoples of Paraguay and the northern provinces, formed a barrier to the stimulation of patriotic fervor along purely nationalistic lines.

Argentina's armed forces in 1864 reflected the conditioning effect of these several factors. The total size of the military at that time has been estimated as high as 30,000.[91] The figure is misleading, however, unless account is taken of internal aspects. Bartolomé Mitre, in Buenos Aires province, could count upon perhaps 10,000 to 15,000 men with which to form an army. The remainder, of about an equal number, represented the soldiers of the provinces. Their availability to the new government at Buenos Aires depended upon the whims and political beliefs of their local chieftains. If these men proved loyal to the new constitution and new government, the adherence of their armies could be counted upon. If they still nurtured resentment and suspicion of Buenos Aires, a call to the colors might generate but little response.

The army, though accustomed to battles and skirmishes, enjoyed neither the stimulation of a unified spirit or tradition such as was the case in Brazil's Imperial Army, nor the benefits of training institutions able to provide a corps of professional officers. Equipment, uniforms, and organization still reflected the same characteristics as those in evidence at the final contest between Urquiza and Mitre at Pavón.[92] The appearances of a regular army establishment were to be observed only at Buenos Aires. This nucleus, together with the availability of *Guardia Nacional* (National Guard) battalions and the yield from recruiting and conscripting efforts in the provinces, formed an army of about 8,000. The force was to be expanded to an estimated 15,000 at the start of the Paraná campaign.[93]

Only about half of the army was available for service against Paraguay. Internal political troubles during the war, coupled with the constant need in the 1860's to meet Indian incursions, required that about 4,000 men, on the average, be withheld from the Paraguayan campaign. One historian has noted that, as the war progressed, there was scarcely a day when some form of revolt or uprising was not underway in the provinces.[94] Later during the war period, provincial Senator Nicasio Oroño was to remark that from June, 1862, to June, 1868, his country had experienced 117 such revolutionary movements, which had, according to his figures, resulted in the death of 4,728 persons.[95] In sharp contrast, Captain Burton was told by Argentine officers that the army's total battle casualties as of August 24, 1868, including killed, wounded, and missing, had amounted to 2,227.[96]

Argentina's navy in 1864 had declined considerably in size and power since the era of Admiral Brown. Insignificant in number of vessels, its scant value as a fighting force was erased during the attack on the port of Corrientes at the outbreak of war. The principal units of the navy in 1864 were the armed river vessels "25 de Mayo," "Gualeguay," and "Guardia Nacional." Troop transports included the "Pavón" and Pampa."[97]

THE GENERALS

As Argentina's citizen-soldier and Hero of Pavón, the command of the armed forces, and indeed the supreme command of the allied armies, was given to Bartolomé Mitre. Though his earlier career had been that of a soldier, and though he had been tried under fire, Mitre's qualifications as field commander of a large, mixed force were not to be compared with those of some of Brazil's professional soldiers.

At the war's outbreak Bartolomé Mitre might have availed himself of the services of Justo José de Urquiza in the organization of Argentina's Army. Urquiza, still the leading personality and hero in the minds of the people of Entre Ríos and Corrientes, had more practical experience in war matters than Mitre, including the management of the allied forces which had finally defeated Juan Manuel de Rosas. The gulf between the two men, however, proved an unbridgeable one. Urquiza was allegedly offered only the "superior command" of the Entre Ríos cavalry, a role which was his in any case.[98] He preferred to play no direct part in the Paraguayan War.

While not up to the military efficiency of Brazil's professional soldiers, Argentina's general officers included men of both great ability and commanding stature. Brief portraits of two may suffice: Emilio Mitre and Juan A. Gelly y Obes. Emilio Mitre, brother of Bartolomé, was to become commander-in-chief of Argentina's forces during the final stages of the war after the fall of Asunción. Captain Burton supplied a succinct pen portrait of him. In 1869 Brigadier Mitre was seen as a tall, stout man, well known for his personal strength. His face, according to Burton, exhibited "the jovial look which often accompanies great physical force." His beard was dark and full, and his hair, though not gray, was becoming "scanty at the poll." Burton concluded that altogether General Mitre was "a prepossessing and military figure which must commend itself to the sex whose commendations he mostly values."[99]

During his trip up the Paraná River Captain Burton also found time to become acquainted with his fellow passengers, the wife and daughter of General Juan A. Gelly y Obes, previous commander of Argentina's contingent and minister of war and marine. From information thus obtained and from a later interview with the general himself, Burton learned that the general had begun life as an auctioneer and that he had been banished to Brazil in the days of Rosas. Burton found him an active and energetic man who appeared to be "the eagle type with a hooked nose, black eyes, long white beard, and waveless gray hair." In all, "a sparse and lithe veteran in magenta-colored kepi, blue frock, and long riding boots."[100] Apparently obsessed with a "mission," Gelly y Obes was later alleged to have denied his Argentine citizenship in order that he might qualify for the presidency of Paraguay on the basis of family origins. He had been born at Asunción and his father had been a secretary to Francisco Solano López.[101]

URUGUAY

As described in Chapter II, Uruguay in 1864 was suffering from a vicious civil war which was, if anything, even worse than the conditions which had prevailed in neighboring Argentina during the period of the struggles between Mitre and Urquiza. The split between the Blancos of the Berro-Aguirre governments and the Colorados of General Venancio Flores naturally encompassed the armed forces. Uruguay was a seething nation in which bloody skirmishing was an almost daily occurrence. Carried on in the customary gaucho style, such fighting was merciless—*tocando el violín* (throat-cutting) was the normal end which prisoners taken by both sides could expect.[102]

Out of such a chaotic situation, it was nigh hopeless to expect of Uruguay any important contribution of an armed force of sizable proportions to the allied war effort. The Uruguayan contingent which General Flores took with him to the Paraguayan War was estimated at about 1,500 officers and men. Only about 500 members of this force were destined to return. The outstanding unit of Uruguay's contingent was the Batallón Florida, a hard-fighting gaucho battalion commanded by Colonel León de Palleja. Killed during the battles of mid-1866, he was promoted posthumously to the rank of general.[103] A further notable Uruguayan unit was the 16th Volunteer Infantry known as the "Garibaldinos," said to be composed of men representing all racial origins to be found at Montevideo. A Brazilian officer commented somewhat caustically that it was likely the majority had never heard of Garibaldi.[104]

When Venancio Flores—"el cabo viejo"—returned to Montevideo shortly after the Battle of Curupaity in 1866, he took with him the remaining 200 survivors of the Batallón Florida. The remnants of Uruguay's contingent, now only a detachment in size, were left under the command of General Enrique Castro.[105] Captain Burton found no trace of the Uruguayan force during his visits to the war theater. Unable to describe General Castro, he confined himself to the observation that the general was said to be a "gaucho ordinario."[106]

Though their number was small, Uruguay's soldiers gave a good account of themselves in Paraguay. Their war service was recorded as being fully in keeping with the traditions of Artigas, of the famous "33," of Lavalleja and Rivera, and of the heroes of the Battles of Rincón and Sarandí.

Chapter 5

A SOUND OF GUNS

To astute observer Captain Richard F. Burton, who left so many discerning portraits of the era, the Paraguayan War was one "waged by hundreds against thousands, a battle of Brown Bess and poor old flintlocks against Spencer and Enfield rifles; of honeycombed carronades, long and short; against Whitworths and La Hittes; and of punts and canoes against ironclads."[1] In essence, it proved to be a war of earthworks and trenches standing against assaults, rather than a struggle of extended sieges and pitched battles.

In its purely military aspects the Paraguayan War could be closely compared with the American Civil War: the early enthusiams were alike, the first offensive actions were similar, the hardening stages into grim, grinding, trench warfare were comparable; the weapons and their employment were about the same, the river operations along the Paraguay suggested those of the Union fleet at Vicksburg on the Mississippi, several of the major actions of each of the wars were remarkably similar, photographs of Brazilian generals reflected but little difference from the dress and poses of Union generals, and finally, the desperate defensive efforts by Paraguay could be compared to the last bitter days of the Confederacy. While both wars featured personalities whose names became bywords among the contending armies, neither Abraham Lincoln nor Jefferson Davis may be likened in other than general terms to Dom Pedro II and Francisco Solano López. The contest between the latter two figures involved not only conflicting views on the role of government but also questions of ambition and honor as well as considerations of national supremacy, territorial delineation, and regional power politics.

The approximately 5½-year period of the Paraguayan War's duration lends itself to division into the three following general phases:

Phase 1: November, 1864-October, 1865: President López ordered the capture of the Brazilian steamer "Marquês de Olinda" in November, 1864, completed recruitment of his army, succeeded with his Mato Grosso invasion, and in April, 1865, moved to the offensive against the northern Argentine provinces. The Paraguayan offensive effort closed in October, 1865.

Phase 2: October, 1865-December, 1868: Following the collapse of his offensive, Marshal López, now commanding his army in person, sought vainly to defend Paraguay's southern frontier, and then slowly retired northward until December, 1868, when he suffered almost total annihilation at Lomas Valentinas.

Phase 3: January, 1869-March, 1870: Despite Brazilian proclamation of the war's end, Marshal López rebuilt an army, carried on limited guerilla operations, and eventually suffered defeat at Piribebuy in August, 1869, in a renewed Brazilian offensive. At the end of a long retreat of delaying actions, Marshal López was finally cornered and killed at Cerro Corá, March 1, 1870.

In order to facilitate reference in the course of the survey of the war which follows there is included in Appendix I an abbreviated chronological record of the major events and their importance.

Uruguay, Powder Keg of La Plata

Only a match was lacking to ignite the fuse of the powder keg represented in 1864 by little Uruguay. The match was not to be delayed in arrival. On the night of April 16, 1863, Uruguayan Colorado chieftain Venancio Flores and several comrades had departed by boat from their Argentine exile and had succeeded in landing safely on the eighteenth at Rincón de las Gallinas.[2] His arrival was soon followed by the outbreak of renewed civil war.

During the remainder of 1863 and the first six months of 1864 the Uruguayan situation grew out of all proportion, inexorably drawing Argentina and Brazil, as well as Paraguay, into its vortex. A review of the diplomatic correspondence between the several nations, transmitting accusations and counterclaims, reflects a level of activity which is little short of amazing for its intensity and volume. Reports of unofficial Argentine support of the movement generated by Flores, given credence by the known friendship between Bartolomé Mitre and the Uruguayan Colorado leader, encouraged Francisco Solano López to question Argentina's new government regarding its policies in the latest La Plata disturbance.[3] His query was rebuffed and shunted off by Mitre, who seized upon the matter of Argentine-Paraguayan border limits as a means of parrying the developing interest shown by López in La Plata affairs.[4]

Until early 1864 Imperial Brazil had maintained a neutral attitude toward the growing civil strife in Uruguay. As complaints of Rio Grande do Sul residents over alleged Uruguayan mistreatment of Brazilian nationals grew, however, the Imperial Government was forced to direct more attention to La Plata. Eventually, the pressure exerted by such Rio Grande do Sul spokesmen as General Antônio de Souza Netto forced Dom Pedro reluctantly to agree to a more positive policy toward Uruguay. In April, 1864, Minister José Antônio Saraiva received his instructions for the presentation of demands for reparations to the Blanco government at Montevideo. In an effort to achieve a peaceful solution to the Uruguayan problem, Minister Saraiva joined with Argentina's Rufino de Elizalde and British Minister Edward Thornton to encourage an understanding between Flores and President Atanasio Aguirre's Blanco government. With the failure of this effort, Saraiva notified the Blanco government on August 4, 1864, that unless satisfaction of Brazil's demands was not forthcoming within six days, the empire's armed forces would undertake reprisals.[5]

In far-off Paraguay President Francisco Solano López had been observing trends in Uruguay with close attention. Kept informed of events at Montevideo by his agents both there and at Buenos Aires, and by Uruguayan special diplomatic representatives as well, López became convinced that Brazil's hardening attitude toward the Blanco government involved a threat to the political equilibrium of La Plata which his own government could not ignore.

In July, Paraguay had offered her services as mediator in the Uruguayan question, an offer which had been declined by Brazil though accepted by the Uruguayan government. Subsequently, on August 24, 1864, the Paraguayan vessel "Paraguarí" had arrived at Asunción bearing as passengers Minister Thornton, on an official visit to Paraguay, and the new Brazilian Minister Resident, César Sauvan Vianna de Lima, as well as the latest news of the Brazilian ultimatum at Montevideo. In a letter of September 6,

1864, to his confidential agent at Buenos Aires, Félix Egusquiza, Paraguayan Foreign Minister José Berges recorded that Minister Thornton had sought with a *destreza admirable* (admirable dexterity) to convince the president of the erroneous stand of the Uruguayan Blancos as well as to put at rest his lack of confidence in the aims of Brazil.[6]

Such efforts proved unavailing. On August 30, 1864, on orders from President López, Minister Berges sent the new Brazilian minister a formal note which deplored the presentation of the empire's ultimatum to President Aguirre and also disclaimed any responsibility on the part of Paraguay for future developments.[7] Minister Vianna de Lima replied on September 1, 1864, that "no consideration would detain the Imperial Government in carrying out the sacred mission which has devolved upon it of protecting the life, honor, and property of the subjects of His Excellency the Emperor."[8]

On September 3, Berges replied to Vianna stating that if the empire should take the measures protested against, the Paraguayan government would be under the painful necessity of making its protest effective.[9] Subsequently, in his report to the National Congress of March 5, 1865, Foreign Minister Berges described these events and pointed to the divergency between the empire's unwillingness to accept mediation in Uruguay and its support of such procedures in the case of its own problems stemming from the Questão de Christie.[10]

No further word was received by Paraguay from Brazil regarding the protest of August 30. Documentation indicates, however, that the reply of its minister resident in Asunción was approved by the Imperial Government on September 22.[11]

In early September, 1864, the Uruguayan steamer "Villa del Salto" was en route to the Uruguay River port of Mercedes with a detachment of reinforcements assigned to defend Mercedes against an impending attack by Flores' forces. On September 8, units of Admiral Tamandaré's Brazilian squadron gave chase to the Uruguayan vessel and forced it to seek refuge at the upriver port of Paysandú. The "Villa del Salto" was there put afire by the Paysandú Blanco army garrison. Once more irritated by Imperial Brazil's apparent disdain of his protest, President López had Minister Berges forward a further note to Minister Vianna de Lima on September 14, which expressed the unfavorable im-

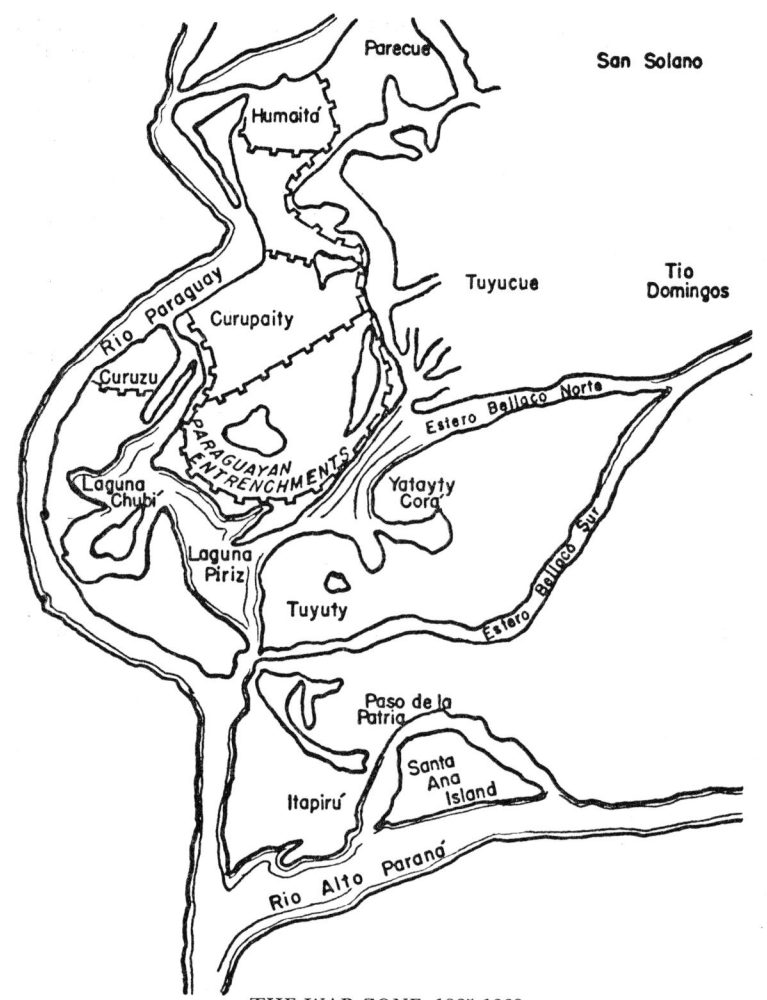

THE WAR ZONE, 1865-1868.
(*From*: William H. Jeffrey, *Mitre and Argentina*, New York, 1952.)

pression made by the attack on the "Villa del Salto" and corroborated the statements made in the August 30 protest.[12]

Announcement of the government's action in response to Brazil's activities in Uruguay made sensational news in Asunción. On September 21, 1864, Minister Berges wrote Félix Egusquiza as follows:

Spirited manifestations on the part of the population took

place in the palace and in the private residence of the president. From the wealthy businessman down to the modest worker, the population banded together to offer both their persons and belongings in support of the protest which our government has presented against the bellicose attitude assumed by Brazil with Uruguay.[13]

On October 12, 1864, a brigade of the Imperial Army composed of the 3rd Infantry Battalion and two cavalry units crossed the Brazilian-Uruguayan frontier at Passo das Pedras. Villa de Mello, capital of the Uruguayan Department of Cerro Largo was occupied shortly thereafter—a development which was to have grave repercussions far north along the Paraguay River.[14]

The Marquês de Olinda

November 10, 1864. The Brazilian river steamer "Marquês de Olinda," put in at Asunción on its usual schedule to load coal en route upstream along the Paraguay River to the Mato Grosso ports. Aboard as its principal passenger it carried Colonel Frederico Carneiro de Campos, newly appointed president of Mato Grosso Province. It also carried the latest news from La Plata, particularly of Brazil's armed intervention in Uruguay.

On the eleventh, its coaling stop completed without incident, the "Marquês de Olinda" proceeded on her way upstream. A special messenger, however, had boarded a waiting locomotive in Asunción's recently constructed railway station and had departed on an urgent run along the new track to Cerro León, the main Paraguayan military base. The message he carried brought to Paraguay's president the news of the commencement by Brazil of active military operations in Uruguay.[15]

According to one version of the event, Francisco Solano López is said to have studied the report for a moment and then to have exclaimed, "If we do not strike now, we shall have to fight Brazil at another time in the future which may be less convenient for us."[16] The special messenger returned to Asunción, and shortly the Paraguayan gunboat "Tacuarí," reported to be the fastest steamer of La Plata, cleared port in pursuit of the "Marquês de Olinda."

The "Tacuarí" caught the slower Brazilian steamer on November 12. The cannon shot fired across the bows of the "Marquês de Olinda," as a sign for her to stop, was the opening gun of the Paraguayan War. On the same day a note was dispatched to Minister Vianna de Lima informing him that relations had been broken between Paraguay and Brazil.

Escorted by the "Tacuarí," the Brazilian steamer returned to Asunción on the evening of November 13. The next morning a Paraguayan detail boarded her, made a thorough search through the cargo and coal bunkers for military consignments, and removed the ship's mail and two cases containing 200,000 milreis in Brazilian paper currency. About a month later, according to the reports of the two crew members who survived the war, Colonel Vicente Barrios, brother-in-law of President López, boarded the ship and had the green and gold colors of the empire lowered. The flag of the "Marquês de Olinda" was made into a rug for the office of Paraguay's president. It was later discovered at Asunción by a Brazilian officer in January, 1869, and returned to Rio de Janeiro for eventual deposit in the National Historical Museum.[17]

After several years of confinement in interior Paraguayan prison camps, the survivors of the "Marquês de Olinda" were transferred to a prisoners' stockade behind the Paraguayan lines near Humaitá. The unfortunate Colonel Carneiro de Campos was reported to have died there on November 3, 1867, from his privations, aggravated possibly by shock upon observing a captured Brazilian battle flag taken at the Second Battle of Tuyuty.[18]

According to United States Minister Charles A. Washburn, Minister Vianna de Lima had previously served his country on diplomatic missions in Europe and was therefore not especially pleased with his new assignment to Asunción.[19] His duty tour was short-lived. His passports were given to him following his protest on November 14 at the seizure of the "Marquês de Olinda." In a typical gesture, however, Francisco Solano López indicated that he was to leave Paraguay by any means other than by the river. This proviso, of course, meant that the only way the minister and his family could reach Brazilian territory would be by overland travel—an almost total impossibility in view of the lack of roads through the nearly impenetrable jungles along the northern and eastern borders of Paraguay. Fortunately for Minister Vianna de Lima, his friend Minister Washburn interceded on his behalf with President López. Washburn wrote later that by threatening Francisco López with withdrawal of his own diplomatic mission, he finally persuaded Paraguay's president to allow Brazil's representative to leave Asunción by river steamer.[20]

No formal declaration of war thus announced the outbreak of hostilities between Paraguay and Brazil. On January 26, 1865, however, Counselor Paranhos at Buenos Aires sent a note to the Argentine government and to the diplomatic corps announcing the existence of a state of war with Paraguay. Theoretically accountable for major state decisions to the National Congress under the terms of Paraguay's Constitution, President López later had his actions approved by Congress in March, 1865.[21]

Voluntários da Pátria

The news of the seizure of the "Marquês de Olinda" and of the arrival of ex-minister Vianna de Lima proved to be events of sensational magnitude in Rio de Janeiro which easily dwarfed the earlier Christie troubles with Britain. Both events, of course, were shortly to be relegated to the background by the even more disturbing news of Paraguay's invasion of Mato Grosso in late December. These first hostile episodes of the Paraguayan War generated the reaction which Dom Pedro characterized as an electric shock to Brazilian nationalism.

As the press of Rio de Janeiro carried the news from Paraguay and of the isolation of Mato Grosso, the Imperial Government in late 1864 busied itself with a task of immediate primary importance —that of building an armed force as soon as possible which would be capable of defending the empire against what was believed to be the immense and modern army of the "tyrant" López. Among the first measures considered was that of mobilization of the Guarda Nacional, the semi-police force of an estimated 200,000 members which was scattered in small detachments throughout the provinces. The Guarda, however, was prohibited by law from serving under that name outside the national boundaries.[22]

To meet this situation and also since the reaction of the Guarda to the call to arms was not entirely enthusiastic, the Imperial Government, on January 7, 1865, issued a call for national volunteers.[23] Enlistments under this decree, later converted into Law No. 3371 of June 28, 1865, were to apply to able-bodied men from 18 to 50 years of age who presented themselves voluntarily for service. These volunteers were to be formed into new battalions of approximately 830 men each, to be called "Voluntários da Pátria."[24]

As news was received of the invasion of Mato Grosso, enlistments for the new Voluntários da Pátria battalions were brisk. In addition to legitimate volunteers, and to the transfer of Guarda Nacional components, the officers of the new battalions succeeded in enticing members of the Guarda Nacional to leave their organizations in favor of the new units. Such pirating activity, in the war's early stages, produced considerable ill-feeling between the officers of the Voluntários da Pátria and the Guarda Nacional.[25]

The newly recruited battalions received only brief training prior to their embarkation at Rio de Janeiro for the army's regular training areas and garrison posts in Rio Grande do Sul. As the new battalions arrived in Rio Grande and as the army steadily grew in size, the first wave of patriotic enthusiasm for the war commenced to subside. On May 23, 1865, for example, Dom Pedro wrote the Condessa de Barral: "Another 1,300 men were embarked the day before yesterday for the Plata. Although quite a number of people appeared, the usual enthusiasm was lacking."[26]

Since the war showed no signs of an early end, and in view of the Imperial Government's goal—"Paz com a victória e a victória com a exclusão de Solano López" (Peace with victory, and victory with the exclusion of Solano López)—it became necessary to devise new methods of obtaining recruits.[27] At first an effort was made to conscript men from among the floating "squatter" populations found in the periphery of the larger urban centers. Since the yield of soldiers from this source proved limited, the recruiting officers turned their attention to the wage-earning classes in the coffee and sugar-cane *fazendas*. Meeting again with but little success, since this class was an essential element in the nation's economy, recruitment was finally focused upon Brazil's slave and freedman population. It was from this latter source that the bulk of recruits and "volunteers" was obtained during most of the war.[28]

INDUCEMENTS TO RECRUITMENT

Measures to persuade men to volunteer ranged from outright press-gang methods stemming from the regulations of 1837 to the inducements represented by offers of land grants and emancipation. During the late war years travelers in interior Brazil not infrequently met with guard detachments transporting men in chains bound for service in Paraguay. J. McF. Gaston, for example, while hunting a home for Americans in Brazil, saw a group of such unfortunates, securely chained, on their way to Rio de Janeiro and the war.[29]

Observer Captain Burton also not only witnessed an attempt at conscription by force in 1867, but was himself considered by people in interior Minas Gerais as never less than the chief of police or a government recruiting officer on a recruiting mission. In the diamond-mine area of the upper São Francisco River he was told quite openly that he was the chief of police of Ouro Prêto.[30] According to Burton, this suspicious attitude by the inhabitants of the interior applied to almost all foreigners traveling in the provinces during this period. In several areas Burton was impressed with the shyness of people. He noted that in certain parts the men had taken to the hills and could be observed slinking about as if engaged in "balking the recruiting officer."[31] At Ouro Prêto he noted that the city's entire 600-man police force had gone "volunteering" for the war. At the port of Januária he had trouble collecting a crew for his river barge because many of the *barqueiros* had been carried off to the war, still others had fled from their homes, and many of those who remained declined to leave the city in the fear that they might be "enlisted" by a recruiting officer in a city strange to them.[32]

When the expeditionary force bound for Mato Grosso reached the city of Uberaba in July, 1865, the future Visconde de Taunay was startled to note that the city police had found it necessary to jail local Guarda Nacional members as a precaution against possible desertion.[33] He utilized the incident later for the background of one of his best-known short stories of the war and Mato Grosso customs entitled, "Juca o tropeiro." Taunay also reported that the expeditionary column had experienced steady desertions from its ranks, with many of its soldiers apparently subscribing to the currently popular cliché, "Deus é grande, mas o mato é ainda maior!" (God is great, but the wide-open country is even greater!).[34]

The inducements held out to entice men into the army were indeed unusual for the empire of Dom Pedro II. Under the provisions of a decree of January 2, 1865, grants of land were offered as a reward to men who would volunteer for the armed forces.[35] Likewise, a law passed on November 6, 1866, granted freedom to slaves who were able and willing to serve in Voluntários da Pátria battalions. A particularly significant feature of this latter law was that the grant of emancipation was also to be extended to the wives of any such slave volunteers.[36] Finally, numerous societies and organizations were formed for the purpose of purchasing the freedom of slaves who were willing to join the army. Dom Pedro himself is reported to have been a subscriber to such projects.[37]

Expansion of the Army

On the basis of Brazil's estimated population of 9 million in 1864 the ratio of the standing regular army to the population in that year was about 560 civilians to one soldier. This ratio was doubtless much larger than that existing in the Spanish-speaking republics, and certainly far greater than that of Paraguay wherein army recruitment had yielded one soldier for each ten persons of the national population. Following the declaration of war by Paraguay and the call in January, 1865 for national volunteers, the Imperial Army was swiftly expanded in size. Whereas in March, 1864, the army had a total strength of only 18,000 men, it showed a total of 67,000 effectives as of April, 1866—its maximum size during the war years. Of this total, 22 battalions comprising about 18,000 men were regular army units. Guarda Nacional mobilization, authorized by Decree no. 3383, had provided 14,700 soldiers from that organization. The remainder of approximately 35,000 men represented the recruits of the Voluntários da Pátria program. Together with the Guarda Nacional transfers, they were formed into 49 new infantry battalions in about one year's time.[38]

Origin

In terms of origin, the new national volunteer battalions directly reflected the systems of recruiting which were then in force, especially those which came to be concentrated on the slave class. Northeast Brazil held the honor of having supplied the bulk of the new volunteers. Of the 49 battalions, 13 were recruited in the province of Bahía alone, 11 battalions were from the Côrte or Rio de Janeiro, 8 came from Pernambuco, and only 3 were formed in São Paulo.[39] Perhaps the most striking contrast in terms of racial composition occurred between these infantry battalions of the Northeast and the cavalry units which were largely recruited in Rio Grande do Sul. While the former were almost totally *gente de côr*, the latter were predominantly of white origin from the Rio

Grande gaúcho class. General Joaquim de Andrade Neves, for example, was a former gaúcho chieftain who in 1864 rounded up all his many Rio Grande male relatives for cavalry service in the war. Only a five-year-old grandchild was left at home.[40]

Chapter 6

¡ VIVA LA REPÚBLICA DEL PARAGUAY!

THE ESTIMATED 90,000 persons comprising the population of Brazil's Mato Grosso province in December, 1864, were indeed faced with a serious situation. Cut off from their usual line of communications by the seizure of the "Marquês de Olinda" and the closure of the Paraguay River to transit by Brazilian-flag vessels, the provincial population could maintain contact with the central government only by means of pack trains over about 1,500 miles of rough trails to the east.

Attack North

Possessing only about 1,300 soldiers as a defensive force, and with borders contiguous with those of Paraguay, the province offered an inviting objective for an attack. The small garrison was distributed among the ports and towns of Fort Coimbra, Corumbá Dourados, Miranda, Nioac, and the capital city of Cuiabá. Of these points, Fort Coimbra was the most important, being the fortified river port closest to the southern provincial border. While its defensive capacity was meager, it had a veteran commander— Colonel Hermenegildo Portocarrero, the officer who had previously served in Paraguay on a special military mission during the presidency of Carlos Antonio López. To the north were located Albuquerque and Corumbá, described by Surgeon Officer Pinheiro Guimarães in 1857 as a "miserável aldeola" (a tiny miserable village).[1] The military colonies of Dourados and Miranda, lying east of the Paraguay River in the zone disputed by Paraguay and Brazil, had been established only shortly before the outbreak of war. They were small, palisaded outposts garrisoned by only a few soldiers.

Representatives of Mato Grosso, mindful of the potential menace to the south, had on several prewar occasions officially voiced their worries over the state of the province's defenses.[2] Events were to show that the Imperial Government had managed to ship substantial stocks of military supplies and equipment to the province. The long distance and communications problems, however, had precluded the sending of garrison reinforcements. In early 1864 the poor state of defenses had been carefully and thoroughly investigated by an innocent-looking "wealthy planter" from Paraguay who bore a name which was shortly to become an ominous one to Brazil—Francisco Isidoro Resquín.[3]

The first offensive operation of the Paraguayan War opened on December 14, 1864, with the departure for Mato Grosso from Asunción of a naval squadron including transports carrying 3,000 troops. Commanded by Colonel Vicente Barrios, brother-in-law of the president, the soldiers of the expedition were dressed in new uniforms featuring scarlet blouses. The enthusiastic farewell given to the force was highlighted by a proclamation issued by President López. Invasion plans called for a combined operation between the river force and a land force composed of 2,500 cavalry and an infantry battalion which was to proceed northward from the port of Concepción under the command of Colonel Resquín, the erstwhile "planter" and competent Paraguayan agent.[4]

The invasion, carefully conceived and ably directed, was a thorough success. Fort Coimbra, besieged on December 27, was evacuated the next night by its small defending force. Hampered by a lack of ammunition, the garrison commander had organized a detachment of 70 women to make cartridges. Caliber 17-mm. lead bullets were pounded out with stones to make them fit the smaller bores of the Minié rifles. For her courage in helping to load cartridges, Dona Ludovina Portocarrero, the commander's wife, was later chosen Patroness of the Mothers and Wives of Brazil's soldiers.[5] Pushing northward, Barrios' force spread both destruction and panic. It captured the only armed vessel on duty in Mato Grosso, the "Anhambay," took the port of Albuquerque, and forced the precipitate evacuation of Corumbá. Unable to proceed along tributaries of the Paraguay River to Cuiabá because of draught limitations, the fleet left garrisons at the captured points and embarked the military stores and equipment which it had captured. News of the Paraguayan advance was brought to Cuiabá on January 7, 1865, by the river steamer "Paranhos." According to to contemporary reports, the news spread terror and demoralization among the provincial capital's population.[6]

The Resquín column, meanwhile, had experienced equal success in its operations. Moving inland it took the small fortified military outpost of Dourados on December 29 and occupied the village of Miranda on January 12, 1865. At the former point, the Paraguayan detachment under Major Martín Urbieta had little trouble in overcoming the resistance of the small 15-man garrison. The Brazilian commander, Antônio João Ribeiro, who was killed in the action, achieved immortality among Brazil's military heroes. His message to his men, copied by Major Urbieta and found later among captured Paraguayan documents, became an inspiration to Brazilian patriotism: "I know that I shall die, but my blood and that of my companions will serve as a solemn protest against the invasion by foreigners of my nation's soil."[7]

Detachments of Paraguayan occupation forces remained in Mato Grosso until April, 1868. Another of the war's many controversies arose later concerning both the amount of military supplies captured by Paraguay in Mato Grosso and the overall strategic worth of the invasion itself. Brazilian historians of the war sought to minimize the military benefits derived by Paraguay from the invasion and claimed that only small amounts of war supplies were in the Mato Grosso ports in late 1864. Evidence to the contrary, however, is found in the memoirs of Minister Washburn, and of Colonel Thompson and G. F. Masterman, both of whom were attached to the Paraguayan army in 1864. Colonel Thompson reported that the captured supplies brought from Mato Grosso represented almost all the military stores consumed by Paraguay during the entire war.[8] Masterman, also an eyewitness, reported that the captured stores included 70 cannon, one steamer, and "an enormous quantity of arms and ammunition."[9] These statements were at least partially substantiated by Brazil's Visconde de Taunay, who wrote in his memoirs that large stocks of war material were taken at Miranda, and that "with reason," Colonel Resquín was said to have declared, "It looks as if the Brazilian government had been expecting to defend the frontier simply with stands of arms."[10] Possibly referring to Miranda, Colonel Thompson noted that at one village Resquín's force took 4 cannon, 500 muskets, 67 carbines, 131 pistols, 468 swords, 1,090 lances, and 9,847 cannon-balls![11]

Many prisoners, including civilians, were brought back to Asunción along with the captured supplies. Some were to remain in Paraguay until 1869. Not the least of the war trophies seized in Mato Grosso was the Patent of Nobility of the Barão de Vila Maria, the government official who had carried news of the invasion to Rio de Janeiro, overland, in a record 47-days time. Colonel Thompson reported that the document was presented by the victorious Paraguayans to Elisa Lynch who used it as a decoration for her anteroom.[12]

Paysandú

Simultaneously with Paraguay's invasion of Mato Grosso, the last events were transpiring in Brazil's undeclared war with the Uruguayan Blancos. In October, 1864, the army which had been stationed along the southern border of Rio Grande do Sul had its status altered from "army of observation" to "expeditionary force." Under the Command of Brigadier João Propício Mena Barreto, it consisted of two divisions commanded by Brigadiers Manoel Luís Osório and José Luís Mena Barreto.[13]

On December 1, 1864, the army left its camps at Rio Paraí-Grande near Bagé and moved toward the theater of operations. Encountering little resistance, the forces under João Propício reached the perimeter of Paysandú on the Uruguay River on December 29, the same day of the attack on the military colony of Dourados in Mato Grosso by the Paraguayan detachment under Major Urbieta. Paysandú, the last stronghold of effective Uruguayan Blanco resistance, was defended by a force of 1,200 men with 15 cannon commanded by Colonel Leandro Gómez. The port had been blockaded by Admiral Tamandaré's gunboats "Araguari," "Parnaíba," and "Ivaí," and a 400-man Brazilian naval detachment had been landed to operate with the 600-man Uruguayan Colorado force of Venancio Flores.[14]

The seige of Paysandú began in earnest with the arrival of João Propício's expeditionary force. It lasted 35 days. During a lull in the operations, according to a report published on January 4, 1865, in the *Jornal do Comércio* of Rio de Janeiro, Leandro Gómez invited a group of foreign naval officers to a luncheon. On entering the dining room the guests were somewhat perplexed on discovering that the rug which adorned the room was in reality a captured Brazilian flag, an innovation strongly suggestive of that of Francisco Solano López of Paraguay. The decorum of the luncheon was swiftly salvaged by the action of a British naval officer who carefully lifted the flag and deposited it with due respect upon a nearby chair.[15]

In renewed operations which featured 52 hours of incessant bombardment, Leandro Gómez was forced to surrender at 8:30 A.M. on January 2, 1865, to Lieutenant Colonel Andre Alves Leite de Oliveira Belo, Mena Barreto's chief-of-staff. Brazil's 1st Mounted Artillery Regiment—later to become famous as the "Bois de Botas" (oxen in boots) for the tall leather boots worn by its members—played a major role in the victory. Under command of Emilio Mallet, the veteran of Passo do Rosário, its 35 guns fired 4,000 rounds of ammunition into the city.[16] Among those of its officers mentioned in dispatches was young First Lieutenant Ernesto Augusto da Cunha Mattos, destined to become a central figure in the "Questão Militar" (Military Question) which was to shake the empire in postwar years.[17] Another young officer to achieve later fame among Brazil's naval heroes was Cadet Luís Felipe de Saldanha da Gama. Only 18 years old at the time, Saldanha da Gama acted as flag-bearer for Admiral Tamandaré's 1st Marine Battalion. He became one of the principal rebels in the Naval Revolt at Rio de Janeiro in 1893-94 and was killed on June 24, 1895, in the final action of the Federalist Revolt. Among the older professional soldiers promoted for bravery was José Antônio Corrêa da Câmara, future field marshal and second Visconde de Pelotas. General Corrêa da Câmara served through the entire war and was commander of the Brazilian forces at the last action at Cerro Corá in March, 1870. A Liberal, he was supported by that party in the postwar era after the death of General Osório. He, likewise, figured prominently in the Military Question for his endorsement of officers embroiled in disputes with the government.[18]

Leandro Gómez, whose heroic defense of Paysandú had made a strong impression upon the population of the neighboring Argentine provinces, met a quick and brutal end. Turned over to the forces of Venancio Flores at his own request, he was executed shortly after his surrender.[19] Since these details were not known at the time, the responsibility for his death was attached to Brazil. The news was a shock to many people in Entre Ríos who had supported the Blancos of Aguirre against the Mitre-backed movement of Venancio Flores. General Urquiza's son, Colonel Waldino Urquiza, for example, had earlier crossed over to Uruguay at the head of a small group of Entrerriano troops to aid the Blancos.[20] The report of the execution of Leandro Gómez also caused resentment in Paraguay. Unaware of all of the circumstances, Colonel Thompson commented that the atrocities committed at Paysandú "form a revolting page in the history of Brazil."[21] Feelings of indignation ran so deep in Entre Ríos at this time that if Francisco Solano López had decided in January, 1865, to attack southward he would have found immediate support within the province and a veritable "war of the races" might then have ensued.[22]

With the fall of Paysandú, Brazil's intervention in Uruguay came to a rapid conclusion. Montevideo capitulated in early February, 1865, and a peace agreement was subsequently signed at Villa de Unión on February 20, the anniversary of the Battle of Passo do Rosário. Venancio Flores became Provisional President of Uruguay.

War against Argentina

On the swift and successful conclusion of the Mato Grosso campaign President Francisco Solano López found himself able to give closer attention to affairs southward in La Plata. Though unwilling to enter into an alliance with the Uruguayan Blancos in their contest with Venancio Flores and Brazil, he, nevertheless, recognized that an excellent opportunity was at hand for Paraguay to strike at the empire. Spending his time about equally between his palace office at Asunción and his headquarters at the Cerro León military base, President López devoted himself to the many problems which comprised the most delicate and momentous period of his career. His directives included an acceleration of mobilization, completion of the railway line to Paraguarí, extension of the telegraph line beyond Villeta southward to the Tebicuary River and on to Humaitá, instructions to Paraguay's European agents for the negotiation of contracts for both modern firearms and armored cruisers, and finally, orders for the transfer of army units to the old Misiones area south across the Upper Paraná River from the town of Itapúa, now Encarnación.[23]

The principal problem faced by López concerned a possible way by which his army could reach the theater of war in Uruguay. In his view Paraguay possessed a valid claim to the old Misiones region which dated back to a Royal Cédula of 1803 establishing a "private" government over the region to be independent of both Asunción and Buenos Aires. Since Bernardo Velasco, the governor of the region, was also appointed Governor of Paraguay in 1806, with retention of his former position, it was the view of Paraguay in the 1860's that its territorial boundaries continued to embrace at least part of Misiones.[24]

López thus had no qualms in sending troops across the Upper Paraná to establish camps at San Carlos in the Misiones district. Argentina entertained a similar claim to the area, however, and earlier negotiations between the two countries had not succeeded in arriving at a boundary agreement. In a decision which has also been the subject of much controversy, President López on January 14, 1865, sent a note to Buenos Aires requesting permission for his troops to transit eastern Corrientes province. The request was received by President Mitre on February 6 and answered by him on February 9. The reply refused Paraguay's request. In a further note of the same date Foreign Minister Elizalde asked the Government of Paraguay for *francas y amigables* (frank and friendly) explanations for the recent increase in the number of troops along the Argentine-Paraguayan border.[25]

Since his inauguration as president, within a few days of that of Francisco Solano López, and especially since November, 1964, Bartolomé Mitre had sought to observe outward neutrality in the questions between Paraguay and Imperial Brazil. While he had undoubtedly furnished unofficial assistance to Venancio Flores, he had also permitted the transshipment at Buenos Aires of military cargo for Paraguay free of any customs declarations or inspections, and had curbed the activities and proclamations of the growing "Comité Revolucionario" of Paraguayans in exile at Buenos Aires.[26] With reports of troop concentrations in Misiones, however, and with the active intervention of Brazil in Uruguay, President Mitre correctly gauged the necessity of assuring for himself either the support or neutralization of General Urquiza. In exchanges of letters with Urquiza in early 1865, Mitre pointed to the possibilities of encroachment or invasion of Argentine territory and eventually obtained Urquiza's agreement to the policy decision that national territorial sovereignty and unity were paramount to Argentina's future. His success in thus neutralizing

Urquiza may have represented Mitre's greatest contribution to the allied victory in the Paraguayan War.

Now associated with the Buenos Aires government, Urquiza sent Benjamin Victorica to Asunción in late February, 1865, on a private mission to persuade President López to avoid complications with Argentina. Victorica wrote later that López had shown him the negative reply to his transit request, and that he had then informed López that General Urquiza could never accept his assistance in Argentine affairs. Francisco López is then alleged to have stated, "Entonces, si me provocan, lo llevaré todo por delante!" (Well then, if they provoke me, I shall push forward at full force!).[27]

Events now transpired in swift succession. Discarding further deliberations, President López had an announcement published on February 25 in *El Semanario,* Paraguay's semiofficial newspaper, calling for a meeting of an Extraordinary National Congress. On March 5 he read a special message to the Congress justifying his actions in November, 1864, toward Brazil, and outlining the status of relations with Argentina. A "Comisión Doble Especial" (the most special of special commissions) then prepared a survey of the situation which it presented on March 17. Its conclusion, which of course supported the president's actions, was approved by Congress on March 18. The Congress also authorized declaration of war against Argentina. The decision was signed by President López and Foreign Minister Berges on March 19. A formal note to Argentina announcing the declaration was signed by Berges on March 29.[28]

Developments at this point assumed a course which has since received contrasting treatment by historians of the nations concerned. According to the most convincing evidence which has become available, Francisco Solano López elected to delay the announcement of his war declaration at Buenos Aires long enough to achieve the following objectives: seize the port of Corrientes by surprise attack, allow time for his agent at Buenos Aires to conclude a sizable loan operation for Paraguay, and assure the arrival of expected military supplies from Europe.[29]

The formal note declaring war on Argentina was reported to have become known to the Argentine government on May 1, 1865, upon receipt of the issue of *El Semanario* in which it had been published. The original was stated to have been finally received on May 3, or 19 days following the Corrientes surprise attack. Documents in the archives of General Mitre, however, suggest strongly that the government learned of the declaration at a much earlier date. The archives show that the declaration came to light at Córdoba, far inland, through some "indiscretion." On April 17, the day after news of the Corrientes attack was received, Minister of Hacienda Guilhermo Rawson informed Mitre that he had actually seen a letter describing Paraguay's decision.[30]

It is also pertinent to refer briefly to the mission of Cipriano Ayala. A young Paraguayan officer and a native of Villa del Pilar, Ayala was sent south as a messenger on April 3 bearing sealed envelopes which had been given to him by General Wenceslao Robles at Humaitá. He left Paraguay on the steamer "Jejuí," transferred to the "Esmeralda" at Corrientes, transferred again at Rosario to the "Pavón," and finally arrived at Buenos Aires on April 8. He delivered his sealed envelopes to the Paraguayan agent at Paraná and to Félix Egusquiza at Buenos Aires. In letters of April 8 and 11, respectively to Agent Juan Brizuela at Montevideo and Candido Bareiro at Paris, Egusquiza wrote confidentially of the war declaration. Egusquiza also believed that the formal note would shortly arrive via the steamer "Salto." This vessel, however had been purchased by Paraguay. Her master, Captain Fidanza, was later a victim of the 1868 conspiracy period.[31]

On April 9 Cipriano Ayala returned to Rosario on the Pavón," where he later transferred again to the steamer "Esmeralda." Meanwhile, Paraguay had attacked Corrientes and Governor Manuel Lagraña had fled downstream carrying the invasion news. The "Esmeralda," with a cargo of arms and ammunition for Corrientes, was detained by Argentine authorities in the vicinity of Goya or Bella Vista just as it was about to be overtaken by the Paraguayan vessel "Ygureí," which had been sent to escort it and its important cargo. Cipriano Ayala returned to Buenos Aires on April 17 where he was promptly arrested.[32] Cleared later of the charges against him, he was reportedly seen in Buenos Aires in 1869 working as a brickmason.[33]

Historians of the war have criticized President López' action against Argentina both as coming too late and as being premature. Those who felt that the war declaration came too late pointed to the probable loss in early 1865 of Urquiza and Entre Ríos as potential allies of Paraguay, and to the time given to Brazil for concluding its undeclared war on the Uruguayan Blancos. Those who believed the declaration to have been premature pointed to the loss to Paraguay of the arms contracted for in Europe which now became unobtainable, to the military advantages which might have been enjoyed in a defensive war against Brazil alone, and to the effect of the war declaration on opinion in the other South American republics which had previously held López as the champion of the Spanish-speaking republics against the Portuguese-speaking slaveholding empire of Brazil.

CORRIENTES AND AFTERMATH

On Good Friday, April 13, at 7 A.M., five Paraguayan steamers appeared without warning off the port of Corrientes. After a brief skirmish, boarding parties seized the old and small Argentine naval vessels "25 de Mayo" and "Gualeguay," which were then towed away with the Paraguayan force. The following day the Paraguayan fleet reappeared at Corrientes, this time to debark an army of 3,000 men under General Robles. The city was occupied without resistance and the army began slowly to move south along the east bank of the Paraná.[34]

In his memoirs Minister Washburn reported that three American citizens were captured on the Argentine vessels at Corrientes. The strange, unsolved fate of one of them deserves mention. Washburn noted that he "was a cook, was a colored man by the name of George Bowen, from the city of Washington, a very powerful, active fellow." The minister related further:

He was released, and came to live at my house. But I soon found that, instead of getting a diminutive white elephant on my hands as in the case of Masterman, I had got a big black one—a fellow who would get drunk every chance he could get, and would steal anything he could lay his hands on to give away to his numerous female friends, of whom he seemed to have almost as many as López himself. When drunk, he was so quarrelsome that the other servants were afraid to remain in the house with him; and, after repeated warnings and threats, all of which were entirely unavailing, I was obliged to send him away. What became of him afterwards I never knew.[35]

The unfortunate, adventuresome George Bowen is not mentioned in the accounts of Martin T. MacMahon, Washburn's successor, nor has any reference to him so far been unearthed in the records.

The news from Corrientes produced an explosion at Buenos Aires. The newspapers *La Tribuna* and *La Nación Argentina* attacked López with renewed fury, using such terms as "fracasado emperador de la nación en patas" (a broken-down emperor of a barefooted nation) and "supremo mercachifle en yerba" (supreme peddler of yerba-maté).[36] Outpourings of patriotic speeches and the singing of the national hymn were heard on all sides. The enthusiasm reached its heights when a crowd gathered before the residence of Mitre, who then voiced his famous but totally erroneous prophecy:

Dentro de veinticuatro horas estaremos en los cuarteles; dentro de quince días en campaña, y a los trés meses en la Asunción, capital del Paraguay! (To the barracks in 24 hours, in 15 days on campaign, and in 3 months in Asunción!).[37]

An urgent call was announced for men to serve in new Guardia Nacional battalions, and a formal declaration of war was approved by decree on May 9.[38] With an international war at hand and with an understanding achieved between the nation's two foremost leaders, Argentina appeared united as never before. Events were to show, however, that the old antagonisms between *crudos* and *cocidos* still remained but slightly under the surface.

THE TRIPLE ALLIANCE TREATY

As of May, 1865, the forces of Argentina, Brazil, and Uruguay became united in a common effort against the Paraguay of Francisco Solano López under the terms of the Triple Alliance Treaty. The negotiation, provisions, and eventual disclosure of this treaty form a chapter in the war's history which is hardly less amazing than some of the most curious and remarkable of the military events. Likewise, the circumstances surrounding the treaty generated a controversy which is still active.

Sent to La Plata in order to conclude an agreement with the Colorado forces of Venancio Flores, and though successful in his mission, Brazil's Counsellor Paranhos fell into the bad graces of the governing Liberal party for alleged soft treatment of Uruguayan Blancos after Pasandú. His place as the empire's chief negotiator in La Plata was assumed in March, 1865, by Counsellor Francisco Octaviano de Almeida Rosa. Counsellor Octaviano's instructions were reported both to have contemplated the negotiation of an alliance with Argentina and the prevention of any action on the part of the Mitre government which might cause complications to the empire's effort against Paraguay.[39]

Many of the details regarding the negotiation of the Triple Alliance Treaty probably remain in confidential state archives. From the correspondence which has come to light, however, its terms had been under consideration at least for some time. Correspondence between Mitre and Flores, for example, shows that a treaty was in preparation in mid-April, 1865.[40] Paraguayan sources indicate that President López and his ministers suspected the existence of a secret agreement between Brazil and Argentina dating back to the early 1860's.[41]

The Paraguayan attack on Corrientes produced a sudden rise in tempo in the conduct of the negotiations. On May 1, 1865, President Mitre met the representatives of Brazil and Uruguay at Buenos Aires and the Triple Alliance Treaty was concluded on the same date—a negotiating feat which must figure among the most amazingly successful and rapid diplomatic performances on record in the Americas if not the entire world.

While it was openly known that the representatives of Brazil and Uruguay had arrived to conduct negotiations with Argentina, the negotiating sessions and the terms of the treaty were kept secret. The treaty was ratified by the Argentine Chamber of Deputies in a secret session on May 24, and ratifications were later exchanged with Brazil and Uruguay, respectively, on June 12 and 13.[42]

In spite of the precautions taken, the tenor of the treaty soon became public knowledge at Buenos Aires. Though it was reported that the three countries had resolved to unite in a common effort against the "tyrant" López of Paraguay, and not against either Paraguay itself nor its people, there were rumors that the longstanding border delineation difficulties had not been overlooked in the treaty. As these rumors persisted, comment became more pointed. The Buenos Aires newspaper *La América*, for example, reportedly carried the following statement, "El tratado es secreto, la sesión es secreta; solo la vergüenza es pública" (The treaty is secret, the session is secret; only the shame is public.)[43]

In a dispatch of April 24, 1865, which was later published by the British government in June, Minister Thornton reported a conversation with Argentine Foreign Minister Elizalde. According to Thornton, Elizalde said that he hoped he would live long enough to see Bolivia, Paraguay, Uruguay, and Argentina united in a confederation forming one powerful republic.[44] Minister Thornton's colleague, H. G. Lettsom at Montevideo, proved even more adept at extracting information. He managed to persuade Acting Uruguayan Foreign Minister Carlos de Castro to give him privately a copy of the new treaty, which he then promptly transmitted to London.[45] Subsequently, in early 1866, the "secret" treaty was published in a British parliamentary blue book as a result of House of Commons proceedings. This action, of course, raised a diplomatic storm between Britain and Uruguay. The storm in London, however, was by no means as great as that generated in La Plata and indeed throughout South America when the text of the treaty was published in Buenos Aires.

An English language translation of the text of the treaty is contained in Appendix II. Its principal provisions were as follows:

(1) The war shall not be against the people of Paraguay but rather against their present government;

(2) The allies bind themselves not to cease war until they have abolished the López government, nor to treat with López unless by common consent;

(3) The independence of Paraguay is to be guaranteed, but Argentina and Brazil shall be entitled to establish the definite limits of their boundaries with Paraguay;

(4) Paraguay shall pay the expenses of the war, the Humaitá fortifications are to be destroyed, and no arms or elements of warfare are to be left to Paraguay;

(5) The command of the allied forces shall remain with General Mitre during operations on Argentine or Paraguayan territory, with Venancio Flores when operations are on Uruguayan soil, and with a Brazilian general when operations are carried out on Brazilian territory.

Publication of the treaty made it clear that the war was to be directed as much against Paraguay and her people as against Francisco Solano López, and that the two largest powers were determined to achieve the maximum of their territorial aspirations at Paraguay's expense. The revelation of these features of the treaty caused a wave of indignation among the other republics and also did immeasurable harm to the allied war effort. In July, 1866, the Peruvian government addressed a protest against the treaty to Brazil, Argentina, and Uruguay, on behalf of Chile, Bolivia, Ecuador, and Peru. Its text was published in *El Peruano* of July 11, 1866. Employing strong language, the protest suggested that the conduct of Brazil was identical with that of France in Mexico and of Spain in the Pacific and in Santo Domingo. In its edition of October 6, 1866, the *Illustrated London News* reported that it had received a copy of the protest and stated: "The document, drawn up with the most consummate ability, attacks the pretensions of the allies to force upon the Paraguayans a new form of government."[46]

Publication of the treaty's text had a decided impact on the peoples of Paraguay. Informed of the provisions through publication of the treaty in *El Semanario* in September, 1866, Paraguayans had little difficulty in calculating that approximately 150,000 square kilometers of what they believed was national territory were now at stake. The popularity of Francisco Solano López rose accordingly. Even those who had been lukewarm or perhaps averse to his government were now persuaded that the war was not a *guerra contra López* (war against López), but more a *guerra contra el Paraguay,* (war against Paraguay).

Counterattack at Corrientes

On May 25, 1865, Argentina's principal independence day, Buenos Aires reflected the usual excitement of patriotic celebrations, heightened this time by the emotional impact of the declaration of war against Paraguay. The anniversary date was also selected for the launching of Argentina's first offensive move. On May 20 the Paraguayan invading force of General Wenceslao Robles, now amounting to 25,000 troops, had occupied Bella Vista, far south of Corrientes, and was heading along the east bank of the Paraná River for Santa Lucía and Goya. Only minor skirmishing had so far characterized the drive. Since the Paraguayan advance threatened to reach the confines of Entre Ríos, the allied command decided upon a diversionary action which might compel the Paraguayan forces to halt and even retreat. A force of 4,000 troops, including a 350-man Brazilian detachment, under General Wenceslao Paunero was embarked on vessels of Admiral Barroso's squadron. Aided by a lack of Paraguayan vigilance along the Paraná and the absence of prepared defensive works, Paunero was able to land an attacking force of about 2,000 men at Corrientes on May 25. He was opposed by Major Martínez' garrison of about 1,600 men. The action, which lasted from 3:30 to 5:30 P.M., was a hard-fought contest which ended in an allied victory. The Paraguayans lost 900 men, three guns, and a battle flag. Aware of the proximity of the large Robles force, General Paunero reembarked his men on the night of May 26 and the diversionary force returned downstream.[48]

In commenting upon this first major infantry action of the war, Colonel Thompson wrote somewhat sarcastically that it was at Corrientes where Brazilian troops "first showed a peculiarity in their tactics which consists in firing whenever they have any guns to fire with, no matter whether they kill friend or foe, or both together, which last was usually the case."[49]

The lesson of Corrientes was not ignored by Francisco Solano López. Recognizing that his invasion forces under Robles would be continually hampered in their advance southward while the Brazilian naval squadron held command of the Paraná, he now resolved to gamble the fate of his own small fleet in a general attack upon the Brazilian fleet. If the result should be successful, the doors to Buenos Aires would indeed be opened. As conceived, the plan also called for the simultaneous invasion of northern Rio Grande do Sul by the 10,000 men of Colonel Antonio de la Cruz Estigarribia camped in the old Misiones district. The overall plan was to represent the peak period of Paraguay's offensive capacity.

Chapter 7

VIVA DOM PEDRO SEGUNDO!

Francisco Solano López, now both Marshal and President of Paraguay, issued a proclamation on June 2, 1865, announcing his decision to assume personal command of Paraguay's forces in the field. He left Asunción June 8 at sunset aboard the "Tacuarí." Though the population of the capital had gathered to see him off, and the crew of the visiting HMS "Doterel" had manned the ship's yards, Colonel Thompson commented that there was no cheering.[1] Arriving at Humaitá the next evening, Marshal López began immediately to prepare a general attack on Brazil's naval squadron, then at anchor slightly below the port of Corrientes near a widening in the Paraná River known as the Riachuelo. According to United States Minister Washburn, López' plans for the battle followed suggestions made to him by Englishman John Watts, engineer-officer on the newly-arrived "Paraguarí" built in England under the Blyth contract.[2] Watts reportedly had served earlier in the Brazilian navy.

Paraguay's naval squadron, commanded by Captain Pedro Ignacio Mesa, consisted of the following vessels: "Tacuarí" (flagship), "Paraguarí," "Ygureí," "Ybera," "Yporá," "Marquês de Olinda" (flying Paraguay's colors since November), "Jejuí," "Salto Oriental," and the "Pirabebé." All units were of the paddle-wheel type except the "Salto" and "Pirabebé" which were propeller-driven. They were all converted merchant ships with the exception of the "Tacuarí," and all had English engineers who had presumably been contracted for by Blyth. The total fire power of the fleet amounted to 30 guns.[3] In addition, six low-lying, flat-bottomed barges each mounting an eight-inch cannon were towed by the fleet. These barges called "chatas," were destined to prove so dangerous to Brazil's ships in later actions that one Brazilian admiral classified them as "monitores de madeira" (wooden monitors).[4]

The opposing Brazilian force lying off Corrientes consisted of the following units: "Amazonas" (flagship), "Jequitinhonha," "Belmonte," "Parnaíba," "Ipiranga," "Mearim," "Iguatemí," "Araguarí," and "Beberibe." All were naval vessels and were screw-propelled, a feature which proved an advantage in the forthcoming battle. Total fire power of the squadron amounted to 59 guns, some of them being of the then modern 120- and 150-pounder Whitworth type.[5] The squadron was under the temporary command of Portuguese-born Admiral Francisco Manoel Barroso de Silva, future Barão de Amazonas and the "Nelson brasileiro." Admiral Tamandaré had remained at Buenos Aires reportedly to complete the organization of an operations base.

Riachuelo

The Paraguayan fleet left Humaitá on the night of June 10. The plan was to strike the Brazilian squadron at dawn, pass along it, and after making a short turn-around, pair off ship-to-ship for an all-out boarding attack. The plan was ingenious and might have succeeded were it not for several factors: a delay in arrival at Riachuelo, an oversight in not supplying the Paraguayan vessels with grappling irons, an advantage in height by the Brazilian ships, and finally, the superior maneuvering ability of the Brazilian screw-driven steamers.[6]

The delays experienced by the Paraguayan fleet, including the disablement of the "Yberá" due to loss of her propeller, caused the force to reach the scene of action at mid-morning rather than at dawn. As the Paraguayan ships arrived they were given added support by the appearance of Colonel Bruguez who stationed the field guns of his artillery units along the shoreline where they could rake any enemy vessels which came in range.

The Paraguayan plan was carried out, but with the ships passing the Brazilian squadron at too great a range to inflict serious damage by their fire.[7] Startled by the unexpected attack, Brazilian seamen were called to battle stations and the squadron moved in pursuit of the enemy vessels. Admiral Barroso sought to inspire his men with a fleet order which ranks high in Brazil's naval annals: "O Brasil espera que cada um cumpra seu dever—atacar e destruir o inimigo o mais perto que cada um puder" (Brazil expects everyman to do his duty—attack and destroy the enemy at as close range as possible.) [8]

On completion of the Paraguayan turn-about maneuver the two fleets met in a general action which proved to be the one great naval battle of the war. It lasted for about four hours and was marked by deadly fighting and heroic actions on both sides. Superior Brazilian fire power, plus greater maneuverability for the Brazilian ships, and the lack of protection for the boilers of Paraguay's converted merchant vessels, gradually spelled victory for Admiral Barroso. The final margin of superiority was narrow, however, for heavy gunfire at close range and the several boarding attempts by Paraguayan crews came close to success. The "Jequitinhonha" ran aground within range of Bruguez' guns which raked the Brazilian vessel mercilessly, the "Belmonte" was holed at the water line and had to be run aground, and the "Parnaíba" was nearly captured by Paraguayan boarding parties. One of the most striking of the many acts of heroism during the battle occurred on the "Parnaíba." Enemy boarding parties, once almost completely in control of the decks, sought desperately to haul down the imperial flag. They were repeatedly beaten off by seaman Marcílio Dias, who managed to keep the flag flying even though he was mortally wounded and had lost his right arm.[9]

On Paraguay's side, the "Jejuí" was sunk, the "Marquês de Olinda" had her boilers shot through and drifted out of action, the "Salto" likewise was put out of action and drifted onto a bank, and the "Paraguarí" was rammed by the "Amazonas" and abandoned. The remaining four Paraguayan steamers broke action and retreated slowly upstream without pursuit by the Brazilians.

Though losses in personnel were reportedly small—only several hundred casualties on both sides—each of the squadrons had been badly mauled. Victory, however, clearly belonged to Brazil—its fleet remained at Riachuelo while that of Paraguay had retired from the scene. Subsequently, the Brazilian squadron moved downstream on June 13, past the positions occupied by the guns of Colonel Bruguez. Brazil could replace its ship losses; Paraguay could not. The Paraná River thus remained under allied control, and Paraguay's land invasion was forced to come to a halt.

Several days after Riachuelo, Marshal López sent steamers to attempt to salvage the vessels which had gone aground. While it proved possible to tow the "Paraguarí" back to Asunción, its damages were too extensive for repair. Its loss was a blow to López for it had been the most modern unit of the fleet. The beached "Jequitinhonha" was stripped of its cannon—the mainyard was removed and taken to Humaitá where it was to serve as the center decoration for a "dancing rotunda."[10] Captain Pedro Ignacio Mesa, mortally wounded during the battle, later died at Humaitá unmourned by Marshal López. John Watts, the English chief engineer of the "Tacuarí," was made a Knight of Paraguay's Order of Merit for his services. He was later to be shot during the 1868 conspiracy trials.[11] At Rosario, several days after Riachuelo, HBM Consul Thomas J. Hutchinson visited some Paraguayan wounded who had been brought down on HMS "Doterel.' He was amazed at both their stoicism and courage. One man, though mortally wounded, refused to utter a sound after being admonished by his comrades not to complain before his nation's enemies.[12]

In Rio de Janeiro, Dom Pedro II wrote the Condessa de Barral on July 8 that he had "shaken with enthusiasm" upon reading the official reports of Riachuelo, and that the account of the maneuvers of the "Amazonas" had recalled to his mind the memory of an excursion that they had made together on board this vessel.[13] The ram of the "Amazonas" and three captured Paraguayan flags were eventually placed in Brazil's National Historical Museum.[14]

Operations along the Paraná River remained quiescent for about two months. In August, Colonel Bruguez succeeded in marching past the anchorage of the Brazilian squadron and emplaced his artillery on high cliffs overlooking the Paraná near Bella Vista and subsequently at Cuevas. Worried by this threat to communications, Admiral Barroso decided to retire south and was forced to run by the Bruguez batteries under heavy plunging fire. The Brazilian squadron then remained downstream until the Paraguayan southern offensives had been finally defeated.

General Robles, who had retired north to positions below Corrientes, was summarily relieved from command in July, 1865. Suspected of having had dealings with the allies, and reported to have shown disrespect to Paraguay's Marshal President, he was imprisoned at Humaitá and later executed. His place was temporarily taken by General Vicente Barrios, the minister of war and lately of Mato Grosso fame. Barrios subsequently transferred command to another Mato Grosso hero, Brigadier Francisco Isidoro Resquín. One of the few Paraguayan general officers who survived the war to write a personal record of its events, Resquín advanced the force once more to the neighborhood of Bella Vista.[15] The army stayed in this area awaiting word from the Estigarribia column and busying itself with collecting and shipping northward immense amounts of supplies and booty.[16]

Uruguaiana

Until June, 1865, the recently declared war with Paraguay had produced relatively little change in the tempo of life in Brazil's Rio Grande do Sul province. The previous tensions over border incidents with Uruguay had evaporated with the departure of João Propício's expeditionary force to Paysandú, and the subsequent surrender of Montevideo had marked the end of the Uruguayan problem.

The departure of the expeditionary forces had left garrison towns such as Bagé somewhat lifeless, though this void was gradually being filled with the arrival from the North of the new Voluntários da Pátria battalions. The men from the North found conditions in Rio Grande do Sul quite different. Aside from the new climate, an important change which caused particular complaint concerned the diet—accustomed to dried or jerked meat and beans, the northerners now had to adapt themselves to rations of fresh meat. A further new item was maté or Paraguayan tea. The Conde d'Eu on his visit to the South, for example, learned to take maté at bedtime as an inducement to sound rest. The natives of Rio Grande do Sul called all northerners "bahianos" (men from Bahía). According to the Conde d'Eu, Riograndenses recognized the existence of only three classes of people: *filhos do paiz* (fellow countrymen), *castelhanos* (their Spanish-speaking neighbors), and *bahianos* (northerners). Recruitment in Rio Grande do Sul itself had experienced some difficulties.[17] The Guarda Nacional units, composed of men accustomed to gaúcho existence and warfare, exhibited slight liking for the rigid discipline of army life as infantrymen. Furthermore, new recruits, volunteers, and Guarda Nacional members, while thoroughly familiar with the old flintlock muskets, proved totally ignorant of the procedures required in the handling of the new percussion-cap Minié rifles being issued.[18] Other problems complained of by the president of the province to the minister of war at Rio de Janeiro concerned the difficulties of recruiting Voluntários da Pátria in May when the original January decree was to be effective only for three months, the possibility of trouble breaking out among foreign-born recruits such as that experienced in the time of the 1852 Rosas war, and the growing shortage of weapons and equipment with which to supply the newly recruited units.[19]

To the northwest, the defense of the more remote zone of the province had been assigned to a force of 5,000 troops under command of Brigadier David Canabarro, the old Farroupilha leader. Though scouts had brought reports of Paraguayan military activity in the Candelaria zone of the Misiones region, the Brazilian commanders did not believe the enemy were capable of sending a large army across two main rivers, the Paraná and Uruguay.[20] On April 17, 1865, however, the President of Rio Grande do Sul wrote the minister of war that he had talked with the Brazilian minister bound for Buenos Aires, who had informed him of Paraguay's declaration of war against Argentina and had warned him of a possible attack on Rio Grande do Sul from the Itapúa (Encarnación) region.[21] For his part General Canabarro showed little worry over a possible Paraguayan attack. On April 24 the commander of the 1st Light Brigade wrote him that he had received word that the Paraguayan force at San Carlos in Misiones now totalled 10,000 men, but that it was composed of "meninos e velhos que quasi nem dentes tem" (children and old men who hardly even have teeth).[22] Canabarro himself wrote to the president of the province on May 13 stating that "there would be no obstacles on the road to Asunción that the Brazilian army could not overcome, and that Brazil instead of being invaded would itself be the invader!"[23]

The "toothless" old men and young boys who were said to compose the Paraguayan force in Misiones came suddenly to life on June 10, 1865. In a movement which caught Brazilian defenders by surprise, advance elements of Colonel Estigarribia's army crossed the Uruguay River at Passo de São Borja and swiftly consolidated a bridgehead. The crossing of the 600-meter-wide river was efficiently accomplished with the use of 20 boats, each with a capacity of 25 men, which had been carried overland from Paraguay. The defending 1st Battalion of Voluntários da Pátria reportedly fired one volley and then fled, leaving its flag which was rescued at the last moment by the courageous action of Sublieutenant Paulino Gomes Jardim.[24] The battalion commander, Colonel João Manoel Mena Barreto, a further representative of Rio Grande's distinguished Mena Barreto family, was later killed in the 1869 assault on Piribebuy. On entering São Borja Paraguayan officers told local citizens that they were counting upon aid from General Urquiza in Entre Ríos which would enable their forces to divide and to undertake the capture of Montevideo and Pôrto Alegre.[25]

News of the invasion of Rio Grande do Sul reached the city of Pelotas on June 16. Official and public Brazilian reaction exhibited some notable contrasts. On July 6 Minister Octaviano, who had signed the Triple Alliance Treaty, wrote to Counsellor José Antônio Saraiva:

If, as it is to be expected, the Triple Alliance crushes these forces, Paraguay can be considered as beaten without the need of any further great effort. The allied armies and Brazil's navy should find little trouble in invading Paraguay. Perhaps even the navy alone, with the intrepid victor of Paysandú at its head, and aided by Brazilian landing forces, can terminate the campaign as soon as the defeat of the enemy's forces on the side of Corrientes is certain.[26]

Minister Octaviano's assessment of the war's status was soon proven overly optimistic both as to the role of the intrepid Admiral Tamandaré and the amount of trouble which still lay ahead.

On July 8 Dom Pedro wrote the Condessa de Barral that "O Rio Grande foi invadido; meu lugar é lá e para lá irei depois de amanhã" (Rio Grande has been invaded; my place is there and I am leaving the day after tomorrow.)[27] On July 17 he wrote again to the Condessa to report that his arrival had proven such a surprise to the people of Rio Grande that upon entering the Church of Carmo to attend Mass he and his group were taken by the faithful within the church as Paraguayans who had just landed in the city! The emperor added that "custou a manter ordem na igreja" (it required much trouble to maintain order in the church.)[28]

The propensity of Brazilians among the provinces to regard unannounced foreign visitors as Paraguayans resulted in other curious situations. For example in 1867 while traveling along the São

Francisco River in northeast Brazil, Captain Burton was mistaken by people of villages along the river as none other than Francisco Solano López himself![29]

On taking São Borja, Colonel Estigarribia split his forces for an advance south along the banks of the Uruguay River. He sent Major Pedro Duarte with a force of 2,500 troops down the right bank (Corrientes side), while he led the bulk of the army, some 8,000 troops, down the left bank (Rio Grande do Sul side).[30] The slow advance of Estigarribia's invasion force met little resistance since General Canabarro, mindful of the inferior size of his own army, adopted the Fabian-like tactics of a retreat in order to draw his opponent deeper into Brazilian territory. Several difficulties began to affect the Paraguayan advance: with only a small cavalry force the Estigarribia column could neither keep an adequate watch on enemy movements nor forage for local supplies, the thin and delicate line of communications back to Itapúa on the Upper Paraná daily grew longer, and finally, the immense body of shallow lakes and swamps comprising Lake Yberá in Corrientes province proved an effective barrier to contact with the Robles expedition along the Paraná. A further difficulty arose when young Brazilian Lieutenant Floriano Peixoto, fresh from the military school at Rio de Janeiro, succeeded in forming a river patrol with two small armed vessels which prevented contact between Estigarribia and Duarte. Lieutenant Peixoto's vessels were manned by the "Zuavos Bahianos," a crack Brazilian infantry unit which attracted the Conde d'Eu later at Uruguaiana. He wrote that the unit was entirely composed of Negroes—no whites, Indians, or mulattoes were allowed. Their uniforms were indeed noteworthy—red trousers, green vest, blue jacket, and red fez![31]

With the news of the continued invasion by Estigarribia, the allied command had speeded up its army concentration. The port of Concordia, on the Uruguay River between Paysandú and Uruguaina, was selected as the operations base, and troops from Buenos Aires and Uruguay, as well as Osório's Brazilian command, began shortly to arrive. Severe winter conditions of rain and mud rendered the Concordia experience a miserable one for the arriving troops.[32] General Mitre departed from Buenos Aires for Concordia in June, leaving the administration of the government to Vice President Marcos Paz; Venancio Flores arrived at the new base in July and was named commander-in-chief of the allied army.

Uruguaiana, high point of the invasion, was evacuated by Brazilian troops on the night of August 4.[33] On entering the city, Estigarribia's column found a considerable amount of supplies, though not sufficient for an extended operation. The only major battle of the Rio Grande do Sul campaign occurred across the Uruguay River from Uruguaiana on August 17 at Yataí (meaning a palm tree having edible fruit).[34] Unable to secure reinforcements from Estigarribia and unwilling to consider retreat, Major Duarte and his 2,500 men were overwhelmed by the advancing Flores forces. For the first time the allies were to experience the ferocity of Paraguayan resistance in the face of certain defeat as well as the characteristic of declining surrender with death as the only alternative. The command was literally annihilated with but few prisoners being taken, Duarte among them.[35] Reported allied losses were small. The actions of young 12-year-old color-bearer Antonio Rivas, and especially his words, sparked new patriotism at Buenos Aires—"Al que me quite la bandera lo mato de un tiro con mi revólver!" (I shall kill anyone who tries to take the flag away from me with one shot from my revolver!)[36]

With the right bank of the Uruguay River now free of Paraguayans, the allies turned to Uruguaiana. General Mitre had arrived in late August with the remainder of the army, and the entire force, now over 17,000 in number, commenced siege operations. Dom Pedro, impatient with the delays and difficulties involved in his overland trip to the front, wrote the Condessa on September 2 that he desired to arrive at Uruguaiana as soon as possible, and that he didn't want to find everything terminated upon his arrival.[37]

Estigarribia's position was hopeless. Lacking new instructions from his chief in Paraguay and completely surrounded, his only alternatives were a fight-to-the-finish or surrender. After much correspondence with the allied command which featured highly patriotic language, he chose the latter course. On August 19, Venancio Flores sent him a message stating that "the allies were not at war with the Paraguayans but rather with the tyrant López who commands them and who treats his countrymen as slaves; and that the allies were going to grant them liberty and institutions together with the right to a government of their own free election."[38] In a later reply of September 5, Estigarribia employed rather pointed and harsh language: "If Your Excellencies are so anxious to grant freedom to Paraguay's peoples, why haven't you commenced by liberating the unhappy Negroes of Brazil who compose the majority of the population and who exist under the hardest and most frightful slavery in order to enrich and provide idle time to some hundreds of the empire's principal figures."[39]

The bombast which marked the beseiged commander's replies changed proportionally with the developing impossibility of his position. By September 18, exactly 100 days after he had crossed into Brazilian territory at São Borja, he was ready to accede to the generous allied terms. These stipulated that the rank and file would be treated as prisoners of war and that the officers might take up residence in any of the allied nations but could not return to Paraguay.[40]

With these terms agreed to on the eighteenth, Estigarribia tendered his sword to Brazilian Minister of War Silva Ferraz who in turn presented it to Dom Pedro.[41] The emperor, accompanied by his two new sons-in-law and by Caxias, wore a poncho and a military kepi bearing the insignia of a colonel of the Voluntários da Pátria. Several articles of this uniform and the Estigarribia sword were later placed in the National Historical Museum. Several unusual sights caught the eye of the young Conde d'Eu. He noted, for example, that Rio Grande cavalry had actually entered Uruguaiana before the surrender had been completed and that they had fraternized almost immediately with the Paraguayans. He was particularly astonished to observe many of the cavalrymen madly galloping about each with an ex-enemy soldier seated behind! Elsewhere he noted that Paraguayan infantrymen took all the loot they could carry with them—each man he saw carried pointed iron bars ripped from fences and windows with which they could prepare *churrasco* (barbecued beef)! The Conde d'Eu wrote that the enemy prisoners could be distinguished from Argentines and Uruguayans by their manner of walking and the nature of their dress. The Paraguayans he saw wore two *mantas* or blankets: the *bichará*, a manta wrapped around the body; and the *chiripá*, a blanket or leather apron wrapped around the lower body including both legs and not around each leg as in the case of Riograndenses, Argentines, and Uruguayans.[42]

Writing to the Condessa de Barral on September 19 Dom Pedro reported that he had visited Uruguaiana the day previous. Referring to the poorly-equipped and starving Paraguayan prisoners, he commented that "o inimigo era mesmo indigno de ser batido—que gente!" (the enemy were not worthy of being defeated—what a people!).[43] Dom Pedro then returned to Rio de Janeiro though not before having a wartime portrait painted at Uruguaiana. The portrait, displaying him attired in gaúcho costume with a wide-brimmed "chambergue-style" hat, was later to cause him some personal vexation.[44]

The taking of Uruguaiana, though a successful combined operation, reflected signs of a developing jealousy and rivalry among officers which were soon to plague the allied high command. On August 31 there had been trouble between Admiral Tamandaré and Venancio Flores regarding overall command of the forces. Subsequently Flores again sought the command in a conference of September 1 attended by the Barão de Pôrto Alegre (Manoel Marques de Souza) and Tamandaré. When Mitre arrived he, too, believed that the supreme command should be his. Finally, in a conference between the three chiefs of state aboard the steamer "Onze de Junho," it was decided that the terms of the Triple Alliance Treaty would not allow Mitre to command the forces while they were on Brazilian territory and that the supreme command should be exercised jointly by Flores, Paunero, and Pôrto Alegre.[45]

Aftermath

His personal participation in the last events at Uruguaiana was a heady experience for Dom Pedro II. It proved the only occasion during the war on which he was able to visit the front—by law he could not leave the confines of the empire without express permission.[46] With an important victory achieved, Dom Pedro condescended to receive new British Minister Sir Edward Thornton, reassigned from La Plata. In presenting both his credentials and Britain's apologies to the emperor Thornton terminated the distant relationships between the two countries stemming from the Questão de Christie.[47]

Old Farroupilha David Canabarro, held responsible by Minister of War Silva Ferraz for the Paraguayan invasion of Rio Grande do Sul, was scheduled for investigation by a council of war. An able report on his part, however, which outlined the weak nature of Brazil's defenses and pointed to the advantages of a strategic retreat, together with the favorable aid given to him by Caxias, caused the proposed proceedings to be suspended. The old gaúcho leader was nevertheless hurt by the accusations and died, a saddened man, in April, 1867.[48]

The 4,113 soldiers and 52 officers who surrendered at Uruguaiana were divided among the allies. The one-third allotted to Brazil were assigned to road construction projects in the interior provinces. Colonel Estigarribia chose Rio de Janeiro for his residence after the fall of Uruguaiana. He then dropped from sight except for a brief, pathetic moment in March, 1869, when he sent a petition to Dom Pedro offering his services as a guide to the Brazilian army in its forthcoming Cordillera campaign.[49] Both the structure and spirit of this letter were in contrast with the colonel's well-written and highly emotional letters to the allies at Uruguaiana. The historian might suspect they were not the productions of the same man. In his account of the war Colonel Thompson claimed the Uruguaiana letters were the work of a priest assigned to Estigarribia as chaplain and secretary. Since the controversial Padre Fidel Maíz later performed such services for Marshal López, there may have been truth in this assertion. The Paraguayan priest could also have been a certain Padre Duarte who, the Conde d'Eu reported, engaged in a bitter post-surrender fight with a Brazilian padre named Gay. In describing the affair the Conde wrote: "Foi preciso que alguns militares separassem á fôrça aquêles dois ministros de Deus—triste espetáculo!" (Several soldiers had to use force to separate these two ministers of God—what a sad spectacle!).[50]

All contemporary sources agree that the news of Uruguaiana proved a deep blow to both the plans and personal vanity of Francisco Solano López. He was said to have become so infuriated over the report of Estigarribia's surrender that even his own son was afraid to go near him.[51] On the one hand his plans for a rapid and successful invasion to the south had evaporated along with the loss of the greater part of his fleet and from 15,000 to 20,000 of his best fighting men. On the other hand, Estigarribia's surrender appeared as a direct flouting of his proud assertion that Paraguayans were prepared to fight to the last man if necessary.

Upon calming down, Paraguay's Marshal President realized that the defeats of Riachuelo and Uruguaiana spelled the end of any hopes for operations in the territory of the allies. He therefore issued orders for the immediate withdrawal of the Resquín forces in Corrientes. Resquín carried out his orders carefully and with foresight. Stringing his men out in a long arc he retreated northward driving an estimated 100,000 head of cattle before him.[52] Apparently wary of the possible presence of further masked batteries of the Cuevas variety, Brazil's fleet slowly followed the Paraguayan army up the Paraná. While it observed the army's crossing of the Upper Paraná to the Humaitá area in late October, it lay idly nearby and may have lost an excellent opportunity to destroy the retreating forces.[53] The promise of adequate army rations held by the immense herd of cattle driven from Corrientes was soon deflated by the effects of fatigue and the appearance of an epidemic among the cattle said to have stemmed from a poisonous herb growing in extreme southern Paraguay.[54]

ADVANCE TO THE UPPER PARANÁ

The withdrawal of Paraguayan forces across the Upper Paraná River after Uruguaiana was followed by the advance of the allies to Corrientes. The movement was hampered by the need to complete the training and organization of arriving new Voluntários da Pátria units, and by heavy winter rains which made the march through Corrientes province a most difficult task.[55]

The Imperial Army, expanding slowly in size, had experienced a number of difficulties. The new volunteer battalions had left Rio de Janeiro at full strength. Sickness and desertion, however, had taken their toll. The 4th Battalion, for example, recruited in Rio de Janeiro and commanded by Lieutenant Colonel Francisco Pinheiro Guimarães, the erstwhile naval surgeon, had left the Côrte in April with a strength of 600. By July, 1865, smallpox and other illnesses had reduced its strength to about 200. Pinheiro Guimarães had trained his men well, however, and at Uruguaiana the 4th Battalion was given the honor of guarding the Paraguayan prisoners. On observing the battalion at drills Dom Pedro commented that it represented one of the finest units of volunteers he had seen.[56]

Other practical difficulties experienced included the need to train volunteers in the manipulation of the new Minié rifles as well as the necessity of standardizing on one rifle caliber only. Faced with the prospect of long marches the artillery units searched for mules and oxen. This proved a serious matter since 6 animals were required to haul each gun, and a further team of 6 were required for the caisson it was estimated that a 20-gun regiment needed 500 animals for its transport.[57] The reorganized engineer regiment under Colonel Vilagran Cabrita soon found itself almost continuously employed in the construction of both stationary and floating bridges across the streams and swamps of Corrientes.

Conditions in the Argentine army under General Mitre were similar. In addition, Mitre's plans for a large Argentine force had been severely curbed by events in Entre Ríos. Resentful over the lack of an offer of high command, General Urquiza was not enthusiastic in persuading his gauchos to join the forces from Buenos Aires. The men themselves could recall that a scant four years earlier they had faced these same Buenos Aires infantry units at the Battle of Pavón. In June Urquiza had succeeded in raising a sizable force, but it had revolted at Basualdo during the night of July 3 and the men simply returned home.[58] Urquiza tried once more but with no better success. Partial to López but unwilling to break his understanding with Mitre, "el vencedor de Caseros" returned to his San José palace and played no active role in the war. In a later interview he informed Captain Richard F. Burton that if López had not invaded Corrientes he would have aided him with 15,000 men against the "macacos" (epithet used by Argentines and Paraguayans referring to Brazilians as monkeys).[53]

The developing allied strength did not pass unnoticed by Marshal López, who believed that the prisoners taken at Uruguaiana were being forced into the Brazilian army. He sent a note of protest to Mitre in November, 1865, which was promptly rejected. Dom Pedro felt the matter to be of sufficient importance for a comment to the Condessa. In a letter of November 23 he stated that he had read the López-Mitre note exchange, that he felt Mitre had given a good answer, and that "happily, there are no Paraguayans serving in the Brazilian army since I gave express orders against such procedure when I was in Rio Grande."[60]

By late 1865 the allied army had reached northern Corrientes and had established camps at Ensenaditas above the port and along the banks of the Upper Paraná The port of Corrientes rapidly assumed an aspect which was strikingly similar to that of City Point, Virginia, General Grant's Union Army supply base during the siege of Petersburg in late 1864 and early 1865. A large hospital was built, a supply depot was established, and the Corrientes roadstead soon became filled with naval and merchant vessels of all flags.[61] Business establishments in the city had swiftly adapted themselves to their new clients. Among the new signs were "Hotel de los Aliados," and "Hotel de Riachuelo." Efforts at rendering restaurant menus more enticing to the new customers featured such suggestions as "Pescado (fish) a la Humaitá," "Riñones (kidneys) de Mitre," "Sesos (brains) de Tamandaré," "Lengua (tongue) de Flores," and "Chauchas (beans) Brasileiras."[62]

Retreat from Laguna

On the outbreak of the war the Brazilian high command had concluded that the most feasible plan for achieving the early defeat of Paraguay would be that of a general attack by Argentine and Uruguayan forces up the Paraná River to be coordinated with a similar offensive by Brazilian forces from Mato Grosso southward down the Paraguay River.[63] This logical plan had to be rejected almost at once because of the relatively small troop strength of available Argentine and Uruguayan forces, the sudden Paraguayan southern offensives, and because of the enormous distances which handicapped the dispatch of a large army from Brazil's coast overland to interior Mato Grosso.

The Mato Grosso project continued to receive study, especially after Paraguay's northern invasion of imperial territory provoked considerations touching on the nation's honor. In early 1865 it was decided that at least a diversionary effort should be attempted in order to reduce possible pressure to the south.[64] The expedition which then took place represented perhaps the most adventurous and tragic military operation of the war. Fortunately, for both the historian and the literary world, the expedition included among its members a young 22-year-old Brazilian engineer officer named Alfredo d'Escragnolle Taunay. Eventually to become one of his country's greatest authors, Taunay began his career with his remarkable account of the Mato Grosso expedition—*A Retirada da Laguna* (The Retreat from Laguna). A further work of even greater renown which stemmed from Taunay's experiences and observations while on this expedition was the novel *Inocência*.

By early March, 1865, the proposed Mato Grosso project had aroused much comment among the cadets of the Escola Militar at Rio de Janeiro. Tentatively scheduled for assignment to Manoel

Deodoro da Fonseca's artillery unit, young Taunay became interested in the expedition when a comrade pointed out that it would represent an opportunity to visit the whole of Brazil's interior and that "with all the required delays the war will be more than over by the time we arrive in the Apa River zone." Taunay approached his father who had no trouble in obtaining his son's appointment by Dom Pedro as adjutant to the expedition's Engineer Commission.[65]

The first detachment of the expedition, including Taunay, left Rio de Janeiro on April 1, 1865, under the command of Colonel Manoel Pedro Drago, ex-chief of police of the Côrte. Traveling by way of Santos and São Paulo, the expedition reached Campinas on April 15. It stayed at this point until June 20 ostensibly to build its strength and to improve equipment. Rumors reaching Rio de Janeiro, however, alleged that Colonel Drago had found his charming feminine hosts at Campinas too great an attraction to relinquish. The expedition finally departed on June 20 with Taunay and his companions having observed a shooting star, considered by them as an ill omen.[66] Arriving at Uberaba on July 18, Taunay noted that it had taken almost four months to travel about 280 miles. Though the force had been increased to about 3,000 men, the inroads of smallpox, malaria, beriberi, and desertion were to cause a steady reduction in its strength.

At Uberaba Colonel Drago received orders from Rio de Janeiro to change the direction of march from Cuiabá, capital of Mato Grosso, to the District of Miranda near the Paraguayan border. On October 18 Drago received further orders relieving him of command because of the impression made by the long delay at Campinas. The second expedition commander, Colonel Galvão, died later near the Rio Negro. After almost unbelievable tribulations, the expedition eventually reached Vila de Miranda in September, 1866. It had taken almost two years to cover 2,112 kilometers and had lost one-third of its original strength.[67]

The expedition remained 113 days at Miranda, from September 17, 1866, to January 11, 1867. Its new commander, appointed January 1, 1867, by the President of Mato Grosso, was Colonel Carlos de Morais Camisão. He had been a member of the garrison which had precipitately evacuated Corumbá during the Paraguayan invasion in December, 1864, and a sonnet had subsequently been circulated which cast aspersion on his name. Taunay wrote that he therefore seized on the expedition's command as a means to vindicate himself. About 47 years old, Camisão was short, robust, and possessed black, piercing eyes. He was serious and preoccupied in manner; his character, however, tended to be marked by indecision. The fact that he was wholly bald was to be availed of by Paraguayans in composing jests regarding his expedition.[68]

Now 1,600 strong and possessing four oxen-drawn La Hitte rifled cannon, the force left Miranda for Nioac on January 11, 1867. On February 25 it began its march toward Paraguayan territory guided by a Mato Grosso sertanejo named José Francisco Lopes, whom Taunay referred to as the expedition's "hawk-eye." The force comprised the 17th Voluntários da Pátria from Minas Gerais, the 20th and 21st Infantry battalions, and the artillery detachment. Some local Indians also were included. Infantrymen carried 60 cartridges in their cartridge boxes; there was no cavalry force with the column, and only a minimum of food and ammunition supplies was carried in carts.[69]

Trouble plagued the expedition almost from its point of departure. Few cattle were found and supplies soon ran low, the delays had enabled the enemy to become informed of the invasion plan, and the lack of cavalry deprived Colonel Camisão of any advance knowledge of the terrain and enemy troop disposition. By late April, however, it had reached the Apa River, the line claimed by Brazil as its southern frontier. On crossing the river, Camisão commenced heading his reports with "Forces in Operation in North Paraguay," and the troops dated their letters home under the phrase "Empire of Brazil."[70]

Only little resistance had so far been encountered, though Paraguayan cavalry had been frequently sighted. On taking Fort Bella Vista, across the Apa, the Brazilians found hides nailed to trees bearing the following message:

Advance, bald-one! Unlucky general who rushes to seek his tomb. The Brazilians think they will reach Concepción in time for the "fiestas;" our troops are awaiting them with bayonets and lead![71]

Colonel Camisão was held to have believed that he could push through North Paraguay to the river port of Concepción where his guns might then form a barrier to traffic on the Paraguay River. Now desperate for supplies he listened to reports that large cattle herds were to be found at a nearby estate called "Laguna" and said to belong to President López. The force reached Laguna on May 1, 1867, but found no cattle—only a burning hut and a further provocative hide message left by the Paraguayans. The first large action occurred on May 8. Known as the Battle of Baiende, it proved to be a Brazilian victory. The supply problem had become so serious, however, that Colonel Camisão now resolved to retreat.[72]

The following 35 days of skirmishing, starvation, and cholera plague formed the epic "Retreat from Laguna." With no supplies and unable to forage for lack of cavalry, the Brazilian force soon experienced starvation. Their plight was rendered even more terrible by the constant attacks of Paraguayan cavalry under Major Urbieta and finally by the outbreak of cholera. Camisão, as well as his second-in-command, the guide Lopes and his son, all succumbed and were buried along the way of the retreat. The long agony endured by the men and the many wives and other female companions who had followed the army, was also marked by the enemy's practice of setting the brush afire along the retreat route. At night, Taunay reported, Paraguayan dogs outside the camp perimeter would set up a loud barking to be answered by Brazilian dogs within the camp. The Brazilian canine defense rapidly dwindled, however, under the pressure of starvation among the troops.[73]

The ordeal eventually ended with the arrival of the remnants of the column at the port of Canuto, June 11, on the Aquidauana River. The survivors were only 700 in number; about 900 men had perished by battle, starvation, cholera, and fire. The remaining troops retained their discipline and had grimly kept their battle flags from enemy hands. They had also managed to haul all four artillery pieces back with them. For their devotion to Brazil and for their undeniable heroism they were acclaimed "Soldados da Constância e do Valor."[74]

Entrusted with the responsibility of carrying the report of the expedition to Rio de Janeiro, young Taunay, in his own words, became for Brazil "the day's man."[75] The Laguna episode, though a defeat, was also a memorable heroic exploit of which Brazil could justly be proud.

Chapter 8

WAR OF POSITIONS

FRANCISCO SOLANO LÓPEZ assumed personal command of the regrouped Paraguayan army on November 25, 1865. It was then about 30,000 men in size. In addition to the 20,000 troops lost during the southern invasions, Assistant Military Surgeon Masterman estimated that almost 50,000 other soldiers had died in South Paraguay from various illnesses including measles, pneumonia, and smallpox.[1] Most of this heavy loss in manpower had been made up by further levies on Paraguay's population. The newer recruits tended increasingly to be either boys in their early teens or older men. Marshal López established his headquarters at Paso la Patria on the banks of the Upper Paraná eastward from its confluence with the Paraguay River at Trés Bocas.

Across the Paraná

By the close of 1865 the allied forces under General Mitre in northern Corrientes province numbered approximately 50,000, of which over two-thirds comprised the Brazilian army. As the allies erected encampments in the area south of the Upper Paraná, Marshal López commenced to plague them with constant raids across the river by groups ranging from but a few men to fairly large-sized detachments. The most serious of these raiding parties turned out to be the first major action of the Humaitá campaign. On January 31, 1866, a 400-man Paraguayan detachment crossed the Upper Paraná and surprised an Argentine army camp near a point on the river known as Corrales. The action, a fierce one, revolved around the stubborn defense by the Paraguayans of their beachhead and the heavy attacks of the 5th Argentine Infantry which went into battle singing the old hymn of General Lavalle.[2] With the result largely a standoff, the Paraguayan survivors retired across the river and young José Díaz, former Asunción police chief, received his first laurels as an enterprising and capable battle commander.[3]

With the near destruction of Paraguay's river squadron at Riachuelo and the retirement to Humaitá of the Bruguez artillery batteries, Brazil's fleet under Admiral Barroso was able to operate as far as the vicinity of Trés Bocas. The construction of heavy batteries at Humaitá and the stretching of a river chain across the Paraguay River presented obstacles to fleet operations further upstream. The squadron, now beginning to receive the new heavily armored ironclads such as the "Brasil" and "Tamandaré," occupied itself in bombardment of the enemy positions at the old brick river fort of Itapirú (meaning dry stone), where the USS "Water Witch" had traded shots with a Paraguayan battery in February, 1855, during the Page scientific expedition. For at least three weeks these operations were opposed by the little "Gualeguay," the former Argentine navy steamer taken by Paraguayan forces at Corrientes in April, 1865. The "Gualeguay," armed only with 12-pounders, provided much amusement for Paraguay's Marshal President who watched its forays against the superior Brazilian warships with a telescope.[4] Sunk purposely when the Paraguayan army retired from Paso la Patria, the "Gualeguay" was later raised and returned to her original owners.

The low-lying wooden barges or chatas once more proved dangerous to the Brazilian squadron. Towed within firing range, the chatas could open a devastating fire with their eight-inch 68-pounders. On March 27 one of these shells hit the "Tamandaré," entering a gun port and causing heavy damage as well as the mortal wounding of Commander Mariz e Barros. He required amputation of both legs, an operation performed reportedly without chloroform—in circumstances strongly reminiscent of the wounding of General Dan Sickles at Gettysburg, the commander died smoking a cigar.[5] His death impressed the emperor, who wrote the Condessa de Barral on April 23 that "the sad event which occurred on the "Tamandaré" hurt me deeply. Mariz e Barros was a brave officer and the Countess should recall him. I believe the ironclads may have drawn too close to the enemy guns without remembering that nothing in this world is invulnerable."[6]

While these events were transpiring the allied high command was busy planning for a crossing of the Upper Paraná into Paraguayan territory. After considerable discussion it was decided to affect the crossing between Itapirú and Paso la Patria. Between the two points, in the middle of the river, lay a low bank called "Banco de Itapirú," to be known later as the "Ilha da Redenção" or "Ilha Cabrita." The action of river currents caused its disappearance after the war. During the night of April 5, 1866, Lieutenant Colonel Vilagran Cabrita landed a force of about 900 men on the island together with a battery of La Hitte cannon and four mortars. Entrenching began immediately protected by the squadron's ironclads.[7]

At about 4 A.M. on April 10 the new advanced Brazilian position was attacked suddenly by an especially chosen force of 1,300 Paraguayans commanded by José Díaz. The force used canoes in order to reach the Brazilian positions undetected. Desperate hand-to-hand combat followed, but by 7 A.M. victory belonged to Colonel Vilagran Cabrita. Some 640 Paraguayan bodies were reported to have been found on the island or floating nearby. Colonel Vilagran Cabrita had but short time to celebrate his victory. That afternoon, while preparing his battle report aboard a launch near the island, he and his aide, Luís Carlos Woolf, were killed by a 68-pounder shell. The gun which fired the fatal round was said to belong to the batteries of José María Bruguez, Vilagran Cabrita's former pupil during his earlier prewar Paraguayan mission.[8]

Success at the Ilha da Redenção provided a bridge for a landing operation on Paraguayan territory. The defending Paraguayan forces retired inland to new positions at the Estero Bellaco, and on April 16, just one year after the news of Paraguay's declaration of war had reached Buenos Aires, Brazilian army units crossed the Upper Paraná. Credit as the first man to reach Paraguay was given to none other than "O Legendário," General Manoel Luís Osório.[9] Accompanying him were two other young officers whose names were to become equally legendary: Floriano Peixoto, regarded familiarly in the army as "o caboclo alagoano" (the countryman from Alagoas), and Manoel Deodoro da Fonseca, the future founder of the republic. The former was congratulated by Mitre, Flores, and Pôrto Alegre for his engineering services; the latter, as a major, commanded a unit composed of companies from the 2nd and 11th Voluntários da Pátria, one of the first detachments to make the crossing and to engage the enemy.[10]

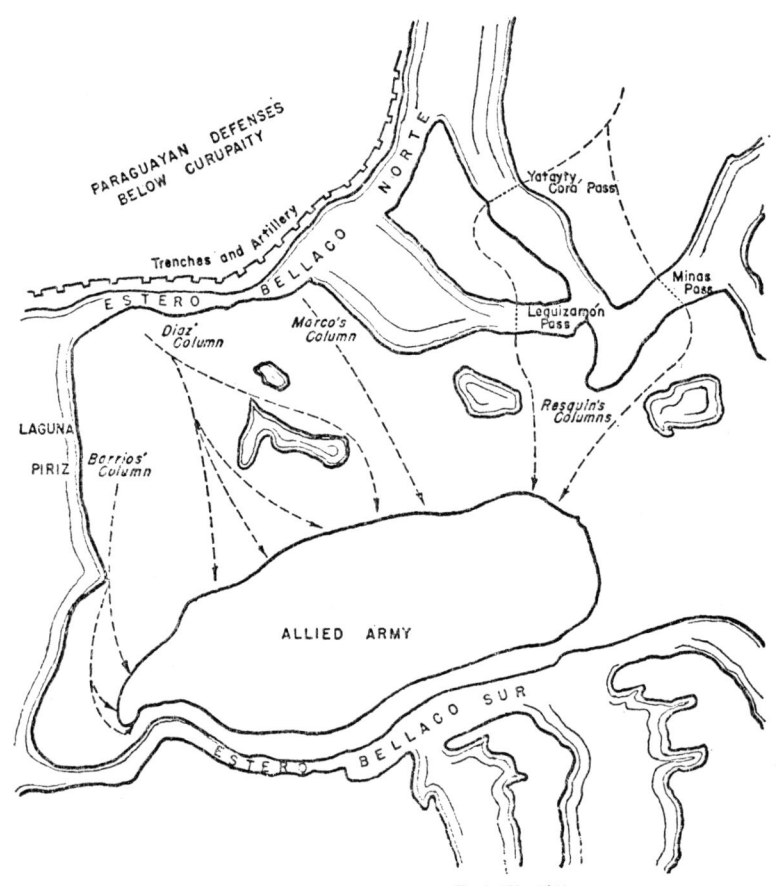

THE FIRST BATTLE OF TUYUTY
(*From*: William H. Jeffrey, *Mitre and Argentina*, New York, 1952.)

Dom Pedro, enthused with these reports, wrote the Condessa de Barral on May 8, 1866, that "the allies will march onto Humaitá and I hope that the war shall soon be ended."[11] His optimistic hopes, to be expressed frequently in his letters, were to require more than two years in fulfillment before the taking of Humaitá.

First Tuyuty

Tuyuty is a place name which figures prominently and frequently among the histories, records, memoirs, and annals of both sides covering the Paraguayan War. It refers to a small area relatively higher than the surrounding marsh land and swamp thickets, dotted by scattered palms, and located a short distance inland from the Brazilian landing point at Paso la Patria. No village or habitations exist in the area, and even today there are no roads which might make it accessible to visitors.

In 1866-67 this isolated point in extreme southern Paraguay was the locale of two battles which rank as the most sanguinary of those in the history of South America. First Tuyuty, fought on May 24, 1866, proved to be a narrow allied victory which assured the permanence of the allied armies on Paraguayan soil. It was also the high-water mark of Paraguay's fighting capacity. Second Tuyuty, which occurred on November 3, 1867, represented the last effort of Marshal López to prevent the encirclement and fall of Humaitá, Paraguay's main defensive bastion.

Following the successful crossing of the Upper Paraná, General Mitre, the allied supreme commander, gradually built up a force of about 35,000 men in the Paso la Patria zone. In early May the allies had been attacked by a large Paraguayan force in the Battle of Bellaco, which resulted in the repulse of Marshal López' forces only after hard fighting among the swamps and mangrove thickets.[12] By late May, 1866, the allies lay along a front extending across the whole Tuyuty area. Facing them in an extremely strong entrenched position which covered the few openings providing passage across the lagoons of the Estero Bellaco lay the Paraguayan army. Aware that Mitre planned an attack, López at first decided upon a defensive action protected by his strong position. In a fatal reversal of this decision, however, he resolved to carry out a well-conceived surprise attack with a force of 22,000 men which might sweep the allies back to the Paraná. His plan called for an early morning frontal assault on the allied positions accomplished simultaneously by a double-envelopment movement on both flanks. The frontal attack was to be made by the forces of José Díaz and Hilário Marcó, and the flank movements by General Barrios on the right and General Resquín on the left.[13]

For his part Mitre had planned a reconnaissance-in-force for May 24 which might yield a victory to be celebrated on Argentina's Independence Day. In general terms the allied troop disposition had Brazilian forces to the left and Argentine units on the right (see end papers). Though the line was only lightly protected, a distinct defensive feature proved to be the deep ditch dug by Emilio Mallet's men, at Osório's orders, in front of the regiment's

28 Whitworth and La Hitte guns.[14] The freshly dug earth was carefully scattered so that the trench, or "fôsso de Mallet" as it was later to be called, became a type of Sunken Road of Waterloo or Bloody Lane of Antietam. Mallet's artillery was supported by the nearby division of General Antônio Sampaio, a 56-year-old Cearense from the Province of Ceará who had been a professional soldier since he was 20. The Mallet-Sampaio combination was to prove as irresistible against the Paraguayan attack as the Rock of Chickamauga was to the Confederates in the fighting before Chattanooga.

Scheduled to begin at daybreak or shortly thereafter, the Paraguayan attack was seriously and inevitably delayed by the difficulties of getting the several units into position along the narrow trails through the Bellaco swamps. The firing of a Congréve rocket was to be the signal for the advance. These rockets, forerunners of the modern rocket-launchers or German *flammenwerfer*, usually fired a 32-pound projectile which caused more fright and confusion by its noise than death and destruction by its explosion. Their use by Paraguay was exactly similar to that by Packenham's British troops at the Battle of New Orleans.[15]

The rocket signalling the commencement of First Tuyuty was not fired until about 11:55 A.M., May 24. Shortly thereafter, a skirmisher of the Brazilian 4th Infantry ran to his commanding officer, Sub-lieutenant Dionísio Cerqueira, and informed him: "Saiba vossa senhoria, sô alferes, que o mato está vermelhando de caboclos!" (Lieutenant! The woods are full of red-shirted Paraguayans!)[16]

For the next four hours this small area was the scene of the most bitter fighting and the worst carnage of the war. Struck repeatedly by the assault troops of Díaz and Marcó, and then by those of Barrios, the Brazilian left flank came close to breaking. The "fôsso de Mallet" and Sampaio's stolid determination, however, proved too formidable for even the fanatic patriotism exhibited by Paraguay's assault troops. Mallet's guns, protected by the ditch in front of them, fired shrapnel with fuses cut to six seconds at such a rate that they were dubbed "artilharia revólver" (repeating cannon).[17] The ditch was swiftly filled with heaps of dead and wounded Paraguayans. Keeping his gunners at their work, Colonel Mallet shouted the phrase for which he became famous: "Por aquí não entram!" (They shall not enter here!)[18]

Antônio Sampaio's 3d Division became known after First Tuyuty as the "Divisão Encouraçada" (armored division).[19] The brevet was well earned. Grimly holding to its task under the orders of its commander, the division fought off seemingly endless frontal charges by the close-packed red-shirted infantrymen of Barrios and Díaz. It alone suffered 1,033 casualties. Among units which especially distinguished themselves were the 42d Battalion of São Paulo under Gomes de Freitas, the 4th Battalion under Pinheiro Guimarães, and the 26th from Ceará under Figueira de Mello. The 4th Battalion went into action with a strength of 490. When the battle was over, only 200 men remained unwounded—it had lost a captain, four lieutenants, two sub-lieutenants, seven cadets and sergeants, and over 100 soldiers. Its commander, former Surgeon-officer Francisco Pinheiro Guimarães, continued to order "Fogo, Batalhão!" (Battalion, Fire!) even after being seriously wounded. His place along the firing line was taken by General Sampaio himself.[20]

Sampaio, mortally wounded by three successive rifle bullets, was finally carried from the field to die on June 8, aboard a transport bound for Buenos Aires. General Osório led a charge of all detached troops he could gather together, which succeeded in stopping a final Paraguayan assault on the survivors of the 26th Battalion. His white kepi, poncho, and silver-inlayed lance—said to have belonged originally to Farroupo leader Bento Manoel Ribeiro—were later placed in the National Historical Museum.[21]

In a letter to the *Semana Ilustrada*, the foremost literary journal of Rio de Janeiro at the time, Colonel Pinheiro Guimarães wrote that one Brazilian feminine camp follower had fought off some Paraguayan soldiers who had managed to reach the rear area. He likened her actions to the famed "Padeira de Aljubarrota" (a Portuguese heroine who was alleged to have brained several Spainards with a bread-oven spatula at the Battle of Aljubarrota in 1385). The observant colonel also quoted a report to the effect that the women of Asunción were stated to have been ready to fight Brazilians with buckets of boiling water. He commented succinctly that such methods were quite unnecessary since Brazilians were to be conquered far more effectively by a "fetching glance or a sly smile!"[22]

With the stubborn defense of the allied left flank and the inability of the Paraguayan cavalry to achieve the planned envelopment of the allied rear, the Battle of First Tuyuty subsided about 4 P.M. Losses had been enormous—between 10,000 and 12,000 for Paraguay and about one-third that amount for the allies. So heavy were Paraguayan casualties, particularly among the best regiments, that the flower of the Spanish race in Paraguay was said to have been obliterated. The famous 40th Battalion, for example, previously riddled in the action of May 2, was once more practically annihilated.[23] Allied troops identified and buried their own dead after the battle. Paraguayan corpses, described as thin and withered, were gathered in piles like logs of wood and cremated. In its edition of June 12, 1866, *La Nación Argentina* carried the story of a mortally wounded Paraguayan flag-bearer who tried to tear his flag to pieces with his teeth in order to prevent its capture by allied troops searching the battlefield.[24]

In a letter to his wife allegedly written the day after the battle, Venancio Flores described how he and General Osório had sought earlier to have the allied camp site changed to a stronger location, and attributed the lack of a greater success to General Mitre. Other details in the letter served to refute Minister Washburn's unfriendly evaluation of him and also provided illuminating comment on relations between the component members of the allied army:

> I can assure you, with all my heart, that during the whole of my campaign against the tyrant Berro, I did not suffer so many annoyances as I have done in the short period we have been on Paraguayan soil. What is passing here does not suit my temper at all. Everything is done by mathematical calculations, and the most precious time is lost in making plans, measuring distances, drawing lines, and looking at the sky: only fancy, the principal operations of the war have been executed on a chessboard.
>
> Everything is left for tomorrow, and the most important movements are postponed. I have seen activity displayed only on levee-days. Then there is plenty of it—regiments, bands of music, compliments, and felicitations everywhere; uniforms and rich swords are shown off. And this happens frequently: for one day is the emperor's birthday, another is the Princess Leopoldina's; tomorrow is the anniversary of the Independence of Brazil; and so on continually.[25]

First Tuyuty had proved an allied victory. Like Shiloh or Antietam, however, it had not been a decisive action. Though the allies were now firmly established on Paraguayan territory, the remnants of Paraguay's army still lay before them within the Humaitá system of fortifications.

Yataity-Corá

During the three months which followed First Tuyuty, until September, 1866, the scene of the war in southern Paraguay was undisturbed by any major action. The first large-scale test of strength had proven a shattering experience both to the allies and Paraguay. During this period Marshal López, now with an army of only about 25,000, occupied himself with the improvement of his entrenched positions, with the emplacement of all artillery which he could discover, and with the dispatch of small detachments to raid allied working parties and lines of communications. One patrol commander, José Matías Bado, achieved such fame for his successful forays that a border village in Northeast Paraguay was later named after him.

On the allied side the combined armies of Brazil, Argentina, and Uruguay preferred to consolidate their newly won foothold on Paraguayan soil. While efforts were made to expand their defense perimeter, the lack of topographical knowledge of the area and of the exact size of the Paraguayan army were factors which curbed any significant offensive moves. Similarly, the river squadron, made wary from its experiences with the chatas and the constant accuracy of enemy shore batteries, exhibited but little disposition for running past the Humaitá fortifications. In a later discussion of allied strategic problems at this time, Mitre told Captain Burton that the possibility of advance by way of Itapúa (Encarnación) had been rejected because of the swamps and deserts reportedly in that area, and also because such a movement would mean loss of the advantage of active support by the Brazilian fleet.

The Paraguayans had constructed a fortified line below Humaitá, the right flank of which rested on a high bank of the Paraguay River known as Curupaity (meaning a tree plantation). Colonel Thompson, now Marshal López' engineer officer, had caused a water battery to be emplaced at this point, which added to the Paraguayan river defenses. Subsequently, a smaller redoubt was built on the river bank south of Curupaity at a point known as Curuzú (meaning a cross).

In addition to these new defensive works, a further innovation in the preparation of obstacles for Brazil's fleet comprised the assembly and laying of river mines and torpedoes. Kruger, the engineer who figured most prominently in this project, was the same unsung American expert of the war who had earlier startled Paraguay's high command at a celebration in Asunción by blowing up a palm raft in the river. Assisted by a Pole named Michkoffsky and a Paraguayan named Ramos, who had received training with the Blyth company, Kruger launched both fake and authentic mines and torpedoes. Unfortunately for Paraguay, he and Ramos lost their lives in the premature explosion of one of these devices.[26] Michkoffsky, suspected of wanting to desert, was assigned to the front lines and later killed in action.[27] The project, however, was a success. On September 2, while engaged in bombardment of the new enemy river positions, the ironclad "Rio de Janeiro" blew up and sank with all hands as a result of contact with one of these torpedoes. It was the only ironclad to be so lost during the war. The event, of course, made Admiral Tamandaré even more cautious in the employment of the squadron.

Curuzú

Following the surrender of Estigarribia's column at Uruguaiana, the Brazilian army units which had fought there were formed into a 2d Army Corps. They were to act partly as a reserve for the main army in Corrientes and as a guard force to watch both the Rio Grande frontiers and to be used if necessary in a diversionary probe at Itapúa in the Misiones area. Under the command of the Barão de Pôrto Alegre, the corps was ordered to move to Itapirú in the active war theater.

In late August, the allied command resolved to use the 14,000 fresh troops of the 2d Corps in an attack on Curuzú. Mitre was reported to have ordered Pôrto Alegre to embark his men for the attack under the command of Admiral Tamandaré. Pôrto Alegre demurred since he felt that the command should be his by virtue of his commission being older than that of the admiral. The disagreement, though finally resolved, turned out to be the prelude of even more bitter haggling over the question of command.[28]

On September 3, Pôrto Alegre's corps debarked and went forward in a general assault upon the advanced Paraguayan Curuzú position. The attack was a swift success, although the troops suffered heavy losses while stumbling through the marshy lagoons which covered the position. An even more signal victory might have been attained had Pôrto Alegre not exhibited undue prudence in halting the pursuit of the retreating garrison survivors.[29] The Curupaity lines were not completed nor was there a strong Paraguayan defensive force at hand. If the Curuzú attack had been maintained on September 3 it might have resulted in a drive straight through the Curupaity line to Humaitá. Pôrto Alegre, however, elected to consolidate his victory at Curuzú. The "Bravo de Curuzú" was shortly to be made visconde for his success.

The Paraguayan survivors of the 10th Battalion which had been stationed at Curuzú received short shrift from Marshal López because of their retreat. They were literally decimated by special firing squads; the remaining men were reassigned to other units.[30]

The López-Mitre Peace Conference

Of the war's many publicized episodes and incidents, few if any reflected the intense drama which was enacted at a small palm grove between the opposing lines on September 12, 1866. On this date Bartolome Mitré, supreme allied commander, and Francisco Solano López, Marshal President of Paraguay, met personally to confer on the possibilities of reaching a peace agreement.[31]

The initiative for the meeting came from Marshal López. He could not have chosen a more auspicious moment for peace negotiations. The Triple Alliance Treaty terms, now made public, had generated indignation among the West Coast republics which had sponsored a protest to the allied governments by Peru, publication of the terms had similarly strengthened the Marshal President's bid for the role of protector of Paraguay and its people, the war showed no signs of an early ending, and finally, the continued prosecution of the war was giving evidence of becoming unpopular among the allied nations, particularly in Argentina. At Buenos Aires only the newspapers *La Nación Argentina* and *La Tribuna* were in favor of continuing the war. Among the others in opposition to the war and in favor of negotiations with Paraguay were *El Nacional, El Pueblo, La América, El Correo Mercantil,* and *La Palabra de Mayo*.[32] The paper *La América*, directed by Agustín de Vedía, was reported to have openly defended López, to have attacked Mitre as incompetent, and even to have reproduced articles from *El Semanario*, the weekly paper at Asunción.[33] Among the Argentine provinces there were rumors that an ugly cry indeed had been frequently heard: "No queremos la guerra con López!" (We don't want war with López!).[34]

There was, however, one factor of which Francisco Solano López may not have been fully aware. This was the intransigent attitude with which Imperial Brazil viewed the war. Its national honor had been impugned, and until the cause of the affront was removed the war would continue. The "cause" was López, and there could be no peace with López. On September 7, 1866, on the eve of the Yataity-Corá conference, Dom Pedro wrote to the Condessa de Barral: "The governments of the republics of the Pacific have protested against continuation of the war; but if the war ends soon the protest will be of no value."[35] He wrote again on October 9, 1866: "Peace is being spoken of in Río de la Plata; but I shall not make peace with López, and public opinion is with me; there is therefore no need for you to be worried over the honorable success of the campaign for Brazil. I fear some possible official intervention from Europe, but we shall know how to conduct ourselves with polish and energy." The public opinion mentioned by the emperor was clearly reflected in the reaction to the peace rumors by the mother of Manoel Deodoro da Fonseca. When informed that negotiations were underway, Dona Rosa Maria Paulina da Fonseca reportedly exclaimed that she would prefer to have her sons buried on Paraguayan battlefields rather than have the nation "saved" by a shameful peace.[36]

On September 11, 1866, Captain Francisco Martínez of the Paraguayan army appeared before the allied lines under a flag of truce, bearing an invitation from Marshal López to General Mitre for a personal interview. Mitre accepted. The famous conference at Yataity-Corá took place subsequently on September 12. General Polidoro, former commandant of the Escola Militar da Praia Vermelha and now acting commander of Brazil's army, refused to attend by citing a lack of instructions to do so. Venancio Flores retired early from the conference due to an alleged uncomplimentary statement by López regarding his role in earlier Uruguayan affairs.

Often described in historical accounts particularly from the aspect of the striking difference reflected by the military splendor of the uniform of Francisco Solano López and the informal, undress attire of Mitre, featured by his old sombrero, Yataity-Corá was the first and most important of the efforts to negotiate a peace between the opposing nations.[37] Other than descriptions of the uniforms of the two men, their exchanges of toasts and riding quirts, little is known of the substance of their historic meeting. Based on correspondence preserved in national archives, and on the accounts of several of the contemporary observers, Francisco López apparently believed that he could convince Mitre of the benefits and need for a peace agreement. His own army had been seriously riddled by losses from both warfare and disease, and his position offered scant optimism. He had, however, fought superior allied forces to a standstill. Besides, as the erstwhile Arbiter of La Plata, he may have believed that his fame stemming from the Pact of San José de Flores may still have been remembered among Argentina's leaders. It was a grim blow to his hopes to discover that the Argentina of Bartolomé Mitre was securely tied to the foreign policy of Brazil which, at that time, was set upon the total disappearance of the López government in Paraguay, as well as the effective neutralization of Paraguay as a potential threat in La Plata.

The conference of Yataity-Corá, therefore, proved both a failure and an education for Paraguay's Marshal President. On the one hand any hopes he may have entertained for an honorable end to the war were thoroughly crushed. On the other hand he came to realize that it was not only the question of his presence at the head of Paraguay's government that was involved in the war. It had become clear that the allies were determined upon a goal which included not only his disappearance, but also the satisfaction of the maximum of Brazilian and Argentine territorial claims against Paraguay, the disbanding of Paraguay's army, the razing of Paraguayan frontier and river fortifications, and a remodeling of Paraguay's form of government. Though these objectives had come to light with publication of the terms of the Triple Alliance Treaty, Francisco Solano López may have held some vain hope for separate negotiations with the Argentina of Bartolomé Mitre.

Paraguay's Marshal President came away from Yataity-Corá in the blackest of moods.[38] Despondent and worried, he faced a most important decision. In this negotiation, as well as in the course of the subsequent discussions with British diplomat Gould, it seemed apparent that a life of ease in Europe might exist for him were he to accept voluntary exile. He realized, however, that by so doing his actions would not spell a return to the prewar status quo for his country. To the Marshal President, therefore, only one course was possible. Paraguay in 1866 was López, and Francisco Solano López was Paraguay. He elected to remain with his country and with his army. So long as he lived, Paraguay would live; the war waged by the Paraguay of Francisco Solano López against its enemies thus became one of "Independencia o Muerte (Independence or Death).[39]

Following Yataity-Corá, General Mitre sought confirmation by the allies of the position he had assumed with Marshal López as well as instructions to cover the preparation of a formal reply to the López proposal. For Brazil's part the confirmation and instructions were contained in a letter from Minister Octaviano to Foreign Minister Elizalde dated November 10, 1866. The letter read:

In accordance with the thoughts of my government, which I have confided to you in showing you the latest confidential instructions I have received, I think you can authorize the General-in-Chief to make the following reply:

"The allied governments are not conducting a war against the nation of Paraguay; it is being conducted against the policies and government of General Francisco Solano López; and convinced by experience that the continuation of this government represents a menace to peace in South America, and to the freedom of commerce and navigation along the Paraguay and Upper Paraná Rivers and their tributaries, *they cannot under any circumstances deal with that nation as long as the aforementioned General López remains on its soil.*"

Any changes to be made in the foregoing will be agreeable to me as long as the text contains the concluding phrase which has been underlined.[40]

No record has as yet come to light regarding the reaction of Paraguay's Marshal President upon receipt of the formal reply of the allies. It might be assumed, that it persuaded him that his earlier appraisal of the situation had been reasonably correct.

Curupaity

In several accounts of the Paraguayan War the suggestion has been made that the peace conference proposed by Marshal López at Yataity-Corá was not without a more subtle motive. López is held also to have evaluated the military situation, and to have perceived that a general attack on Curupaity was being planned by the allies. He therefore sought to obtain as much extra time as possible in order to construct a strong line of defenses.

In his memoirs Colonel Thompson stated that both he and the Marshal made a personal inspection of the new front along the Paraguay River facing Curuzú, and that on September 8 López decided to order the immediate construction of a heavily fortified line. In Thompson's words, "López was now quite persuaded that the allies were about to give him the coup de grâce, and he thought of trying to come to terms with them, or, at any rate, to gain a little time to fortify Curupaity."[41]

Working night and day under Thompson's able direction, Paraguayan engineer details dug a trench about 2,000 yards long, running east from the river, protected on its left flank, and six feet deep and eleven feet wide. All trees in front of it were felled to make revetments for gun positions and for the erection of a line of *abatis*—tree branches with their sharpened ends pointing towards the enemy—and a forerunner of barbed-wire entanglements. Forty-nine artillery pieces and two Congréve rocket-stands were emplaced along the line, all in positions selected to provide the greatest enfilading fire possible. The most powerful guns were eight 8-inch 68-pounders capable of firing charges of grapeshot (like a sack of iron tennis balls) which could decimate an entire platoon with one round. These guns and the 5,000 infantry assigned to the trench were placed under command of José Díaz, now Marshal López' favorite officer.[42]

Paraguay's Marshal President was entirely correct in his assessment of the military situation. After a conference of the allied high command which was again marked by much bitter controversy, Mitre finally won the honor of directing the attack. The original plan contemplated a general assault on the supposedly weak Paraguayan line on September 17, the anniversary of the Battle of Pavón. Heavy rains, however, caused postponement of the movement until September 22.[43] The attack was to be made after a preliminary bombardment of the enemy positions by Armiral Tamandaré's squadron. The admiral, upon being advised of his role, was said to have commented, "Em duas horas descangalharei tudo isso!" (I shall blow the earthworks to pieces in two hours!).[44]

The fleet opened its bombardment as scheduled on the morning of September 22. Though awesome in aspect, the rain of shells on the Paraguayan earthworks did little damage. Lying in trenches situated about 30 feet above the river level, the defending troops were securely protected against shellfire. At noon the signal for the assault was given and some 11,000 Brazilian troops and 7,000 Argentines advanced upon Curupaity.

The assault is best and most briefly described as being similar to the attack by Packenham's British regulars upon Jackson's line at Chalmette, or the attack upon Lee's Confederate positions at Cold Harbor by Grant's Union troops in June, 1864. It was a gigantic and bloody failure. Though the assault began in good order, the swampy ground and lagoons together with the Paraguayan fire, shortly disrupted any efforts to maintain organization. Carrying fascines and scaling-ladders with which to cross the trenches, the attacking force came under artillery fire almost at once.[45] As they neared the Paraguayan line, Argentine troops now almost shot to ribbons by the concentrated blasts of grape and canister fired at them, attempted a final, hopeless charge upon the earthworks. It was met by Paraguayan infantrymen who emerged from ditches and fired point-blank with short-ranged, flintlocks.[46]

The carnage was so dreadful that Bartolomé Mitre gave early orders for a general retirement. The proud Argentine 6th Infantry, still commanded by the wounded Major Luis María Campos, marched backward from the trenches in order not to show their backs to the enemy.[47] If the flower of the Spanish race in Paraguay was said to have been obliterated at First Tuyuty, the same might nearly have been said of the finest of Buenos Aires aristocracy at Curupaity. Among the many dead on the marshy ground and in the lagoons between Curuzú and Curupaity were 21-year-old Dominguito Sarmiento, only son of Argentina's minister to the United States and the future successor to Mitre as president, and young Francisco Paz, son of the vice president, who had foregone studies in Europe in order to join the army.[48] About a week later, when the transports "Susan Bearn" and "Río de la Plata" reached Buenos Aires with the news and bearing hundreds of wounded, almost the entire city went into mourning. Subsequently in the United States, Mary Mann was upset by a letter from Domingo F. Sarmiento's sisters in Buenos Aires, who wrote that they feared the news of Curupaity might affect their brother's mind.[49]

Curupaity was a stunning victory for Paraguay—it was its greatest military feat of the war. When the firing ceased and an account was made of the results, it was found that Paraguayan losses had been incredibly small—only about 50 killed and wounded. In comparison, and though official reports showed much lower figures, the allies had lost about 9,000 soldiers. According to Thompson, an eyewitness, more than 5,000 killed and wounded were left on the field alone. Jubilant Paraguayan detachments scoured the battlefield tossing corpses into the lagoons or the river, dispatching most of the wounded, and collecting enormous amounts of trophies including the welcome addition of more than 3,000 new-model Liége Enfield rifles. Paraguayan soldiers also stripped the dead of their clothes and equipment—whole Paraguayan detachments later appearad dressed in new Argentine and Brazilian uniforms.[50]

José Díaz, excited by his easy and complete victory, sent a telegraphic report to Marshal López at his Paso Pucú headquarters, in Guaraní, which possibly failed to indicate the magnitude of the allied defeat.[51] Had López been aware of all details, he might have mounted a counterattack which would have compounded the allied disaster. Retiring Brazilian and Argentine units, however, were allowed to resume their former positions at Curuzú. Francisco Solano López celebrated his success with an all-out victory dinner; José Díaz became Paraguay's man of the hour; the troops had their own victory dance around the main yard of the "Jequitinhonha."[52]

The Quadrilátero

Following the Battle of Curupaity the front in southern Paraguay saw no more major battle actions for fourteen months. This long period could not be called a quiet one, however, for patrol duty, entrenching tasks, skirmishing, sniping, and almost daily bombardments, kept the armies of both sides constantly on the alert. It was the period of the war most similar to the Union Army's siege of Petersburg in 1864-65.

The system of trenches and strong points which comprised the defensive position of Paraguay's army appears on maps of the time like a rectangular trapezoid in shape. It was for this particular reason referred to among the allied armies and by their military historians as the *quadrilátero*. Its entrenched lines ran along the crests of the few small slopes in the area, and were expressly laid out to cover all openings or passages through the Estero Bellaco swamps. The strongest point of the system, of course, was the Humaitá fortification commanding a sharp horseshoe bend in the Paraguay River. It had been originally designed by a Hungarian soldier of fortune, Colonel Enrique Wisner von Morgenstern, who had earlier served Brazil and had been captured by Caxias for having participated in the Minas Revolt of 1842. Humaitá was largely a "Sebastopol" in name only. It had only one brick revetted battery, the famed "Batería Londres," and most of the parapets and barbettes were of dirt construction. Its aspect, armament, and location were nonetheless menacing. Other than by attack by frontal assault, the quadrilátero could be taken only by the fleet's passage of Humaitá or by an extensive flank movement to the east. The former maneuver, though it eventually proved possible, faced the combined obstacles of river obstructions and mines and torpedoes as well as the direct, concentrated fire of the powerful Humaitá batteries. The latter possibility would involve the maneuver of a large force over unknown and difficult terrain together with the danger of enemy attack upon a supply line which would be both long and vulnerable.

Under the direction of Colonel Thompson, the quadrilátero was made into an extremely strong position. An account of its defenses was contained in a report by British diplomat G. Z. Gould, who visited the Paraguayan lines during 1867:

The riverside batteries of Humaitá at present mount only 46 guns, namely one 80-pounder, four 68-pounders, eight 32-pounders; the rest are of different calibers. The battery of Curupaity towards the river mounts thirty 32-pounders. The center is defended by about a hundred guns. On the left are 117 guns, including four 68-pounders, one 40-pounder rifled Whitworth (recovered from the wreck of the Brazilian ironclad after the Battle of Riachuelo), one 13-inch mortar; fourteen 32-pounders, and many rifled 12-pounders. Humaitá, on the land side, is protected by three lines of earthworks, on the innermost of which 87 guns are mounted. Total on the left, 204 guns. The grand total is, therefore, 380 guns.[53]

Marshal López established his headquarters at Paso Pucú, near the eastward end of the line, and had a large earthern bombproof shelter constructed for his protection. Tall lookout towers called "mangrullos" were built at intervals along the lines which facilitated both observation of enemy movements and the direction of artillery fire.[54] Similar towers were built by the allies.

The relative inactivity along the front in late 1866 and 1867 provides an opportunity for a brief survey of conditions within the two opposing armies.

THE PARAGUAYAN LINES

Rebuffed at Yataity-Corá yet possessing an enormous victory to his credit, Marshal President López elected to remain on the defensive. The possibility of foreign intervention to stop the war still existed as events were to prove, and the allied losses at Curupaity assured further clamor for peace among the allied nations. His own army, though confident from its recent success, now numbered only about 20,000 men.[55] Most of the earlier elite units had been lost in action and their places were now being filled by the last manpower resources available to Paraguay—the young boys and the "toothless" old men.

Artillery practice.—Aside from the constant raiding parties, the principal military activity of this period comprised the endless artillery bombardments. Since the Paraguayan army was of necessity handicapped in this field by supply considerations, its artillery practice was reserved for occasions when obvious good targets presented themselves. The allies, however, were under no such restraints. Both the land artillery and the fleet poured an almost continuous fire upon the Paraguayan positions. The fleet was particularly active. The rain of shells it fired at the quadrilátero became a daily occurrence—General José Díaz, the "Vencedor de Curupaity," referred to this activity as the "fiesta diaria de los Negros" (the daily fiesta of the Negroes).[56] His disdain for the fleet's efforts was to prove his undoing. In early January, 1867, José Díaz decided to go out on a river scouting patrol in a canoe and was mortally wounded by a shell fired from the fleet. His death on February 7 was a severe blow to López. Fidel Maíz was to write after the war that it represented the only occasion on which Paraguay's Marshal was seen openly to reflect grief.[57]

As the daily allied bombardments continued, the Paraguayans hit upon a unique system of replenishing their ammunition supplies. Many of the allied shells failed to explode, and Paraguayan soldiers were ordered to collect them for re-use by their own artillery. Marshal López himself found artillery practice to be an excellent diversion. While at his Paso Pucú headquarters he had an elaborate sign system developed whereby he could be advised at once of the target for the new rounds from his batteries. He could then train his telescope on the target and observe the result of the salvo. General Osório's headquarters became a favorite target for the Marshal in this pastime.[58]

The Turututús.—Hampered by supply shortages, the Paraguayans were not always able to return the allied fire in kind. They were still able to express their feelings, however, with use of strange local horns called "turututús" which were said to have emitted a singularly derisive sound.[59] Each blast of allied gunfire came to be followed by the odd wail of the turututús indicating the lack of a successful hit. Though perfectly harmless, of course, this unusual custom was alleged to have irritated the Marquês de Caxias after he assumed command.[60] Brazilian troops were also reported to have adopted the strange custom.

Telegraph services.—The use by Marshal López of telegraphic communications impressed several foreign observers. Consul Hutchinson at Rosario commented that the Paraguayan system followed that employed by Napoleon III at the battles of Magenta and Solferino—"telégrafos ambulantes," or movable telegraphs comprising batteries, wires, and poles sufficient to cover a 15-mile circuit.[61] The system, still operated by Fischer von Truenfeldt, centered upon the López headquarters and included the original line to Asunción as well as the circuit along the front. Attracted to the new device, Paraguay's Marshal requested daily reports from every sector of his defensive position. Von Truenfeldt was even reported to have undertaken the invention of Morse instruments from local materials, in view of the inability to obtain replacements from abroad.[62] Unfortunately, this enterprising German technician left no known memoirs of his Paraguayan experiences.

During his visits to the Humaitá area Captain Burton observed the Paraguayan telegraph lines and noted that each pole was of fine hard wood with a lightning conductor on top—an innovation which he felt might have represented a "wrinkle" for the Brazilians.[63]

Supplies and equipment.—With use of the Paraná River effectively blocked by Brazil's squadron, the Paraguayan army could draw only on the supplies accumulated prior to the war and on the stores taken in Mato Grosso and Corrientes. An effort was made to open a road through the Chaco to Bolivia, but only a small trickle of supplies was received over this route. Although Bolivian strong man Melgarejo was held to be sympathetic toward López, his sympathies were never transformed into concrete assistance.[64]

As the war progressed the army was therefore forced to rely solely upon supplies captured in battle or upon locally made substitutes. The original red blouses soon gave way to the use of any clothing which was available, the rough chiripás came into use, the former French Guard caps were replaced by poor leather copies, hospital equipment and medicines simply became nonexistent, and rations, once equal to a cow for every 80 men, eventually shrank to a one-per-500 ratio.[65] Women who had come to the lines to be near their men sought to grow corn and manioc for the army's supply on ground that was not suitable for agriculture. The farming areas to the north had now lost their normal field hands to the army, and local production thus declined. Like the Union blockade of Confederate ports, the allied grip on the Paraná was slowly achieving more success than had military actions.

Morale.—The one element of Paraguay's defensive capacity which reflected no noticeable signs of decline was the army's morale. In addition to the strict disciplinary measures that he enforced, Marshal López sought to maintain the loyalty and morale of his men at a high level. Exceptional service and heroism in battle on the part of his officers were recognized by promotions, the award of special medals, and appointment to one of the orders of merit which had been established at the outbreak of the war.[66] The men were eligible for promotion from the ranks. It was also the custom of Paraguay's Marshal President to hold informal, impromptu meetings after Mass on Sundays during which he would give effective speeches in Guaraní regarding the status of operations to the men gathered about him. Jokes at the allies' expense were especially appreciated by the soldiers. Perhaps in retribution for the disparaging remarks concerning their president which were printed in the allied press, the following derisive terms were coined by López' men:

    Caxias—el viejo bragueta
    Dom Pedro—el caraí de la macacada
    Mitre—el desplumado cisne del Plata
    (Caxias—the old "so-and-so"

Dom Pedro—chief of the monkey tribe
Mitre—the "deplumed" swan of La Plata).[67]

Large celebrations, including banquets and dances, were always held to mark the president's birthday, July 24, and on October 16, the date on which he assumed the presidency.

For those of the troops who could read there were several newspapers in circulation. The semiofficial *El Semanario*, directed by Natalicio Talavera, printed the texts of decrees, proclamations, and speeches, as well as war reports. Further weekly newspapers were *El Centinela*, which began publication in April, 1867, and the *Lambaré*. A particular favorite within the army proved to be *Cabichui* (the name of an especially vicious black wasp), which appeared in May, 1867, and which was published in both Spanish and Guaraní. Copies were occasionally passed into the allied lines. Young Dionísio Cerqueira reported that in one such issue the allies were tauntingly described as follows:

Orientales—general sin ejército
Brazileros—ejército sin general
Argentinos—ni general ni ejército!
(Uruguayans—general without an army
Brazilians—army without a general
Argentines—neither general nor army!).[68]

Later during the Cordillera campaign a portable press was used to publish the army's last paper, *La Estrella*. As newsprint became impossible to obtain, telegraphist von Truenfeldt developed a paper factory able to produce a satisfactory substitute from local materials.[69]

In his account of his Paraguayan experiences, George F. Masterman related that the Marshal ordered a peep show and a magic lantern set from Europe for the distraction of the troops, and that the set, minus directions for its installation and operation, arrived just before the Paraná River was blockaded by war. In the absence of the directions, López had Masterman and Thompson put it together. Fortunately, the two Englishmen succeeded. Its first showing, which featured "The Bay of Naples by Moonlight" and "A Chasseur d'Afrique Engaging Ten Arabs at Once," together with other comedy acts, was a tremendous success. While battle scenes of the Franco-Italian War evoked only mild applause, a comic scene which featured a dwarf's nose growing steadily to immense size, produced an uproar. Masterman reported that Bishop Palacios, in particular, came close to total collapse from glee at the dwarf's plight.[70]

Peace overtures.—Commencing with the ill-fated conference at Yataity-Corá, there were several peace overtures made during 1866-67. None of them succeeded, but on each occasion hopes were raised on both sides that the war might soon be terminated.

Acting on instructions from Washington, ministers Asboth at Buenos Aires, Webb at Rio de Janeiro, and Washburn at Asunción, sought in late 1866 and early 1867 to convince the governments to which they were accredited of the advantages of a peace to be attained possibly through the good offices of the United States. Marshal President López was agreeable to the proposal; none of the allied governments were in favor. Washburn, who went so far as to cross the lines in order to interview Caxias, found that Brazil's position toward López was adamant. A later effort by Webb was similarly unavailing even though several newspapers at Buenos Aires, notably *La República* and *Pueblo* had openly urged the advisability of concluding a peace with Paraguay.[71] The key to these negotiations lay with Dom Pedro. On March 23, 1867, he wrote to the Condessa de Barral that "the good offices of the United States do not give me reason for concern, and everybody knows the nature of my firm resolution."[72] On May 23 he wrote again: "Above all we must continue forward and finish the war with honor. It is a question of honor and I will not compromise."[73]

The failure of the United States effort, which was marked by an alleged dubious negotiating skill, and the refusal by the allies to consider the proposal, represented a signal exception to the usual Western Hemisphere policy of the peaceful settlement of international disputes.[74]

In August, 1867, G. Z. Gould, a British diplomatic officer from Buenos Aires, arrived within the Paraguayan lines in order to conduct negotiations for the repatriation of British subjects in the service of Paraguay. Partially successful in this effort, he also tried his hand at negotiating a possible basis for peace. His efforts foundered on the same obstacle that had caused failure at Yataity-Corá—"peace with victory and victory with the exclusion of López." The terms were refused by Paraguay's president.

By the fall of 1867 Brazil could detect an optimistic turn in operations which augured well for the future. Regarding the

Gould incident Dom Pedro wrote the Condessa de Barral on October 8, 1867: "The secretary of the British legation at Buenos Aires, entirely *motu proprio,* went to Humaitá to protect British subjects and returned from there with peace proposals. Brazilian agents only listened to him. They were inadmissable; even López through his own declarations ruined the efforts of the secretary whose failure may counsel greater circumspection in the future in the matter of intervention into alien affairs."[75]

Manlove and von Versen.—Of the numerous foreigners who were in Paraguay during the war there were none whose adventures presented more curious circumstances than those of James Manlove, an American, and Max von Versen, a German. Both came through the allied lines during the quadrilátero period—no mean feat considering that the allies had established a strict blockade against almost all outside communications with Paraguay. Minister Washburn, himself, was forced to employ every conceivable means short of force by the United States Navy in order to return to his post at Asunción after home leave.[76]

Manlove and von Versen were the only foreigners, so far as history has recorded, who were able to traverse the allied lines and enter Paraguay during the war without benefit of diplomatic or other official status. Both were partial to Paraguay. Manlove was a soldier of fortune who believed his services could be utilized by Paraguay, and von Versen was a professional soldier who merely wished to view the war as an observer at close range.

In his memoirs Minister Washburn claimed that James Manlove was a Marylander and an ex-major in the Confederate army who had been with General Nathan Bedford Forrest's command at the massacre of Fort Pillow.[77]

Manlove succeeded in entering the Paraguayan lines in August, 1866. According to Masterman's account, he is said to have discussed with Marshal López a proposal to finance the purchase of privateers which, under his command, would then embark upon high-seas raids against Brazilian merchant vessels. For some reason Paraguay's Marshal President mistrusted Manlove, rejected his proposal, and had him sent to Asunción. Later during the conspiracy period, the major fell at odds with the local police, was arrested, and met his end before a firing squad in company with Britisher John Watts, the man who had advised López on the eve of the Battle of Riachuelo.[78]

If López had accepted Manlove's services, he might have added an additional novelty to the war's character. The major's scheme was by no means fantastic, and assuming that he could have fitted out a privateer in the Caribbean, his probable depredations among Brazilian shipping would undoubtedly have heightened public distaste for the war.

Max von Versen was a major in the Royal Prussian army who became so interested in the conflicting reports of the war in far-off Paraguay that he determined to visit the scene as a private, unofficial observer. He obtained temporary retirement from the Prussian army and, armed only with a letter of recommendation from Paraguayan agent DuGraty in Paris and a letter of reference from General von Moltke, he sailed for South America in February, 1867. The account of his difficulties in reaching Paraguay are nearly as fascinating as his adventures within the war zone. Almost constantly mistaken for a Paraguayan spy, he was jailed in both Brazil and Argentina—in all, he was arrested a record five times during his two years in La Plata!

Von Versen finally reached the Paraguayan lines in July, 1867. Though his description of himself as a simple observer was plausible, the Paraguayans had found in his pockets a photo of Colonel Susini, commander of the 1st Argentine Infantry. This cast enough suspicion on him to induce Marshal López to order his semidetention. Although his movements were thus curtailed, von Versen managed to obtain an excellent impression of Paraguay's army before the fall of Humaitá and during the period up to the allied victory of Lomas Valentinas. Freed from his captivity along with Brazilian Major Cunha Mattos in December, 1868, von Versen returned to Prussia in time for the Franco-Prussian War. His later account of his Paraguayan experiences ranks with the memoirs of Colonel Thompson as the most reliable and competent eyewitness record of the war.[79]

The Allied Lines

The two-month period following Curupaity represented the nadir of the allied war effort. The heavy losses suffered in the frontal attack at Curupaity had generated consternation and anger, especially at Buenos Aires. The high command again quarrelled over the responsibility for the recent battle disaster. It was obvious that the army required a period for both recuperation and reorganization. Significant changes in command were not to be delayed—Venancio Flores was soon called to Montevideo to face growing disturbances at home; Bartolomé Mitre began to experience similar pressures which required his subsequent return to Buenos Aires; the need for a more positive and experienced commander at the head of the Imperial army had now become evident to the government at Rio de Janeiro.

Although Luís Alves de Lima e Silva, Marquês de Caxias, was a staunch Conservative, it was obvious even to Brazil's Liberal government that he was the only military figure available who might achieve the reorganization task now urgently required in the conduct of Brazil's war effort. Caxias was offered the command and accepted at once. During a Senate appearance in October, 1866, government leader Zacarias praised Caxias' action and noted that the war effort had not lacked as much of men as it did of a good leader.[80] The choice for commander of such a prominent Conservative as Caxias, however, resulted in political repercussions. In July, 1868, by use of his *poder moderador* (moderating power), Dom Pedro managed a form of coup d'état which toppled the Liberal government of Zacarias and returned the Conservatives to power. The event is also held as the first evidence of the entry of the military class into politics.

Like his earlier performances in the service of the empire, Caxias' assumption of command provided the leadership and stimulation required for attainment of Brazil's goals. The 64-year-old Field Marshal arrived at Corrientes in November, 1866, and assumed command of the army on November 18. According to an anecdote he is said to have placidly announced, "Hei de fazer alguma coisa" (I expect I shall accomplish a thing or two). Polidoro was relieved of the command of the 1st Corps; Pôrto Alegre, ill since the Battle of Curuzú, returned temporarily to Brazil and relinquished command of the 2d Corps to General Argolo; Osório, now Barão do Herval, was ordered to build a 3d corps in Rio Grande do Sul. In December, 1866, old Admiral Tamandaré turned command of the squadron over to Admiral José Joaquim Ignacio.

Changes within the army and navy.—In striking contrast to Paraguay's army, wherein the question of equipment and supplies as well as manpower grew daily more serious, Brazil's army daily became stronger. Losses from battle and disease were replaced by a steady flow of new recruits, shiploads of supplies moved unhindered up the Paraná to Corrientes and Paso la Patria, and important improvements were made to equipment. By the end of 1866 several infantry units had been issued the new German needle rifles, and cavalry units were receiving Spencer repeating carbines. Even before Curupaity, Paraguayan soldiers had captured Minié rifles stamped with the Tower of London mark and dated 1866.[81] Captain Burton, on his visit to the war zone, met an enterprising businessman at Corrientes named Edouard Peterkin, of Scottish-Belgian extraction, who was busy contracting for the supply of new Liége Enfield rifles.[82] Artillery units were likewise receiving new Whitworths, La Hittes, and even Krupp guns. Adequate ammunition supplies were assured by the operation of a cartridge factory at Corrientes under the direction of Lieutenant Américo de Vasconcelos. Finally, the older ships of the naval squadron were being substituted by new armored monitors—a change which was soon to enable the squadron to attempt the forcing of the Humaitá batteries.

Life at Paso la Patria.—A contemporary sketch which appeared in the *Illustrated London News* showed Brazilian troops in the trenches before the quadrilátero to be almost exactly like the Union troops in Matthew Brady's celebrated photograph of the trenches before Petersburg. Uniforms, forage caps or kepis, rifles, and even the grim countenances of war, were unbelievably alike. Frontline duty was equally as dangerous in Paraguay as in Virginia. A particularly notorious section of the allied lines was the "linha negra" (black line) and the nearby "chapas de fêrro" (iron-sheets), a lightly protected position noted for its proximity to the enemy and for its record of heavy casualties from sniping. Brazilian infantrymen soon learned to distinguish Paraguayan rifle fire because of its similarity to the explosion of skyrockets—a feature ascribed to the larger caliber of Paraguayan smoothbore rifles. Similarly, the men could distinguish between spent bullets since Paraguayan ammunition was usually of the round, musket-ball type. In addition to the normal dangers of war, frontline duty was made even more disagreeable by the miasma of the swampy terrain, the intense summer-time heat, and the continual harassment by clouds of mosquitoes.[83]

Bothered by few supply difficulties, the Marquês de Caxias slowly succeeded in building an effective fighting force. On a visit to Brazilian camps Captain Burton noted that infantrymen were in excellent condition, well clothed, well fed, and "only too well armed." The soldiers wore shoes, fatigue suits of brown drill, and white forage caps with red bands.[84] Other units which Burton did not observe, especially the 2d Corps, wore black wide-brimmed hats which made them known to the Paraguayans as "los paisanos de Puerto Alegre" (Pôrto Alegre's country boys).[85] The infantry seen by Burton were all armed with Belgian Enfields and sword bayonets. He noted that the ranks had ample meat rations, and that each squad of six men enjoyed a daily ration of one bottle of the fiery Brazilian rum known as *cachaça*.[86] A singular feature of Brazilian camps, according to Burton, was the low army pay standard which seemed to him to have encouraged the practice of "begging" among the troops. He also noted that "with some brilliant exceptions, no ranks were free of corruption," and that the prevalence of waste in the camps "appeared excessive even to an eye familiar with the loss and recklessness of the Crimean campaign." On a visit to Asunción, Burton met a *fornecidor* (supply contractor) who openly boasted that in three days' time he had made a profit of $30,000 in silver from army contracts.[87] When given leave or on Sundays, officers and men found ample facilities for relaxation at the Paso la Patria army base. Now a city in size, the base sported suttler's huts, billiard halls, a theater, dance halls (where such numbers as La Habanera and the polka were popular), taverns, barber shops, photo studios, and even a branch of the Banco Mauá. Later in the war Captain Burton estimated the female population at a main Brazilian campsite at 4,000, all of whom appeared to enjoy dashing about on horseback "en amazon."[88] Ships coming up the Paraná brought the latest news from Rio de Janeiro in the papers *Diário de Rio de Janeiro*, *Correio Mercantil*, *A Reforma*, and *O Jornal do Comércio*. An odd feature was the number of dogs around the camp. Those which were fat and sleek were eyed as veterans from the Siege of Uruguaiana; thin hungry animals were held to be Paraguayan "deserters." When more than half the army left the base in late 1867 for the grand flank movement, the dog population found that its usual source of food had suddenly vanished. In circumstances reminiscent of episodes of the Retreat from Laguna, the wailing of starving dogs became such a nuisance to the remaining soldiers that the camp's military police mounted an all-out offensive against them which swiftly solved the problem. One war anecdote held that from this event stemmed the later custom in cities of Northeast Brazil of referring to policemen as "mata-cachôrros (dog-killers).[89]

Complaints and desertion were uncommon in the Brazilian army. The troops, mainly from the empire's lowest social and slave classes, possessed little or no notion regarding their rights. Disciplinary measures, moreover, were severe. The use of the *vara de marmelo* (a thick stick for flogging) served to punish any offenders.[90] Though frequent while the troops were within the empire's territory, desertion became almost nonexistent once the army reached Paraguay. Distances home were too great and the Paraguayan army exhibited absolutely no interest in receiving and providing for allied defectors.

Such circumstances, however, did not erase the homesickness which naturally affected the troops. As evidence of nostalgia (*saüdades*) for the homeland, the following rhyme circulated among Brazilian units at Paso la Patria:

Foi o Marquês de Caxias	(It was the Marquês de Caxias
que mandou-me chamar,	who called me up,
mode ir ao Paraguai,	in order to go to Paraguay,
mode aprender a brigar.	in order to learn to fight.
Vou-me embora, vou-me embora,	Now I'm leaving, I'm leaving,
Vou-me embora para o mar!	I'm leaving for the sea!)[91]

With Caxias in command and with the departure of the testy Admiral Tamandaré, the former bitterness and jealousy in the high command temporarily subsided. Worried over domestic problems, Bartolomé Mitre proved willing to allow the new Brazilian commander to assume the overall direction of the allied army. Petty jealousy and rivalry, however, still existed among the lower echelon of officers. Colonel Francisco Pinheiro Guimarães, for example, had learned an early lesson—as the correspondent for one Rio de Janeiro newspaper he had been falsely accused by an officer jealous of him as being the author of an article in another paper which was critical of General Osório.[92] Subsequently in April, 1868, Pinheiro Guimarães became embittered at the rapid promotion of other officers of inferior rank who had been sent home ill while he had remained at the front. Fortunately, his own promotion was approved at about the same time and he continued to serve as one of the most capable of the volunteer officers.[93]

Relationships between the lower ranks of the Brazilian and Argentine units were also not always cordial. Observer Burton noted that at one large camp a trench had been dug to separate the troops of the two nations. He concluded that the wartime alliance was like that of "dog and cat."[94]

Cholera.—In early 1867 one of the worst of war's evils—cholera—appeared in the Brazilian camps. Closely following an extended epidemic of malaria, the new plague proved to be a nightmare. Within a short time the number of sick men entering hospitals rose to about 280 daily. Hospital conditions were frequently grim. Dionísio Cerqueira, in his reminiscences, recalled a tale which alleged that one doctor, on entering a ward, would automatically prescribe *purgantes* for patients on the right side and *vomitórios* for those on the left. He would reverse the order of the prescription on his next visit![95]

Fortunately for the allies, the plague was almost simultaneously communicated to the Paraguayan lines so that offensive operations by either side became temporarily an impossibility. Aware of the normal peacetime profession exercised by Dr. Francisco Pinheiro Guimarães, Caxias had him ordered at once to the task of combatting the cholera outbreak. The erstwhile doctor swiftly isolated all known cases, caused a special hospital area to be reserved for plague victims, and calmed the fears of the population at Corrientes. The measures adopted by Pinheiro Guimarães and his corps of doctors eventually halted the plague, though not until it had caused the death of a heavy number of soldiers. Impressed by the doctor's versatility, Caixas subsequently gave him the added assignment of searching through the hospitals at Paso la Patria and the Saladero hospital near Corrientes for malingerers and excess army personnel. It was estimated that as a result of the doctor's efforts about 2,500 able-bodied men were promptly returned to active frontline duty.[96]

Revolts in Argentina.—In late 1866 and early 1867 serious revolts broke out in Argentina's western provinces over the Mitre government's determination to continue the war against Paraguay. Argentina's Federalist sector, never satisfied with the apparent peace between Mitre and its former hero Urquiza, decided that the grave defeat at Curupaity presented an excellent opportunity to foment discontent in the provinces.[97]

In addition to the repercussions of Curupaity, provincial feelings had been aroused by the unpopular efforts of the government to conscript army recruits. No better description of these conscription methods nor of the reaction they generated can be found than that of eyewitness HBM Consul Thomas Hutchinson at Rosario:

> About this time there came down one evening by the railway train to Rosario, a contingent of soldiers, 96 in number, from Tucumán and Salta, for the Paraguayan War. Amongst them were thirty others—the most forbidding countenances I ever saw—who were handcuffed and fettered. The latter came under the title of "Voluntarios," or volunteers, for the 96 were soldiers of the line. The manacled part of this corps d'armee was got safe on board the steamer; but when the soldiers were being brought by their officers, they stopped just after passing the customhouse, and two of them shot two of the officers through the brain. The whole group then dispersed, passing up through the principal plaza, and by the door of the Gefatura, escaping to the camp. No attempt—nor even pretense at attempt—was made by the rebels in power to capture them; for the Paraguayan War is becoming so unpopular, that the sympathy of the people is with every one who can draw out of it. The appearance of these poor fellows at the railway station brought to my mind a tale which had been told to me some time previously by a gentleman, who assured me he saw the letter in question, written by the Governor, whose name it would not of course be prudent to give. The Minister of War had written to one of the provincial potentates for another lot of volunteers to send to Paraguay; and the answer was, that a large troupe would be sent down as soon as the Minister would remit back the fetters and handcuffs that had been ornamenting the first contingent forwarded.[98]

On November 9, 1866, mob disturbances and attacks upon government buildings and authorities were reported in Mendoza. The trouble spread swiftly to Corrientes, to Salta and Jujuy in the north, to Cuyo in the west, and to central Córdoba. On January 5, 1867, it was learned that armed rebel forces had gained a victory over a government detachment at Pocitos. With subsequent reports of uprisings in San Juan, La Rioja, and Catamarca, President Mitre was finally forced to take strong measures. He detached General Wenceslao Paunero and almost half the Argentine contingent—eventually about 4,000 troops—from Paraguay to form an "Ejército Pacificador" (Army of Pacification).[99] Mitre wrote to Vice President Marcos Paz on January 24: "Quién no sabe que los traidores alentaron al Paraguay a declararnos la guerra?" (Who doesn't know that by declaring war upon us the traitors have given new heart to Paraguay?) [100]

Pozo de Vargas.—The rebel uprising in the western provinces was soon curbed with the arrival of the regular troops. At the Battle of San Ignacio on April 1, 1867, the 4,000 men of General Juan Saá (alias "Lanza Seca"—Dry Lance) were defeated by Colonel Arredondo, Paunero's second-in-command[101] The major action of this renewed period of internal revolt, however, occurred near the city of La Rioja on April 10. In two hours of heavy fighting on that date at a place known as Pozo de Vargas, the 2,100 government troops of General Antonino Taboada soundly defeated the 4,000 men of Felipe Varela, a native of Catamarca. Pozo de Vargas was a battle—not simply a riot or mob demonstration. One of Varela's units was named "Batallón Urquiza," and the flag captured by the victorious Taboada forces bore the following slogans: "Federación o muerte. Viva la unión americana. Viva el ilustre Capitán General Urquiza. Abajo los negreros brasileños!"[102]

Losses of the rebel forces included 300 dead, 400 prisoners, 500 rifles, 2 cannon, and the battle flag. Battle reports stated that many of the prisoners were Chilean nationals who had been recruited by Varela.[103] The defeated rebel leader was forced to flee to Bolivia and later to Chile. A feature of the Pozo de Vargas affair of more enduring significance proved to be the victory song played by a Catamarca band. It was a *zamacueca de chile* (a new Chilean rhythm) which became so popular that it was remembered as late as the 1940's in northwestern Argentina as the *Zamba de Vargas*.[104]

The news of such events acted as Bartolomé Mitre had suspected —it encouraged Marshal López and his army to believe that help from Argentina's provinces might still be forthcoming. Colonel Thompson commented that these revolts may have persuaded López to have adopted his intransigent attitude during the August, 1867, peace discussions with British diplomat Gould.[105]

South America's first aeronautical service.—Brazil's famed Santos-Dumont is usually credited with the honor of being the pioneer of flight in South America. His achievements, however, were preceded by the little-known exploits of two American balloonists during the Paraguayan War. Their efforts on behalf of Brazil marked the first appearance in South America of a military aeronautical service.

In early 1867 the offensive plans of the allied army under Caxias were hampered by the lack of precise knowledge of both the extent of the Paraguayan entrenched lines and of the nature of the terrain to the east of the quadrilátero. To resolve this difficulty the Brazilian command decided to experiment with balloon observations. The original project involved the services of a French aeronaut. His experiments at the front ended in early disaster with the destruction by fire of his balloon and possibly as a result of a suspicion that he may have sought to blow up Brazilian ammunition dumps.[106]

Having learned of the American Civil War performances of Professor Thaddeus S. C. Lowe, the Imperial Government had its representatives in the United States contact the professor in order to contract for his services. Busy with a new project for the invention of an ice machine, Professor Lowe declined the offer and suggested instead that his former assistants, James and Ezra Allen, be consulted.[107] The Allens accepted; James was appointed engineer captain in the Brazilian army, and Ezra received the title of assistant aeronaut. The two brothers left New York in March and spent only four days in Rio de Janeiro while en route to the Paraguayan front. The Brazilian minister of war promised to forward a supply of iron filings and sulphuric acid with which to produce hydrogen gas required for filling the balloons. The order subsequently failed to appear, however, and Caxias had to send a special assistant urgently to Montevideo to purchase the essential raw material. Unable to find iron filings, the agent purchased zinc sheets instead—a highly dangerous substitute since the lead in the sheets also contained arsenic. The Allens were thus forced to use lumps of scrap iron gleaned from the nearby army camps.[108]

Undaunted by these practical difficulties, the two enterprising Americans eventually were able to devise a system whereby they could generate the necessary 30,000 cubic feet of gas to fill a balloon. In the first ascent, made on June 24, 1867, the balloon reached a height of 270 feet. Captain Allen was accompanied by Major Robert A. Chodasiewicz, special engineer of the Argentine army. On the second ascent made on July 8, Allen was accompanied by Chodasiewicz and a Paraguayan lieutenant named Céspedes, an exile who was acting as chief of guides in the Argentine army. The trio spent three hours aloft and Chodasiewicz drew a map of the previously unknown area of the Paraguayan left flank while Céspedes searched for trails through the marshes and thickets.[109]

In a letter of July 14, 1867, to Professor Lowe, Ezra Allen reported that the Marquês de Caxias was highly satisfied with the project, that they had by then made about 12 ascents, that they were even planning to take Caxias himself on an elevation, and finally that the entire affair had been successful beyond all expectations.[110] No record has come to light as yet which might confirm whether the Marquês de Caxias went up with the Allens. (An airplane baptism ceremony in Minas Gerais in July, 1942, however, indicates that his aide, Dr. Francisco Pinheiro Guimarães, added "flight by balloon" to the already long string of accomplishments to his credit—a recently received aviation club airplane was given his name and the speeches marking the occasion referred to the doughty doctor's aeronautical exploits in Paraguay.)[111] Newspapers in the United States commented that Dom Pedro II had been so pleased with the success of the balloon project that he had presented aeronaut James Allen with a handsome bonus of $10,000 in gold at the close of his operations with the Imperial Army.[112]

The balloon project, of course, was a sensational event in the war's theater. On the allied side the project elicited precisely the topographical information which Caxias required for his forthcoming strategy aimed at flanking the quadrilátero. On the Paraguayan side Marshal López had his men fire artillery at the balloons and build giant brush fires which might mask his lines from observation. He also sought to utilize the enemy balloon ascents for propaganda purposes by spreading the rumor that the balloons were actually infernal machines filled with a deadly substance aimed at spreading a frightful disease among the Paraguayan troops.[113]

As an epilogue to the account of the balloon project it may be of interest to include a brief portrait of Chodasiewicz, the courageous map-maker. According to Captain Burton, who met him during his war-zone visits, he was a Pole who had quit the Russian army in May, 1853, and had been made a captain in the secret service of the British Crimean forces. In 1857 he had gone to England where he published a book entitled *A Voice from the Walls of Sevastopol*. He later served with the Turks in the Hejaz campaign, became an American citizen, resided in Philadelphia, served in the Union army in the Civil War, and finally joined the Argentine army in the Paraguayan War. When Burton interviewed him he had transferred to the Brazilian army as a lieutenant colonel and was engaged in preparing a map survey of all fortified positions and campaign plans.[114] Young Lieutenant Dionísio Cerqueira wrote later of his admiration for the ingenuity of the skillful Polish officer in his use of the samovar method for preparing *maté* (Paraguayan tea), a refreshing drink to which many northern Brazilians became accustomed while in Paraguay.[115]

Chapter 9

WAR OF MANEUVERS

By July, 1867, the allied army was ready to resume its offensive against the forces of Paraguay. Under Caxias' command the army now numbered about 45,000, of which 40,000 were Brazilians, 5,000 were Argentines, and only a few hundred were Uruguayans. Their opponents' strength was only about 20,000 men, of whom 15,000 were infantry, about 3,500 were cavalry, and 1,500 were artillerymen.[1]

Second Tuyuty

With the odds in numbers more than two to one in his favor, the Marquês de Caxias decided upon a full-scale flanking movement based on his newly acquired knowledge of the terrain to the northeast. Though Mitre returned to the front in July, he preferred to leave the direction of the forthcoming operation to Caxias. In a postwar *Memoria Militar* Mitre inferred that lack of cooperation by Brazil's fleet prejudiced his own strategic plan for the reduction of Humaitá. The new plan called for the concentration of the 1st and 3d Corps, respectively under Argolo and Osório, for use in the movement, while the 2d Corps under Pôrto Alegre would remain at the Tuyuty base area near Paso la Patria. The squadron, now equipped with the new monitors, was to maintain pressure on the Paraguayan right with its bombardments and maneuvers to run past the Curupaity and Humaitá fortifications. The only sour note in the overall allied strategy came from Rio de Janeiro in the form of news of the failure of the Laguna expedition in Mato Grosso.

The extreme allied right flank was now secure. Brazilian

forces under Colonel José Gomes Portinho had cleared the banks of the Upper Paraná River of Paraguayans up to the falls of the Sete Quedas; and Osório, now a lieutenant general, had concentrated 7,000 troops in the Candelaria or Misiones zone. Orders were sent to Osório for his corps to join the main army and it arrived at Paso la Patria in mid-July. The flank movement, with the 3d Corps as the spearhead, began on July 22. The 28,000 troops involved in the movement faced marches over most difficult terrain. At times the soldiers moved across swamps with water up to their waists. By nightfall of the twenty-second, however, they had reached an area known as San Solano (see Figure 4), and the advance guard reported it was in sight of the shell-blasted towers of the Humaitá church, which marked the location of the main Paraguayan defensive bastion.[2]

By August the slowly moving force had established a strong position near the small inhabited point of Tuiucué, and the squadron had succeeded in running past the Curupaity batteries. Rio Grande do Sul gaúcho cavalry patrols had cut the existing telegraph line to Asunción and had effectively stopped use by Paraguayans of the old highroad to the north. In his memoirs Dionísio Cerqueira recalled an anecdote which held that a Brazilian general officer, upon observing a roll of telegraph wire along the highway, lamented that it could not be used by the army since it was Paraguayan wire and therefore could only transmit messages in Guaraní![3]

In order to maintain communications northward Marshal López had a road built through the Chaco on the west side of the Paraguay River from Timbó, about nine miles above Humaitá, to Monte Lindo, a small landing place about five miles north of the mouth of the Tebicuary River. This 54-mile-long road through the marshes and thick forests along the Paraguay, and the new telegraph line which was also built along it, became the last communications link between the quadrilátero and Asunción. With the gradual encirclement of his position Paraguay's Marshal President ordered all civilians still living in the area to move north of the Tebicuary River.[4]

On November 2, 1867, Brazilian troops successfully attacked Tayí, a small fortified position on the east bank of the Paraguay River about 15 miles north of Humaitá. The flank movement had achieved its objective and the Paraguayan positions in the quadri-

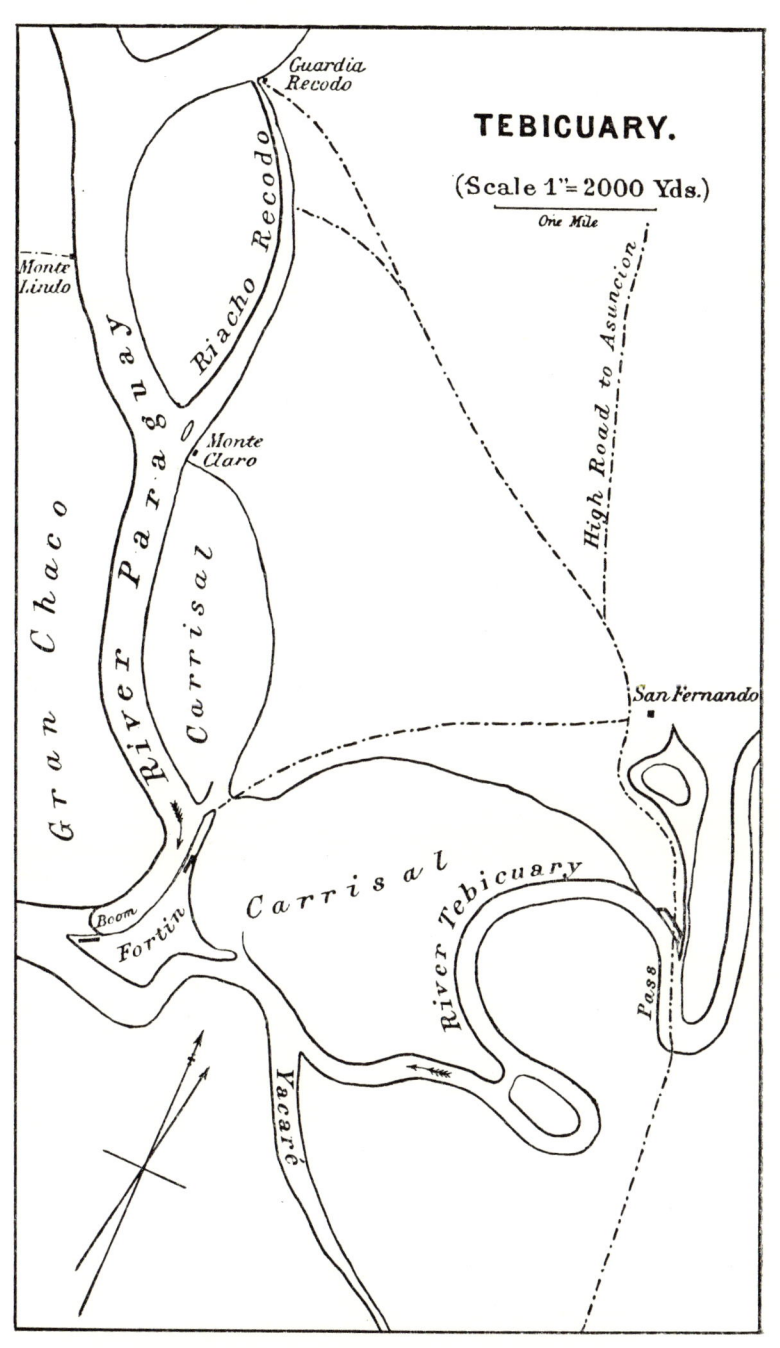

THE TEBICUARY RIVER AND SAN FERNANDO
(*From*: George Thompson, *The War in Paraguay*, London, 1869.)

látero were now surrounded, with the exception of the one escape route across the river from Humaitá at Timbó. The difficult and long flanking operation, like that of the Siege of Petersburg in 1864-65, had involved construction by the allies of 51,375 meters of trenches.

Second Tuyuty.—Since commencement of the allied flank movement pressure on the left of the Paraguayan entrenched lines had gradually increased. From strong positions near Tuiucué, allied batteries fired continuously at the quadrilátero. In order to relieve this pressure, and possibly to capture some of the new Brazilian 32-pounder Whitworth rifled cannon, Marshal López now decided upon a strong surprise attack against the 2d Corps of the Brazilian army at Tuyuty. He had Colonel Thompson survey the enemy lines and subsequently ordered General Barrios to attack with 8,000 men at daylight on November 3. The original plan called for a swift assault and the immediate return of the force with all captured artillery. According to Thompson these orders were later amended to allow the attacking force time to pillage the enemy camps.[5]

The element of surprise, which had been lost at First Tuyuty in May, 1866, was definitely in Paraguay's favor at Second Tuyuty in November, 1867. Barrios' heavy force succeeded in reaching its assault departure positions on schedule, and at daylight, November 3, it launched a full-scale attack on the Brazilian trenches. It was a swift success—charging Paraguayan infantry overran both lines of earthworks and punched a wide hole clear through to the allied camp sites. To the Paraguayan left the cavalry under Bernardino Caballero, who had begun his career as a sergeant in Mato Grosso and who was later the founder of Paraguay's Colorado Party, charged up to the Brazilian redoubts, dismounted, and captured the positions after brief but vicious hand-to-hand fighting. Among the approximate 250 prisoners taken was Brazilian Major Ernesto A. da Cunha Mattos, who figured prominently in the "Questão Militar" of the empire's last years.[6]

With permission having been granted them to pillage, the attacking soldiers lost all organization on reaching the allied camps. The sudden deflation of the assault proved fatal. To the rear of their camps, retreating, panic-stricken Brazilian troops were brought up short by the remarkable efforts of Manoel Marques de Souza, Barão de Pôrto Alegre, the 63-year-old hero of the Battle of Monte

Caseros. Battle reports noted that Pôrto Alegre, with his long white beard and bare sword, proved an inspiration to his men. Much like Phil Sheridan at Winchester in the American Civil War, he succeeded in reforming the retreating infantry and in encouraging them to mount a counterattack. Two horses were killed from under him and his uniform was perforated several times by bullets.[7]

With Pôrto Alegre at their head, the nearly smashed Voluntários da Pátria battalions, including the famous 41st from Bahía, reformed and charged upon the Paraguayans engaged in plundering the camp. The tide of battle changed abruptly, and by 9 A.M. Barrios' men were forced to retreat under heavy fire. They carried with them enormous amounts of booty including, in Thompson's words, "two very seedy Brazilian flags and a beautifully embroidered Argentine one."[8]

In Brazil, Second Tuyuty was hailed as a victory since the Paraguayans had been finally repulsed. In a comment on these claims in the Rio de Janeiro press, British legation secretary J. J. Pakenham wrote, "A curious circumstance connected with the recent engagement is that the vanquished (Paraguayans) seized, and were able to carry off several pieces of artillery belonging to the victors." Fourteen cannon were actually hauled back to the Paraguayan trenches including a new Krupp 12-pounder breechloader which was still loaded, and one of the new 32-pounder Whitworths which López had coveted. Battle casualties were estimated at about 2,000 on each side.[9]

Second Tuyuty was a militarily inconclusive battle. It served, however, to remind the allied high command that the outnumbered and poorly equipped Paraguayan army was still capable of mounting heavy attacks. On Paraguay's side the quantity of captured material brought back served as a distinct boost to morale. Colonel Thompson's account of the nature of the trophies is worthy of transcription:

The spoil brought from Tuyuty by the Paraguayans was immense, and consisted of articles of every conceivable kind. The only artichokes I ever saw in Paraguay were brought from the allied camp that day. A mail had just arrived from Buenos Aires, and was taken to López, who, on reading one of the letters said, "Poor Mitre! I am reading his wife's letter," and then stated what the letter was about. A box was brought to López, which had just arrived for General Emilio Mitre, containing tea, cheese, coffee, and a pair of boots. New officers' uniforms were brought from a tailor's. Parasols, dresses, crinolines, shirts (Crimean shirts especially), cloth, were brought in large quantities, every man carrying as much as he could. A tripod telescope was brought from one on the watchtowers, and gold watches, sovereigns, and dollars were abundant. One man, who found a bag full of the cut half and quarter dollars, threw it away as not sufficiently valuable for him.[10]

The 32-pounder Whitworth proved a particularly valuable acquisition among the Tuyuty trophies. Marshal López had his men renew their collection of unexploded allied shells and the gun was soon being fired with exasperating accuracy at the Brazilian Tuiucué positions. Prized by López, it was to be carried on the retreat from Humaitá to Lomas Valentinas, where it was finally retaken by its original owners.[11]

The Fall of Humaitá and San Fernando

The effects of Second Tuyuty were not as lasting as those of the first battle of that name nor of Curupaity. The allies held to their Tuiucué and Tayí positions and the vise remained clamped about the quadrilátero. In January, 1868, Paraguayan hopes for an end to the war were aroused by the observance along the allied lines of flags at half-mast. Thought to be in mourning for the death of Mitre, the event turned out to concern the demise of Argentine Vice President Marcos Paz.[12] Mitre, however, was forced to leave the war zone permanently in mid-January in order to assume direction of the government and also to cope with further provincial disturbances, notably in Santa Fé. Venancio Flores, who had long since departed from the war zone, was assassinated at Montevideo in February. Argentina's continued internal troubles had not gone unnoticed by Dom Pedro. On January 6, 1868, he wrote to the Condessa de Barral: "A revolution has occurred in the Argentine Province of Santa Fé along the Paraná. Even though it is only for a brief time, I do not like such neighbors for our recruits and our ammunition ships which travel up the Paraná bound for the army and the squadron."[13]

Now formally in command of the allied army Caxias resolved to tighten his encirclement of the quadrilátero. Two movements were planned to occur simultaneously: the passage of the Humaitá batteries by the navy's monitors, and an assault on the La Cierva or Estabelecimento redoubt only two miles north of Humaitá near the Paraguay River. Both actions took place on February 18 and both were successful. The fleet's ironclads and new monitors, though battered by direct Paraguayan plunging fire, took advantage of an exceptionally high water level and passed the batteries and sunken river boom without loss. The feat was hailed as a signal naval victory by Brazil.[14] In a series of direct frontal assaults, Brazilian infantry finally took the La Cierva redoubt. The action was highlighted by the charge of the 5th Brigade, now commanded by the veteran Dr. Francisco Pinheiro Guimarães. Once more in the role of an infantry officer, Dr. Guimarães led his troops in person and was credited with hauling down the Paraguayan flag at the climax of the action.[15] Both the flag and the doctor's sword scabbard, dented by bullets, were later placed in the National Historical Museum.[16]

After passing Humaitá, units of the fleet proceeded up the Paraguay River to Asunción, which was briefly bombarded on February 24. The city had been evacuated several days earlier at the orders of Marshal López, and the government was moved to the nearby village of Luque. López soon received strange reports indicating that a controversy had arisen among officials as to whether or not the Asunción batteries should return the Brazilian fleet's fire.[17]

Now facing a situation which was hourly growing more serious, Paraguay's Marshal President resolved once more to attempt one of the ingenious offensive stratagems for which he had already achieved fame. On the night of March 1 he sent a fleet of canoes carrying a force of picked men under Ignacio Genés to surprise the Brazilian squadron. The force actually succeeded in boarding the ironclads "Herbal" and "Cabral," but was unable to pry open open the steel hatches before being riddled by the canister fired at them point blank by guns of the other ships.[18]

The failure of the canoe fleet to inflict serious damage on the squadron was interpreted by López as the disappearance of his last hope to stave off the allied pressure on the quadrilátero. He immediately ordered the evacuation of the bulk of his army across the Paraguay River to Timbó and the gradual withdrawal of a holding force within the confines of the Humaitá fortifications. The Marshal himself left Humaitá on March 2 and traveled over the new Chaco road to Monte Lindo. The Brazilian squadron, thrown temporarily on the defensive by the unusual canoe attack, did not interfere with the evacuation.

The Paraguayan army, now only slightly over 10,000 in strength, struggled through the Chaco to Monte Lindo with its best artillery and remaining supplies, and then recrossed the Paraguay River to assume new positions on the north bank of the Tebicuary River. Colonel Thompson was ordered to construct a water battery at the confluence of the Tebicuary with the Paraguay, which was armed with the remaining heavy eight-inch and 32-pounder cannon. When the Brazilian ironclads again sought to ascend the river, Thompson's guns blasted them at the extremely short range of only 18 yards. Though no monitors were sunk, the Brazilian vessels suffered heavy damages each time they passed the Tebicuary position.[19] Marshal López established his new headquarters slightly north of the Tebicuary at a point called San Fernando, a small piece of elevated ground only about 30 yards square.[20] The surrounding area was quickly drained of marsh water and the army soon built a new campsite. Conditions at San Fernando were somewhat more healthy since the higher ground of Paraguay's more habitable zone commences north of the Tebicuary.

While at the Tebicuary position, Marshal López decided to repeat the strategy of a canoe attack on the fleet. He had his picked men organized into a special *Cuerpo de Bogabantes* (Canoe Paddlers Corps) and ordered a new attack on July 9. The Paraguayans, camouflaged by the floating river hyacinths or *camelotes* which are common in the Paraguay River, sought to board the ironclads "Rio Grande" and "Barroso" lying off Tayí. The attempt was again beaten off, though not until after the "paddlers" had succeeded in boarding the "Rio Grande."[21]

The impact of the canoe attacks on the fleet, the skill with which the withdrawal from Humaitá was performed, and the employment of dummy "quaker" guns along the quadrilátero lines, were factors which effectively masked the true state of affairs at Humaitá.[22] Left with only a garrison of 3,000 men, Colonel Paulino Alén managed to display a sufficient show of strength to delay an all-out final assault on his position. Starvation, however, proved to be a more implacable foe than allied bombardments. Faced with a completely hopeless task, and unable to expect any reinforcements or even supplies, Alén eventually sought relief from his trials through suicide. Unsuccessful in the attempt he was carried back to San Fernando to die slowly from his wounds.[23] Colonel Francisco Martínez, the second-in-command, fared slightly better. He held on grimly at Humaitá, beat back a strong allied assault, and finally sought to lead his remaining force through the new allied lines around the Timbó area. He evacuated Humaitá the night of July 24, 1868, the birthday of Francisco Solano López. The ragged and now ill-equipped band, whose final musical efforts were clearly audible to the Brazilians, was the last unit to leave.[24] The allies entered Humaitá the next day.

Caught in a merciless cross fire, Martínez surrendered the remaining 1,300 starving members of his garrison on August 5. It had taken the allies 13 months to reduce Humaitá, considered by Colonel Thompson to have been the weakest of all of Paraguay's defensive positions.[25] Estimates of the total killed on both sides during the long campaign were as high as 100,000.[26] Though personally safe from retribution for his action, Martínez suffered the loss of his wife, Juliana Ynsfrán de Martínez, who was executed on the orders of Paraguay's president for no other apparent reason than her connection with the colonel. In later years the heroic actions of Martínez were justly recognized by the baptism with his name of a central street in Asunción.

The fall of Humaitá was the motive for enormous celebrations in the allied nations. It proved, however, to be no more indicative of the war's early end than had the final collapse of Vicksburg in the American Civil War. More than a year and a half of bitter fighting still lay ahead. For at least one person, nevertheless, the date and event were definitely memorable. Dom Pedro was never to forget what was for him perhaps the most joyous time of his life. While he never specified particulars, he recalled the "night of the fall of Humaitá" three times in his letters to the Condessa de Barral. On December 2, 1879, for example, he wrote as follows: "What a wonderful time it was on the occasion of the fall of Humaitá. I was never so happy in my life as then!"[27] On December 19, 1880, he wrote: "How hot it was today. What I would give for the moonlight of Humaitá!"[28]

SAN FERNANDO

To the student of the era of Francisco Solano López the most controversial phase of his life is generally held to have commenced at the time of his withdrawal to the San Fernando position. For want of an accepted term, this phase in Paraguay's wartime record might be entitled "the disintegration period."

By March, 1868, the best of Paraguay's fighting men had been lost in battle or by disease, and the remaining army of about 10,000 was now definitely composed of old men and young boys, and of wounded who had recuperated sufficiently for return to duty.[29] Supplies, especially foodstuffs, were next to nothing, and most of the artillery had been left within the Humaitá fortifications. In addition, Brazil's river squadron was now able to operate almost at will along the Paraguay River.

These circumstances combined to make it almost impossible to maintain further hopes for eventual victory. There may have been some among the elite of Paraguay, therefore, who felt that further resistance was useless. At all events, San Fernando marked the advent of the so-called period of conspiracy. It is difficult to believe that any antiwar or anti-López movement could have originated either among the common people of Paraguay or within the army. The people, conditioned against knowledge of popular, spontaneous political demonstrations through their years of rigid obedience to Dr. Francia and the two Lópezes, appeared to accept leadership by their president without question. Likewise, the fanatic loyalty of his troops reflected no visible reason for any doubt by Paraguay's Marshal regarding their dependability. The sector which stood to lose most by continued allegiance to Francisco Solano López in the face of impending allied victory may have been that comprised by the Marshal's own family members, some among the middle and merchant classes, and some in high government posts.

The precise origins of the 1868 conspiracy period are still not definitely known. Controversy among authors and students of the era continues over the question whether a conspiracy against López did, in fact, exist. The persons accused as accomplices were, in the majority, executed, and the record of their movements disappeared with them. The few accounts left to history are those written by survivors of the Marshal's staff who took part in the trials, and by the several foreigners who were involved in the accusations and who sought to exonerate themselves through memoirs of their Paraguayan experiences. Chief among such accounts are those of Fidel Maíz, López' early opponent and later his favored chaplain of the army; Francisco Isidoro Resquín, the tough and capable general who served López throughout the entire war; and the memoirs and accounts of Minister Washburn, Porter Bliss, George F. Masterman, and Max von Versen.

Although their reliability has been questioned, the memoirs of General Resquín contain possibly the most specific references to the existence of treason and conspiracy plots. According to his account, Resquín believed that Minister Washburn had originally mapped out a secret conspiracy plan with the Marquês de Caxias during his visits to the allied headquarters in late 1866 and early 1867.[30] Resquín stated that it was later discovered that Washburn was implicated with a group conspiring for a revolutionary movement which included Minister of Foreign Affairs José Berges, and both Venancio and Benigno López.[31] Washburn was vehement in his denials of complicity in any such plot. It proved difficult for him, nevertheless, to offer convincing explanations for his decision to retain his legation in Asunción instead of moving to Luque where the government had been transferred, and for his action in transforming the legation into a haven for more than 40 persons, many of whom were among the conspiracy suspects. Mrs. Washburn, moreover, in an apparent slip of the tongue, later to be duly recorded in a sworn deposition, told an officer of the United States Navy that both she and her husband had been aware of a plot to overthrow President López.[32] The Marquês de Caxias, for his part, always maintained a correct, dignified silence regarding the entire controversy.

Resquín stated further that letters were intercepted from Benigno López to the Marquês, which referred to the poor condition of Paraguayan river torpedoes and to the removal of artillery batteries from Curupaity to Humaitá.[33] Toward the end of March, 1868, according to Resquín, a letter addressed to Caxias was found in Benigno's handwriting, and in the names of his accomplices, which gave full details covering López' situation and which also implicated Bishop Palacios, Dean Bogardo, Generals Barrios and Bruguez, and the more than 80 other persons.[34] Also in mid-March, in an exchange of letters with Vice President Francisco Sánchez in Asunción, President López learned of the meetings at the time of the appearance of the Brazilian squadron when the strange question was discussed whether or not the enemy vessels should be fired upon.[35]

In the face of such evidence, Marshal López called a council of war by a decree of August 2, 1868, at which it was decided to try those under suspicion by military courts under the ordinances or *Leyes de Partida* then in force in Paraguay. A series of five two-man tribunals were appointed to handle the investigations, and General Resquín was designated as the official responsible for carrying out the sentences of the tribunals.[36] Police and army units were ordered to arrest all suspects, and within a short time San Fernando took on the appearance of a grim detention camp.

Marshal López, himself, does not figure in any of the accounts as having taken a personal hand in the work of the military tribunals other than to have acted as a judge of last resort in the cases of the prime suspects. These two-man teams effectively combed Asunción in their efforts to root out a conspiracy. Under justice as it was then held, methods involving torture were still countenanced as a means of encouraging confessions by prisoners. Those who had the misfortune to have their names appear on the tribunals' lists found themselves securely fettered by the hated *grillos*—iron bars riveted to their legs—and counted themselves indeed lucky if they were not subjected to the *Cepo Uruguayo*, an extremely painful form of bucking which involved the use of muskets tied to the neck of the victim who had been forced into a cramped, sitting position.[37]

Through the use of such measures an almost endless stream of confessions was obtained which tended to implicate still more unfortunates. The roll of those in custody came to read like a roster of Asunción's first families. Foreigners were not overlooked. In addition to Masterman and Porter Bliss, those apprehended by the police included Leite Pereira, the former acting Portuguese consul; Antonio de las Carreras, former Uruguayan diplomat; Alonzo Taylor, the stonemason; John Watts, the engineer; Manlove, the soldier of fortune; von Truenfeldt, the telegrapher; and hapless Max von Versen, the Prussian observer.[38]

In all, according to an allegedly captured record, more than 500 persons may have been executed for complicity in the treason plot.[39] Those whose names were most prominent among the victims included Benigno López, Bishop Palacios, Generals Barrios and Bruguez, Treasurer Saturnino Bedoya, Ministers Berges and Benítez, and Juliana Ynsfrán de Martínez.

Not all the confessions of those arrested were obtained through duress. In his account, contained in the memoirs of Fidel Maíz,

Juan C. Centurión noted that many of the prisoners, including Venancio López, confessed without the use of torture.[40] There is also reason to believe that Francisco Solano López may not have been fully aware of the extent to which his tribunals went in their hunt for suspects. At Lomas Valentinas on December 25, according to Masterman's memoirs, the Marshal and Mrs. Lynch came upon a group of prisoners. The Marshal is said to have shown surprise on recognizing Alonzo Taylor among them, and to have ordered his immediate release along with several others.[41] In commenting upon Max von Versen's account, Brazilian General Ernesto A. da Cunha Mattos also recalled that he and other prisoners at Lomas Valentinas were given gifts of sweets, cigars, and Paraguayan rum by Elisa Lynch.[42]

Among the records of this period two are considered of particular significance for their bearing on the question whether or not a conspiracy actually existed. In his account, General Resquín stated that Foreign Minister José Berges confessed that a revolution had been planned for July 24, 1868, upon the scheduled forcing of the Tebicuary batteries by the enemy squadron.[43] Likewise, in the deposition of Juan Esteban Molina, the prime conspirators were held to have been Berges, Benigno López, and Saturnino Bedoya, with the date for the outbreak also set for July 24.[44] Curiously enough, the Brazilian monitors actually forced the Tebicuary batteries on that date, and Colonel Thompson reported he had seen someone aboard a monitor apparently attempting to make signals to the shore. Thompson also noted that he was requested by Marshal López to render an immediate report of the circumstances.[45] More strangely still, July 24 was the birthday of Paraguay's Marshal President as well as the date of the final evacuation of Humaitá by the Paraguayan garrison.

Marshal López showed little mercy or pity in his attitude toward the members of his family who were implicated in the conspiracy trials, nor did he extend to them any special consideration. Already aware of Benigno's ambitions since before his own election as president, he countenanced his execution in December, 1868, along with that of his sisters' husbands, General Barrios and Treasurer Bedoya. López may also have been aware of his mother's attitude toward continuation of the war. Colonel Thompson related that Doña Juana came to the Paso Pucú headquarters after the first Battle of Tuyuty, and that it was afterwards rumored she had attempted to persuade her son to give up the war and to retire to Europe.[46]

From the reports of persons such as Padre José I. Acosta, chaplain of the López family, Marshal López probably realized that both Doña Juana and his sisters had known of a plot being hatched against him.[47] Though lenient with his mother, for whom he continued to hold sincere affection, he had his sisters placed in arrest and kept near his headquarters. Unlike Benigno, his brother Venancio was kept in custody like a common prisoner until his execution during the final retreat to Cerro Corá[48]

Lomas Valentinas

On August 26, 1868, following the successful passage of the Tebicuary batteries by the Brazilian monitors and the fall of Humaitá, Marshal López decided to withdraw his forces a distance of about 140 miles further north to new positions near the small river port of Villeta. He had Thompson prepare a new riverside battery at Angostura, a point located where the small stream named Pykysyry (the shrimp stream) flows into the Paraguay. An entrenched line to defend the Pykysyry was also begun, and a strong, semicircular fortified position was built at Itá-Ibaty (high-stone) in the Lomas Valentinas hills immediately east of the Villeta river port.

After a brief reorganization period following the capture of Humaitá, the Marquês de Caxias again resumed his offensive. He left the 2d Corps of his army temporarily at Humaitá under the command of General Argolo and began a slow advance northward along the Paraguay with about 26,000 men of the 1st and 3d Corps. By September 1, 1868, the allied army had crossed the Tebicuary after a sharp skirmish in which the famed Paraguayan patrol leader José Matías Bado was wounded and captured. Apparently unwilling to become a prisoner, Captain Bado reportedly pulled off his bandages to assure his death. As the advancing troops reached the former Paraguayan positions at San Fernando discoveries were made of the bodies of persons executed during the conspiracy trials.[49] These discoveries were given much publicity in the allied press as evidence of cruelty by Marshal López. In his report of his wartime visits Sir Richard Burton described how six such corpses were found, each with a paper pinned to the breast bearing the words: "Así perecen los traidores" (Such is the death for traitors). As Burton related the incident, the number of corpses found gradually increased in press reports from six to 64, to 74, and finally to 400 and then to 800, by the time he had returned to Buenos Aires.[50]

The Lomas Valentinas Campaign

The battles in the vicinity of the low-lying hills known as the Lomas Valentinas during December, 1868, marked the last phase of the allied advance which had begun nearly three years earlier at the crossing of the Upper Paraná River. During these years the military power of Paraguay came close to extinction. At their end the allies believed the war to have been won.

From September to December Marshal López continued with his defensive plans and attended to problems presented by the constant arrival of French and Italian naval vessels as well as by the closing events of the conspiracy period and the angry departure from Paraguay of Minister Washburn. In the bad graces of President López for his refusal to abandon Asunción, for his action in transforming his legation into a place of refuge, and for his generally suspect activities, the minister had his worries compounded by yet a further incident. Reportedly among the persons and belongings which had collected at the legation were several large macaws and parrots. One of these birds had apparently acquired the ability to speak, for it was alleged to have screamed most clearly from the legation confines, "Viva Dom Pedro Segundo!" The birds were swiftly dispatched on Washburn's orders.[51] The incident, however, must have impressed the secret policemen who had been posted about the legation by López.

Washburn departed on September 12, and his successor, General Martin T. MacMahon, arrived by the USS "Wasp" on December 3. MacMahon, a keen observer who also possessed a sense of humor, carefully recorded his impressions of his river trip aboard the "Wasp." The entry below illustrates his descriptive ability:

The officers amused themselves with occasional shots at birds or beasts on the shore. In one instance a most extraordinary transformation was wrought by the rather questionable rifle practice of a gallant captain, who fired at a white crane on the shore, and was astonished to behold the strange bird suddenly assume the shape and proportions of a native of the country, who had been stooping in the bushes by the waterside, and disappear with great rapidity toward the interior.[52]

Familiar with battle conditions from his own experiences in the Civil War, MacMahon was to leave a striking eyewitness account of the Lomas Valentinas campaign. He also became a staunch and capable defender of Paraguay's cause. His description of the López headquarters at Itá-Ibaty might easily be compared to portraits of similar American Civil War command posts:

At one end of this line the side walls had been omitted, leaving a large open shed, which seemed to serve as military office, dining-room, and observatory. Under this shed were three large telescopes on tripods, through which, from morning until night, aides were constantly observing the movements of the enemy, and reporting them from time to time to the President, who generally sat at a large table near the further end to receive reports or attend to the military business of the day. Three aides remained outside the "galpon" or shed, but always in full sight. Their business seemed to be to deliver to López the telegraphic dispatches which were constantly coming from the office nearby, or to communicate his orders from time to time to the other officers of the staff. These latter, when not occupied on military duties, spent their time chiefly in little groups pitching coins—a practice in which all had acquired singular skill.[53]

After reconnaissance had revealed the strength of the new Paraguayan positions at Lomas Valentinas and Angostura, Caxias decided upon a flank movement through the Chaco along the west bank of the Paraguay River. Utilizing practically the same methods employed by Marshal López in his withdrawal from Humaitá, he had an eleven-kilometer corduroy road built paralleling the banks of the Paraguay to a point opposite the small river port of San Antonio, four miles north of Villeta. While a holding force demonstrated before the Pykysyry lines Caxias and 19,000 troops of the 1st and 3d Corps moved over the Chaco road and crossed the Paraguay to San Antonio on December 5.

Ytororó.—Moving inland on December 6 along the road to Villeta, Brazilian troops found their way blocked by the enemy at a bridge over a small stream known as the Ytororó (meaning cascade). Built of wood, the bridge was only three meters wide. On being informed of the successful allied flank movement, Marshal López had ordered his reserves of about 5,000 men under Bernardino Caballero to defend the bridge at Ytororó. The late morning battle which followed was one of the most hard-fought actions of the war.[54] The bridge was the only means for crossing the stream and the Brazilian forces were thus required to take it by direct assault. The task became one for Argolo's 1st Corps alone. Although Osório's 3d Corps was expected to lend support, it had become lost on a left-flank movement under the direction of guide Céspedes, the former balloon observer, and did not arrive in time for the action.[55]

Caballero's outnumbered Paraguayans stubbornly defended their positions and the struggle for possession of the bridge became a seesaw affair marked by bitter hand-to-hand fighting. Paraguay's 23d Battalion, commanded by Captain José Romero, went into action with 300 effectives; when the battle ended only nine men remained unwounded. With the decision in balance, only a last charge by the reserves headed personally by Caxias finally produced an allied victory. The 65-year-old marquês led his men into the enemy rifle fire shouting: "Sigam-me os que forem Brasileiros!" (Follow me those of you who are Brazilians!)[56] Postwar anecdotes also held that he wore an ancient curved sword which had remained unused for so long in its scabbard that when finally drawn at Ytororó it emerged along with a cloud of rust, spiders, and crickets![57]

Ytororó was recorded in Brazil's history as Caxias' greatest hour. His personal inspiration turned the tide, and Caballero's remaining troops were forced to retire in disorder leaving six field guns behind them. Brazilian losses were serious—estimated at about 3,000 killed and wounded. Among the long list of officers wounded in the battle were generals Argolo and Antunes Gurjão. The latter, known in Brazil's military annals as "O Sacrificado de Ytororó," had been regarded as the most famous soldier produced by extreme northern Brazil. Badly wounded in the left arm, he was taken to the Humaitá base hospital where he died from a hemorrhage on January 17, 1869.[58] Manoel Deodoro da Fonseca, Brazil's future "Proclamador da República," was hit by a rifle bullet in the lower left side. He had earlier seen two of his eight brothers killed at Curupaity. A third, Major Eduardo Emiliano da Fonseca, was killed at Ytororó while leading his 40th Voluntários da Pátria. Yet a fourth brother, João Severiano da Fonseca, was engaged in his grim duties as field surgeon with the Army Medical Service.

He was the only army doctor to receive the distinction of being named Knight of the Imperial Order of the Cruzeiro. The seven Fonsecas who served in the war fully merited the brevet later given them in Brazil—"The Seven Swords of Alagoas."[59]

Avay.—The close decision at Ytororó and the heavy losses suffered forced Caxias temporarily to suspend his offensive. With Osório's 3d Corps now on hand, however, the allied advance again moved southward toward Villeta on December 11. The summer day was a blistering one, and the troops, using tree branches as protection for their heads from the sun, gave the impression of a forest on the march. The advance was shortly halted by the remnants of Caballero's force, now about 4,000 in number, which held a strong position across the road along a stream known as the Avay (the Indians' river). The ensuing battle lasted four hours in a heavy rainstorm. Considered one of the bloodiest battles in the military records of South America, Avay was a vicious struggle in which quarter was neither asked nor given by the two armies.[60] The Paraguayan force was almost totally destroyed. Only a few prisoners were taken since it was literally necessary to wound Caballero's men before they would drop their weapons. Caballero, himself, was among the few who returned from Avay, having miraculously escaped capture by not being recognized by his enemies. His cavalry commander, Colonel Valois Rivarola, managed to escape with him though shot through the throat. Despite his serious wound, Colonel Rivarola led his remaining men in a desperate charge on December 21, which prevented an early Brazilian victory at Itá-Ibaty. Wounded again, he was carried back to Cerro León where he died on December 25. Paraguayan histories list him as the nation's greatest cavalryman.[61]

Like Ytororó the Battle of Avay was an action decided only by superior Brazilian manpower. The 3d Corps absorbed heavy punishment—at one point only the charges of the cavalry under General José Antônio Corrêa da Câmara, future second Visconde de Pelotas, saved three infantry battalions from almost certain annihilation.[62] Among the units which distinguished themselves was the 44th Voluntários da Pátria commanded by Major Floriano Peixoto, Brazil's future Iron Marshal and second president.[63]

The most grievous loss to Brazil proved to be the wounding of Osório, "O legendário." Hit in the jaw by a bullet, he refused to leave the field and insisted upon being carried about in a cart so that his men could still see their general. The wound was serious, however, and Osório was forced to leave the army after Avay to recuperate in Rio Grande do Sul. When he subsequently returned to the army he was forced to wear a black silk cloth tied around his jaws both to support them and to cover the wound.[64] The cart of Avay was later placed in the National Historical Museum.[65]

Brazilian casualties were so heavy at Ytororó and Avay that Caxias ordered the 26th, 28th, 42d, 44th, 48th, and 55th Voluntários da Pátria battalions to be disbanded and the survivors incorporated into other units. In his memoirs Colonel Thompson commented that the decision to carry the fight to the allied army had been a serious mistake by Marshal López. Thompson believed that had López maintained his army in the strong Itá-Ibaty defensive positions he might have inflicted a repulse even more disastrous to the allies that that of Curupaity.[66]

Itá-Ibaty.—Though his forces had been badly mauled, Caxias correctly estimated that Paraguay's losses in the early December battles had been proportionately more serious. Patrols gave him reports of the semicircular entrenched Itá-Ibaty lines, and on December 20 the army, now rested, was alerted for a direct attack on the Paraguayan positions.

The movement on Lomas Valentinas began at 2 A.M. on December 21. The Brazilian force, composed of about 25,000 men, was divided into two columns commanded by generals Machado Bittencourt and J. L. Mena Barreto. The infantry left their packs at Villeta and began the march in their best uniforms with their rifles freshly cleaned.[67] By noon the columns had reached the perimeter of the Paraguayan positions. The defenders had built a shallow trench about two feet wide and two feet deep, which ran in a semicircle about the hill but which was open to the rear in the direction of Cerro León. The position was held by the remnants of Paraguay's army, estimated to have been from 3,000 to 8,000 in number, with the former figure probably being more correct in view of the heavy casualties at Ytororó and Avay.[68]

During the halt before these lines at noon, Caxias detached Mena Barreto's force to attack the Pykysyry line in the rear, and the cavalry under General Andrade Neves to explore the rear of the main Paraguayan positions. Mena Barreto's men quickly took the Pykysyry line, killed or captured most of the 1,500 defenders, and forced the few survivors to withdraw to Thompson's fortified position at Angostura.

Apparently unaware of the absence of defenses to the rear of the Paraguayan lines, Caxias ordered a direct frontal assault on Itá-Ibaty at 3 P.M. For three hours Brazilian infantry and cavalry repeatedly charged the light trenches in the face of all the fire power which Marshal López could still muster. Witnessed by Minister MacMahon, the fighting was in his opinion as desperate as any he had himself observed in the Civil War.[69] Paraguay's troops were not of the caliber of those who had formed the army earlier in the war. The boys and old men, nevertheless, gave a good account of themselves. They beat back all of the attacks and often fought on, even though wounded several times. Both the famous 40th Battalion and the Escort Battalion were annihilated. Artillery pieces, dismounted by the continuous Brazilian bombardment, were placed on mounds of earth in order that they could still be fired.

The action was broken off by the allies at 6 P.M. Although attacking troops had captured fourteen Paraguayan guns including the famous 32-pounder Whitworth from Second Tuyuty, and had stormed almost to the López headquarters area, they had not succeeded in breaking the defense line. Losses on both sides were heavy. By the night of December 21 Paraguay's army had dwindled to less than 2,000 men. Brazilian casualties numbered almost 4,000. The wounded were sent to the field hospital behind the lines where most operations were performed without the benefit of anesthesia. Among the wounded was Sublieutenant Dionísio Cerqueira, struck by a glancing blow in the head while leading his infantrymen. In his later memoirs he wrote that the Tuyuty 32-pounder had felled 13 men of the 16th Infantry with one round, and that the battalion's total losses at Itá-Ibaty amounted to 78 per cent of its officers and 58 per cent of its men (22 out of 28 officers and 209 out of 358 men)—a ratio comparable to losses suffered by Union and Confederate units at such desperate battles as Antietam and Shiloh.[70]

The most serious loss among the officers was the mortal wounding of cavalryman Andrade Neves, the 61-year-old Barão do Triunfo. Known both as "O Vanguardeiro" (the advance scout) and "Os Olhos das Fôrças" (the eyes of the army) for his reconnaissance feats, he was wounded while fighting on foot. Taken later to Asunción, he died of fever on January 6, 1869. His last words were reported to have been: "Camaradas, mais uma carga!" (Comrades, one more charge!).[71]

During December 22 and 23 Brazilian infantry and artillery poured an almost continuous rain of fire upon the Paraguayan trenches. In the comparative lull from the heavy frontal attacks Marshal López received some few reserve troops from Cerro León and was able once more to reform the famous 40th Battalion. His position, however, was hopeless.

On December 24, believing that the Paraguayan army had collapsed, Caxias sent a note to López advising his surrender. The Marshal's reply, prepared in about eight hours time and after consultation with his officers, was delivered to the Brazilian lines by staff aide Colonel Silvestre Aveiro and the Marshal's eldest son, young Major Juan Francisco López, shortly after 3 P.M. on December 24.[72] Its text, a translation of the major portion of which is contained in Appendix III, exhibited in the clearest terms the stamp of character which had made Francisco Solano López Paraguay's Iron Marshal. In it, Francisco López referred to the conference of Yataity-Corá in which he had sought "the reconciliation of four sovereign nations of South America which had already begun to destroy each other in a remarkable manner," and went on to state:

My initiative met with no answer but the contempt and silence of the allied governments, and new and bloody battles on the part of their armed representatives, as Your Excellencies call yourselves. I then more clearly saw that the tendency of the war of the allies was against the existence of the Republic of Paraguay and, though deploring the blood spilled in so many years of war, I could say nothing; and, placing the fate of my country and its generous sons in the hands of the God of Nations, I fought its enemies with loyalty and conscience, and I am disposed to continue fighting until that God and our arms decide the definite fate of the cause.[73]

In renewed Brazilian infantry and cavalry assaults which were witnessed by Minister MacMahon, the Paraguayan positions rapidly crumbled. Sensing defeat, Marshal López ordered Mrs. Lynch, his children, and MacMahon to leave for Piribebuy, an interior village to the east of Cerro León, which was soon to become the third of Paraguay's wartime capitals.[74]

The Paraguayan line fell to pieces on December 27. Under the personal command of López, now directly within range of enemy rifle fire for the first time in the war, the remains of his forces, some 60 men including his staff, withdrew eastward toward the old training area at Cerro León. The allied cavalry, though fresh and in number, was not ordered to pursue them.[75] In storming Itá-Ibaty the allied forces found and took the Marshal's correspondence files as well as his carriage bed, which Captain Richard Burton later saw and described as a kind of *fourgon* similar to the old wagons of the Suez Road in Egypt.[76] The Marshal's famous gold-embroidered kepi was also found and later placed in a Rio de Janeiro museum.[77] Among the prisoners liberated were Max von Versen and Major E. A. da Cunha Mattos. In celebration of the victory Caxias had his bands play the National Anthem.

Surrounded, and with but little provisions and ammunition left, Colonel Thompson at Angostura had no recourse but to surrender. He did so on December 30 upon verifying the extent of the defeat at Itá-Ibaty. Granted most liberal terms by the allies, he was allowed to board a British naval vessel which took him to Buenos Aires and away from the war. He was the only foreigner to have learned Guaraní fluently and to have been given actual command of a large Paraguayan army detachment. With no little pride George Thompson could later note in his memoirs that he was a Knight of the Order of Merit of Paraguay. To young Lieutenant José María Fariña, already a hero for his exploits as a commander of chatas along the Upper Paraná in early 1866, surrender of the Paraguayan flag was impossible. He hauled it down, wrapped it around a cannon ball, and threw it in the river rather than deliver it to the enemy as a trophy.[78]

By December 31, 1868, the allies believed that the long war against the Paraguay of Francisco Solano López was now ended. They had overlooked the one prime essential for complete victory—the subjugation or death of the Marshal President. Though the avowed objective of the allies had been "war to the death against López," he had almost miraculously escaped both death and capture. The failure to cut off his retreat after Lomas Valentinas was to prove a major tactical error by Caxias. While her president still lived Paraguay remained unconquered.

Chapter 10

CAMPAIGN IN THE CORDILLERA

A BRAZILIAN LANDING FORCE commanded by Colonel Hermes da Fonseca, another brother of Manoel Deodoro, reached Asunción on the night of January 1, 1869. On January 5 the bulk of the army, which had marched northward from Villeta and Lomas Valentinas, entered the city dressed in their best uniforms and with the bands playing.[1] They found Asunción to be abandoned. On the orders of Marshal López the civilian population had been evacuated to Luque, Piribebuy, and other interior points; the government had been removed first to Luque and subsequently to Piribebuy, and all machinery at the arsenal which could be transported had been taken to Caacupé, about 35 miles to the east.[2]

Fall of Asunción

The allied army swiftly occupied the city. The commanding officers were assigned to the best private residences, many of the troops were quartered in the new railway station, and Mrs. Lynch's private residence in the suburbs was converted into a hospital. Argentine troops, under their new commander Emilo Mitre, were moved through Asunción to camps at Luque. Allied patrols were pushed forward along the railway to Areguá, on the shores of Lake Ypacaraí in the direction of Pirayú and Cerro León.

Three days after he had entered Asunción, Caxias fainted during a victory *Te Deum*. The effects of his weakened physical condition were aggravated subsequently by the news of the death of his secretary, Colonel Fernando Sebastião Dias da Motta.[3] These circumstances, together with his belief that the war had ended and the somewhat unfavorable views which had been expressed in Rio de Janeiro regarding his conduct of the last campaign, caused him to decide to retire from active duty. He asked to be relieved on January 12, issued Order of the Day No. 272 on the fourteenth proclaiming the war to have ended, and transferred command on the eighteenth to Field Marshal Guilherme Xavier de Souza.[4] On his return to Brazil Caxias was called to face a Senate inquiry into the reasons for the successful flight of Marshal López from Itá-Ibaty and for his proclamation that the war had ended.[5] Though his explanations were accepted, the old commander was reportedly disillusioned with the turn in events. In recognition of his undeniably valuable services, however, the Imperial Government conferred upon him the Medal of *Mérito Militar* and the *Grã Cruz da Ordem de Pedro*, a decoration which was customarily given only to princes of royal blood. On March 26, 1869, "o maior soldado da pátria" (the nation's greatest soldier) received the title of Duke—the only Brazilian to achieve this imperial distinction.[6]

Conditions in occupied Asunción deteriorated after Caxias' departure. The troops, with few military duties to keep them occupied, engaged themselves in the pillage of the residences of the former inhabitants. Immense quantities of booty including silver and furniture were reported to have been loaded on departing ships.[7] Although some of the previous inhabitants returned, the impression began to spread among allied officers that so long as Paraguay's president still lived the civilian population would continue to identify itself with him. Some sectors of Brazil's officer corps were convinced that the time was ripe for the negotiation of a peace treaty since it might prove necessary to kill every Paraguayan in order to reach López.[8]

Disheartened, disillusioned, and perhaps bored with the deflation in military activity, many officers sought to be relieved from command and transferred home, alleging illness or other compelling factors. Their requests were usually granted by Xavier de Souza, himself a sick man.[9]

The trend toward demoralization which had set in was effectively countered by the arrival at Asunción of Counsellor José Maria da Silva Paranhos, future Visconde do Rio Branco. At a formal banquet given in his honor as the empire's chief civilian authority, Paranhos was sobered by the comments of Major Anfrísio Fialho, former commander of the Rio Grande do Sul German artillery battalion. In reply to arguments regarding the need to continue the war, Major Fialho pointed to the advantages of an early peace which would end the lassitude now affecting the army and which would also terminate the heavy financial burden that the war had placed on Brazil.[10]

Paranhos reported the circumstances prevailing at Asunción to the Imperial Government. Allegedly after some vacillation it was decided to renew the war effort. Dom Pedro himself was said to have hinted at abdication if his rigid opinion regarding prosecution of the war did not prevail.[11]

A further problem arose with regard to the direction of the renewed effort. The decision was finally reached to appoint Luiz Felipe Maria Fernando Gastão de Orléans, the Conde d'Eu, as the new commander of Brazil's forces. A young French nobleman only 26 years old, and grandson of Louis Philippe, the Conde d'Eu in appearance was blond, and had a beard and blue eyes. He was also somewhat deaf. Never fully accustomed to Portuguese, his pronunciation of the language became the subject of jokes in his army.[12] He had frequently sought an appointment to the war zone but his status as the emperor's son-in-law, together with the circumstances of his youth and his slight acquaintance with military affairs, had kept him at the court. His sole wartime adventure had been his "viagem militar" (military trip) in 1865 to Rio Grande do Sul and the surrender of Estigarribia at Uruguaiana. In early 1869, with the war obviously turning in the allies' favor and with but apparently slight trouble to be expected from Francisco Solano López, the pleas of Gastão de Orléans for an active duty post were finally satisfied. He was named to the high command on March 22, 1869.[13]

To his credit, the Conde d'Eu displayed a disposition to assume command of the army with a firm hand and to achieve the long-awaited victory over Marshal López as quickly as possible. News of the government's decision served to rekindle public enthusiasm for the war. By 1869, moreover, Brazil's economic situation, which had suffered a heavy burden of war expenditures, was showing signs of improvement under the direction of the Visconde de Itaboraí.[14]

The Conde d'Eu left Rio de Janeiro on March 30, 1869, aboard the steamer "Alice." The staff which he took with him to Paraguay had at least two notable members who left somewhat contrasting reports of the war. They were Colonel Dr. Francisco Pinheiro Guimarães and Captain Alfredo d'Escragnolle Taunay, of *Retreat from Laguna* fame. Doughty Pinheiro Guimarães, hardly recovered from the effects of the Humaitá campaign, was soon appointed deputy adjutant general. Captain Taunay was appointed as the official reporter of the new campaign with the express assignment of writing a *Diário do Exército* (an official daily record of events).[15] Both men experienced vicissitudes in their return to war. Dr. Pinheiro Guimarães, a vehement Liberal party member, became disliked by Counsellor Paranhos for his suspected influence upon the Conde d'Eu.[16] The Conde himself exhibited leanings toward the Liberal party which culminated in estranged relationships with Taunay, always a staunch Conservative. During the voyage to Asunción, the Conde d'Eu sought to persuade Taunay to send his news reports to the Liberal Rio de Janeiro newspaper *A Reforma*. Taunay politely but firmly refused, pointing out that he planned to write for the impartial *Jornal do Comércio*.[17]

The Conde d'Eu arrived at Asunción on April 14, 1869, and replaced the ailing Xavier de Souza as commander of the army on April 16. On the twenty-eighth a large celebration took place at Luque in honor of his birthday. Though careful not to arouse the new commander's ire, Captain Taunay steadfastly refused to allow his reports to be sent to Liberal newspapers. The Conde soon had his enthusiasm for the Liberals quashed by an article which appeared in *A Reforma* complaining that an untried young man who had been only a simple French adjutant in Morocco was now to hold command over an officer like General Osório.[18] His liking for Dr. Pinheiro Guimarães did not cool, however, and the versatile doctor was eventually named as chief of staff.

As Brazil's "General da Pena" (General of the Pen), Counsellor Paranhos was busily engaged on the political front. With the occupation of Asunción and the temporary pause in military operations, the time seemed propitious for the return to Paraguay of some of the exiles who had formed the Revolutionary Committee at Buenos Aires. Many of these men had also served in the Paraguayan Legion attached to the allied army—a unit composed of exiles which was particularly hated by Marshal López.

During early 1869, therefore, Asunción's population witnessed the return of the Decouds, the Recaldes, the Machains, and even of Félix Egusquiza, who was said to have held hopes for becoming

Paraguay's new president.[19] A further person who appeared and who became prominent in the immediate postwar period was Cirilo Rivarola. A Paraguayan sergeant who had been a López political prisoner, he was captured by the allies in May and placed at liberty in Asunción.[20] In April the newly formed *Club del Pueblo* sent a note to the allies proposing the formation of a provisional government, and in June a triumvirate was nominated composed of Rivarola, Carlos Loizaga, and José Díaz de Bedoya.[21] General Emilio Mitre had also raised a new special force of Paraguayans opposed to López and had allowed the unit to use Paraguay's flag—an act which was angrily challenged by President López.[22]

By the end of June, 1869, the Conde d'Eu had completed the reorganization of the Brazilian army, and the allies were ready to renew the war. The new effort, however, was to be almost wholly a campaign on the part of Brazil alone. A token Argentine force under Mitre still remained at Luque, but Uruguayan participation in the allied army had practically disappeared. By June the Brazilian army comprised 26,000 battle-hardened veterans who were well equipped and divided into two corps each commanded by experienced and famous generals—Osório the legendary, and Polidoro the former Commandant of the Escola Militar.

Though his jaw wound suffered at the Battle of Avay had not healed, the famous Osório felt it his duty to return for the final campaign. He arrived at the army's camps on June 6 and received an ovation from the troops which may have had no parallel in the war.[23] "O legendário" still had his chin bound in the black silk scarf and was forced to follow a diet of liquids because of his wound.[24] While the admiration bestowed upon him was reported to have made Counsellor Paranhos jealous, it was clear that the return of the army's most popular general represented a distinct psychological factor which would be valuable in the forthcoming campaign.

Regeneration at Azcurra

The remarkable events which transpired on Paraguay's side after the debacle at Lomas Valentinas in December, 1868, form a major feat of the war over which there has been no controversy. His army thoroughly smashed at Itá-Ibaty and left only with his staff and a few members of his escort, Marshal President Francisco Solano López was definitely a defeated general. He lived, however, and no amount of proclamations by the allies declaring the war to be ended could be considered valid while Paraguay still possessed her Marshal.

Retiring on horseback with no artillery or baggage salvaged from Lomas Valentinas, the Marshal and the survivors of his army reached the former army training base at Cerro León in late December, 1868. At this point he found Minister of War Luis Caminos with about 1,500 troops from the Asunción garrison. While the allies occupied Asunción, López set about to rebuild an army. He ordered the equipment saved from the arsenal to be put back in operation at Caacupé, had the remaining state archives and treasury moved to Piribebuy which became the third capital of Paraguay, and drew a defense line along the Cordillera escarpment, the westward edge of the Paraná plateau which falls just to the east of Lake Ypacaraí and the railroad. This Azcurra position was a strong one, though a large force would be required to defend the flanks.

Minister MacMahon, meanwhile, had found his new residence at Piribebuy much to his liking. His description of his accomodations there and of the village itself represent an excellent portrait of a mid-nineteenth-century Paraguayan town. The description likewise casts light on the minister's own amiable and adaptive personality:

Late in the afternoon we arrived at Piribebuy, the provisional capital—a town of about three or four thousand inhabitants—and took possession of a house which had been hospitably prepared for our reception. It consisted of two principal rooms, one floored with brick, the other with a hard earthern floor. The windows were without glass, and opened, as did the doors, on both sides on wide corridors, as the open space sheltered by the overhanging eaves is generally called in these countries. The furniture consisted of a circular center-table, quaintly carved of native wood, a large writing-desk with drawers, and a side-table with a decanter, several glasses, and a bundle of cigars. The tables, like all others in the country were uncomfortably high. The decanter was comfortably full of caña (Paraguayan rum).

The village of Piribebuy consists of four streets intersecting each other at right angles, and enclosing an open space or grass-covered plaza, about a quarter of a mile across. It is situated on a gentle slope or knoll, with higher ground or crests on all sides at a distance of about a mile and a half. The houses are of one storey, and generally roofed with thatch. On the crown of the knoll was the cemetery, enclosing about an acre of ground, and marked by a single large wooden cross in the center. The market-place was under a dense orange grove at one extremity of the village, and always presented during the day a spectacle full of life. Scores of women, old and young, assembled there to sell their wares, and kept up an incessant chatter all day long. The Piribebuy—a clear and rapid stream, very sudden in its rises and falls—passed at the foot of the slope on which the town was built. The whole population bathed here every day, the women generally after nightfall.[25]

Dividing his time between Piribebuy, Cerro León, and Azcurra, Marshal López performed the near miracle of organizing a new Army of Paraguay. With the few Lomas Valentinas survivors and the Asunción garrison as the nucleus, the new army grew steadily. Soldiers who had escaped capture at Itá-Ibaty, prisoners who had been released by the allies, convalescents from army hospitals, and the youth of Paraguay—respected their Marshal's call and reported for further duty. By the end of January, 1869, the new army along the Azcurra escarpment had grown to an estimated 13,000 effectives. Thirteen light field guns had been cast by the make-shift Caacupé arsenal under the direction of General Resquín.[26] Arming the reformed infantry units was a more difficult problem. The only sources for weapons were the gleanings of former battlefields, allied prisoners, and the few relics and antique firearms owned by civilians.

By April, Marshal López felt himself able to plan offensive engagements. He mounted light field guns on a railway car and sent the first armored train in Latin America's history down the line toward Areguá. While this ingenious scheme failed to produce any notable military success, it impressed the allies that the enemy still possessed the capacity for innovation for which he was already famous. López also sent out patrols to burn railway bridges and crossties on the track behind the Brazilian advanced positions.[27] Reports reaching the Conde d'Eu in June indicated clearly that he had a cunning and capable adversary with whom to contend, and that Paraguay's army, considered effectively dispersed by Caxias, had exhibited a totally unexpected ability for regeneration.

Piribebuy and Campo Grande

On July 7, 1869, the Conde d'Eu held a council of war at his field headquarters at Pirayú, the small station on the railroad lying in front of the Azcurra escarpment. The strategy which evolved from the meeting was known as the "Plano de Pirayú." It called for a holding force at Pirayú to convince López that an attack would be made against the Azcurra heights, while a strong flanking force commanded by the Conde and Osório would seek to turn the extreme Paraguayan left flank.[28]

The plan worked smoothly and efficiently. The envelopment movement began on August 1. A small Paraguayan force was routed at Sapucay, and a road was found through the village of Valenzuela which led to the strong point of Piribebuy to the south and well behind the flank of the positions at Azcurra. The flank force reached the vicinity of Piribebuy on August 11. The next day, after a crushing early morning bombardment by Emilio Mallet's 47 guns, Brazilian troops rushed the trenches, killed or captured the defenders, and occupied the city. They found most of Paraguay's remaining state archives and treasury. Among Brazilian casualties was the veteran General João Manoel Mena Barreto, killed during the last phase of the action. Reporter Taunay, an on-the-spot observer, noted that the general's *china* (mistress) suffered an emotional breakdown from her loss.[29]

It was at Piribebuy that allied troops sensed the tragedy which had befallen Paraguay—many of the dead Paraguayans turned out to be women and extremely young boys. So fierce was the resistance of the defenders that their actions have since been described as "scenes from Saragossa," in a reference to the heroic Siege of Saragosa in Spain against French troops during the Peninsular Wars. Sublieutenant Dionísio Cerqueira, now recovered from his Lomas Valentinas wound, was especially impressed by the sight of a mother and her young son lying dead at the entrance to the church, apparently killed by the same bullet.[30] In postwar accounts Paraguayan historians bitterly referred to Piribebuy as a massacre. Brazilian sources, including the Conde d'Eu, have refuted such allegations.

The Conde d'Eu, with victory in his grasp, moved north toward Caacupé on August 13. Marshal López, however, appreciated the sudden danger to his position. He immediately evacuated his Azcurra camps and retired northeastward toward Campo Grande. Some 1,200 wounded were left at Caacupé under the direction of Dr. Diego Domingo Parodi, an Italian physician to whom Resquín reported López gave most of his remaining money for the care of the patients.[31] The Paraguayan wounded, some 70 Europeans, Dr. Parodi, and the abandoned arsenal were found by pursuing Brazilian troops at Caacupé on August 15. A portable press was also discovered which still contained the unfinished August 12 edition of the Paraguayan army's last newspaper, *La Estrella*.[32] The strain of active campaign conditions proved too exhausting for Manoel Luís Osório and he asked to be relieved at Caacupé. His place in command of the 1st Corps was assumed by General J. L. Mena Barreto. General Polidoro, the former commandant of the Escola Militar, also became ill and was substituted in command of the 2d Corps by General Victorino Carneiro Monteiro, future Barão de São Borja

Campo Grande.—The Battle of Campo Grande, or Acosta Nú as it is known in Paraguay, proved to be the last major action of the war. Realizing that he had succeeded in his strategy and that his opponent was now attempting to retreat to a new position, the Conde d'Eu ordered an immediate, full-scale pursuit of Marshal López. Brazilian troops found the rear guard of Paraguay's army under Bernardino Caballero entrenched at Campo Grande. Again the poorly equipped and untrained Paraguayans were no match for Brazil's veteran infantry and cavalry. Many of Caballero's "men" were found to have been boys as young as ten years who wore false beards in order to inspire caution among their adversaries.[33]

The ruse did not work and the "men" suffered terrible losses. Captain Taunay noted that the ineffective Paraguayan fire was due probably to the poor quality of their arms and poor aim on the part of the soldiers.[34] He also commented that the types of weapons left on the field were amazing for their variety and age— many were of the old flintlock type, long since outmoded; some were so primitive that they were not recognizable, and others were of the ancient blunderbuss style which, Taunay claimed, "can only be seen in archeological museums."[35] Among these discoveries, however, Brazilian troops also found Wilhelm Wagener's modern Congréve rocket-launcher, which impressed them by its ingenious construction.[36]

Bernardino Caballero's stubborn holding action at Campo Grande provided time for Marshal López to withdraw his remaining forces to the less-populated and more-forested area of northeastern Paraguay. At Campo Grande, however, the army ceased to exist as an organized and effective unit. Casualties were so heavy that fewer than 2,000 troops now remained. Marshal López had lost almost all his baggage train, some 42 carts loaded with supplies, and 23 cannon.[37] Young Lieutenant Dionísio Cerqueira, who finally received a promotion after the action, was shocked by the appearance of the battlefield, which he described as being covered with dead boys, most of whom had not yet reached the age of adolescence. He noted that his infantrymen had commented that "não dava gosto à gente brigar com tanta criança" (there is no pleasure in fighting with so many children).[38]

Chapter 11

CERRO CORÁ

THE HAMMER BLOWS represented by the allied victories at Piribebuy and Campo Grande spelled the end of any expectations by Francisco Solano López of a military success. There was still the possibility that the allies would tire of the prolonged struggle, however, as well as the chance, though now remote, that foreign diplomatic intervention might yet stimulate peace negotiations. Hopes for action by the United States had disappeared in late May with the recall to Washington of Marshal López' friend, Martin T. MacMahon. Apart from these possibilities, Paraguay's president remained staunchly adamant in his decision that the war was one of Independencia o Muerte. There would be no bargaining with the enemy and he would continue the fight to his last breath if necessary.

Unlike the campaigns by Juárez against Maximilian in Mexico, it proved impossible for the remnants of Paraguay's army to conduct guerilla operations in late 1869. The land features in northeastern Paraguay were not suited to hit-and-run tactics, the people were not of the nomadic gaucho type such as those of the Argentine pampas, and the Paraguay River was the nation's economic artery along which the principal population centers were located.

Following the Battle of Campo Grande the survivors of Paraguay's army retreated northeast to the small interior villages of Caraguatay and San Estanislao. They were closely followed by allied units, and on August 19 the Conde d'Eu and his forces entered Caraguatay only hours after López' departure.[1] In Asunción, meanwhile, a provisional civil government had been installed and had declared Francisco Solano López to be an outlaw.[2] Brazilian cavalry detachments, spreading out through central Paraguay, raided the former iron foundry at Ibicuí and executed the Paraguayan commander, Captain Julio Ynsfrán, for alleged mistreatment of allied prisoners.[3]

As Brazilian patrols passed through Paraguay's small villages it was evident that wartime propaganda had created some curious beliefs among the inhabitants. At one point women reportedly exclaimed: "Santo Dios! Los macaquitos no tienen cola!" (Holy Father! the monkeys have no tails!).[4] The terms *macacos* and *cambas*, signifying monkeys and blacks, were commonly used in Paraguay and its army in referring to Brazil's Negro soldiers. Brazilians, for their part, usually referred to Paraguayans as *caboclos*, or mestizos.[5]

Since the advancing troops were under strict orders against pillaging there were only a few isolated incidents of depredations against the civilian population. Villagers, once their original surprise and curiosity had vanished, usually developed friendly relations with the allied soldiers. Dances and parties were common in occupied towns, and more lasting unions between Brazilian soldiers and Paraguayan women were by no means infrequent. Dionísio Cerqueira noted that the most popular tunes at local dances attended by Brazilian officers were "Palomita" and the "London Carapé." Captain Taunay, perhaps with a more appraising eye, wrote that many of such dances were popularly classified by his colleagues as "bailes sifilíticos" since the feminine guests were frequently "chinas e mulheres do comércio (women of easy virtue).[6]

Caraguatay became a temporary base for the allied army and heavy patrols were sent out to locate and pursue López. The Conde d'Eu learned that the last six small vessels of Paraguay's navy had been brought up the Manduvirá River to escape capture by Brazil's squadron, and he ordered cavalry General Corrêa da Câmara to seize the ships. General Câmara arrived too late. Informed of the allied advance, Paraguayan soldiers set fire to the "Apa," "Anhambay," "Guairá," "Yporá," "Paraná," and "Pirabebé." When the Brazilians arrived, several of them were killed by the explosion of the magazine of one of the burning vessels.[7] The rusted remains of the hulks are still visible in the river, and the event is still remembered in a Paraguayan folksong.

Allied troops camped at Caraguatay soon began to experience supply difficulties. By reason of a dispute over contract terms between the Conde d'Eu and the established contractors, Lesica and

Lanus, the flow of rations was suddenly halted and food shortages began to occur. The Conde d'Eu was forced to renew the Lesica and Lanus contract, but not before the firm had suffered a financial loss which was later the basis for a long dispute with the Imperial Government.[8] The lack of food in the allied camps caused problems among the troops. Argentines, reportedly not averse to horseflesh for their sustenance, displayed an attraction to the mounts of Rio Grande do Sul cavalrymen. As their horses began to disappear nightly, the cavalry complained. According to reporter Taunay, only threats of execution as thieves persuaded the suspect Argentines to cease their unusual supply forays.[9]

For his part, the Conde d'Eu attempted to ease the food problem through the issue of emergency supplies in the form of his private stock of canned "sardinha de Nantes." The appearance of this new item in the army's diet engendered renewed efforts at rhyming among the troops. Dionísio Cerqueira noted down the following popular verse of unknown authorship which sarcastically compared the wartime trend in rations from the roast meat of Osório's time through the manioc flour and beans of Polidoro and Caxias, to the sardines of the Conde d'Eu:

> Osório dava churrasco,
> E Polidoro farinha.
> O Marquês deu-nos jaba
> E sua Alteza sardinha![10]

As the patrols brought reports of the retreat northward of Francisco Solano López toward the Amambay-Maracajú low mountain plateau, the Conde d'Eu ordered a force to occupy the port of Concepción, about 200 miles north of Asunción along the Paraguay River, and established a new temporary base at Rosario, midway between the two larger ports.

Marshal López, meanwhile, evacuated San Estanislao in early September and renewed his march through the wilderness of extreme northeast Paraguay by way of the small inhabited points of Curuguaty and Itanará. In the early stages, his few soldiers were accompanied by so many hundreds of civilians that the march assumed the appearance of an exodus. Most of these were women. They were divided into two groups: *residentas* and *destinadas*. The former were members of families loyal to López and had simply obeyed his orders to evacuate their homes and accompany the army.

The latter were members of families whose loyalty to the Marshal had become suspect; their lot was scarcely better than that of prisoners.[11] The trek through the most remote region of Paraguay soon became a tragedy. With no food supplies and dependent upon the few edible roots and wild fruits which could be found, and constantly plagued by insects, the unfortunate civilians underwent terrible sufferings. Through the early summer months of November and December, pursuing Brazilian troops found hundreds of the *residentas* and *destinadas* prostrate along the trail either dead or in the last stages of starvation. To rescuing allied officers the pathos of these scenes was indescribable.[12]

Paraguay's *via dolorosa* was led by Marshal López. His army had now dwindled to less than 1,000 men. Many were unable to face the severe privations of the march and either gave way to their exhaustion or left the column to surrender to the pursuing allied patrols. The march was also featured by a renewal of the treason trials. Though evidence of suspect activities was not always fully convincing, the Marshal and his remaining staff believed that sufficient grounds existed for the execution of several officers including his brother Venancio, Lieutenant Aquino, and Colonel Mongelós. His mother and sisters who were carried with the force were also suspected of a poison plot against the Marshal.[13] At some point along the march a large part of the remaining treasury of Paraguay may have been secretly buried. The stories regarding this possibility proved so enticing that for years afterwards enterprizing adventurers dug many deep holes along the López trail in the hope of discovering the treasury chests.[14]

The optimistic news from Paraguay proved gratifying to Argentina's new president, Domingo F. Sarmiento. In a letter of December 30, 1869, to his good friend Mrs. Mary Mann, he wrote: "La guerra está concluida aunque López queda como Blackeagle en los bosques" (The war is ended even though López keeps on like Blackeagle in the forests). The new president also noted that he had read the pro-Paraguay statements of ex-minister MacMahon, which he felt had caused indignation among all in Buenos Aires who knew the "truth" about Paraguay. He added, "Such representatives of the United States produce a deplorable effect upon public opinion."[15]

In the extreme northeastern region of Paraguay, about 30 miles along the Concepción road west of the border cities of Pedro Juan

Caballero and Ponta-Porá a natural bowl is located in the foothills of the Amambay mountain range which is known as Cerro Corá, or Corral of Hills. As its name implies, the area is a natural ampitheater surrounded by small round hills with sharp cliffs, similar to the *mogotes* of Cuba. It lies near the Aquidaban-Niqüí River, a tributary of the Aquidaban River and a small and shallow stream which is normally easy to ford. There are no towns or villages in the vicinity. Cerro Corá is still one of the most wildly beautiful scenic attractions in Paraguay.[16]

The surviving members of Paraguay's army, now only about 500 in number, together with their Marshal and Elisa Lynch and her sons, reached Cerro Corá in early February, 1870. Due to its isolated location and defensive features, Marshal López decided to use the area as a base for the recuperation and reorganization of his small army. Some historians have suggested that he may have been hoping to march across the Chaco to Bolivia, or northward into Mato Grosso. No definite evidence of such plans, however, has come to light.

One of the Marshal's first actions at Cerro Corá was to have a medal designed to commemorate the long and arduous six-month march from Piribebuy and Campo Grande. The medal, the last to be authorized by Francisco Solano López, bore the following words, "Venció Penurias y Fatigas" (the bearer overcame the most difficult of trials and tribulations).[17] The surviving soldiers fully merited this last decoration. While apparently safe in their new camp, the soldiers still suffered from the lack of food. There were no farms in the area and daily rations had now reached the slim ratio of one cow or ox for 500 men. Even the hides were reportedly consumed by the hungry men.[18]

The Death of Marshal López

Like so many of the major incidents in his life, the final moments in the career of Francisco Solano López have been given varied and often contradictory treatment in the numerous accounts of his era. In some studies he committed suicide, or was killed in the Chaco while attempting to flee to Bolivia. In others he is said to have been executed after having been taken prisoner, of having died while clutching a dozen lances thrust into his chest, or of having been killed in a swamp with his body left to rot in the sun. Descriptions in later historical studies reflected such wide variation that scarcely two accounts are to be found which are similar.

Reports of the whereabouts of Marshal López were soon brought to General Corrêa da Câmara's Brazilian patrols by captured Paraguayan prisoners and possibly, by deserters. By the end of February, 1870, a strong force of Rio Grande do Sul cavalry and some infantry units including the 9th Battalion under Lieutenant Colonel Floriano Peixoto had gradually converged upon Cerro Corá. The final action of the Paraguayan War began at daybreak March 1, 1870. In an efficient surprise thrust, General Câmara's men, under the immediate command of Peixoto, Francisco Antônio Martins, and João Nunes da Silva Tavares, overwhelmed the small Paraguayan outpost at the Chirigüelo gateway to the area and pushed forward toward the Paraguayan camp.

At about 6 A.M. a survivor of the outpost detachment brought word of the Brazilian attack. The group with Francisco Solano López then included about 400 of his soldiers, Elisa Lynch and her children, Vice President Francisco Sánchez, Secretary of State Caminos, Padre Fidel Maíz, General Resquín, and others of his staff. The report from the outpost was swiftly followed by the appearance of enemy cavalrymen who immediately charged upon the camp. In a short but violent action of about 15-minutes duration the defenders were scattered and all organized resistance ended.[19]

The Marshal President and members of his staff were a special target for the cavalrymen. Most eyewitness reports agree that credit for the mortal wounding of Francisco Solano López belonged to a corporal named José Francisco Lacerda, nicknamed "Chico Diabo" by his comrades. Corporal Lacerda, possibly enthused by the reward of 100 pounds sterling which had been offered for the death of López, succeeded in hitting Paraguay's president with a lance thrust in the abdomen. In the flurry of the attack López may also have received a saber slash through his straw hat.[20]

Badly wounded and bleeding profusely, Francisco Solano López managed to escape momentarily from his assailants, and in company with several of his staff, to reach the banks of the Aquidaban-Niqüí. Helped by his remaining aides, he stumbled across the shallow stream. His severe wounds and the steep slope of the opposite bank then halted him. While his aides ran in search of an easier slope, the Marshal lay, half in the water, grasping a small palm tree at the water's edge. It was in this condition that his Brazilian pursuers found him.[21]

Upon being informed that López had been located, General Câmara hastened to the banks of the river and called upon the Marshal to surrender. In a gesture which must be classed as fearless, Francisco Solano López flung his sword at his enemies. Then, in terms which even his most outspoken critics have declined to belittle, he uttered the words for which he shall always be remembered: "Muero con mi Patria!" (I die with my country!).[22]

A Brazilian cavalryman, who was reported to have been a Riograndense named João Soares, waded across the stream, spun López around, and fired a shot into his back at close range from his Spencer carbine.[23] So died the only chief executive in South America's history to have met his fate in battle against his country's enemies. The era of López and El Supremo had ended.

Aftermath

Blood-spattered and muddy, the body of the Marshal was tossed over two poles and carried back across the river. A brief unofficial autopsy was performed by a Brazilian doctor, probably Surgeon Manoel Cardoso da Costa Lôbo.[24] The report showed mortal lance wounds in the abdomen with final death coming from a gunshot wound in the back. Though accounts of the event are understandably confused, the corpse was then apparently thrown on the ground for exhibition to the troops. Among the objects removed from the body were a watch bearing the official motto of Paraguay—"Paz y Justicia," and a ring inscribed with the words "Vencer o Morir" (Conquer or Die).[25] Brazilian souvenir hunting soldiers were also stated to have pulled out some of the hair from the Marshal's scalp, with one officer allegedly cutting off an ear to satisfy a pledge he had made on joining the army.[26] Other López souvenirs from Cerro Corá which history has mentioned included the Marshal's manta, or horse blanket, taken by young Colonel Floriano Peixoto, who was eventually to become Brazil's Iron Marshal and second republican president; the Marshal's sword with its point broken off, and the map prepared by Lieutenant Thomas Jefferson Page of the United States Navy, now in the possession of a Swedish historian.[27] For his part, Corporal "Chico Diabo" Lacerda probably received his 100 pounds sterling. In any event his actions were widely publicized within Brazil's army through the popular verse which ran as follows:

"O Cabo Chico Diabo
ao Diabo Chico deu cabo."

Corporal Chico [Little] Devil has
killed the Little Devil [López].

During the final skirmish at Cerro Corá, Vice President Sánchez and Secretary Caminos were shot dead, and Padre Fidel Maíz and General Resquín were made prisoners. Bernardino Caballero, the stout defender at Avay and future founder of the Colorado Party, was away on a foraging expedition on March 1. As his position was hopeless, he surrendered later to Brazilian troops. Fidel Maíz, apparently high on Brazil's list of war criminals, went through a hair-raising mock execution ceremony in which he later claimed his life was spared by Floriano Peixoto.[29] Elisa Lynch, attempting to escape by carriage, was caught by Brazilian cavalrymen. Her eldest son, Juan Francisco, now a colonel at fifteen, refused to surrender and was killed while resisting capture. Mrs. Lynch asked for and received permission to bury her dead. According to one account she was aided in her task by her lady companion, Isidora Díaz, sister of General José Díaz, the Hero of the Battle of Curupaity.[30]

In his memoirs Fidel Maíz wrote that the Paraguayan prisoners were then forced to march over the grave of their leader.[31] In spite of such grim scenes, history has recorded that not all those present succumbed to the intense emotion of final victory. Ernesto A. da Cunha Mattos, returned to active duty after his escape from Paraguayan custody at Lomas Valentinas, and now commanding Brazil's 12th Battalion at the gateway to Cerro Corá, remembered the kindness previously shown him by Mrs. Lynch, who had offered him sweets and Paraguayan rum while he was a prisoner. A thoroughly correct gentleman, Cunha Mattos placed himself at Elisa Lynch's orders, with the observation to her that by doing so he would not be suspect by his colleagues since, as he put it, "all we Brazilians are above such suspicions."[32] Both Mrs. Lynch and the few Paraguayan prisoners later received further demonstrations of Brazil's ability to respect the fortunes of war through the actions of Counsellor Paranhos in denying the existence of treasures in Mrs. Lynch's possession, and in his refusal to remand the captured former López officers to summary justice at the hands of the new Asunción provisional government.[33]

The victory celebrations in the Brazilian camps at Cerro Corá were wild and prolonged. Though Doña Juana Carillo de López was stated to have wept at the news of her eldest son's death, her two widowed daughters, Inocencia and Rafaela, whose husbands Vicente Barrios and Saturnino Bedoya had died during the 1868 conspiracy trials, allegedly displayed no similar grief. In one reliable account Inocencia reportedly entered into an immediate friendship with General Corrêa da Câmara of which a daughter was eventually the evidence. The *laços de amor* stemming from Cerro Corá may have gone even further. A Commander Pedra was reported to have formed a union with Rafaela López de Bedoya, and Captain Teodoro Wanderley was said to have become more than entranced with a daughter of Venancio López.[34]

On March 4, 1870, the Conde d'Eu boarded a steamer bearing his name at Rosario and proceded toward Concepción. At noon the supply ship "Davidson," flying the American flag at the stern and the Brazilian flag at the bows, stopped the "Conde d'Eu" and communicated the news from Cerro Corá. The Brazilian commander-in-chief continued on to Concepción and a victory celebration featuring a dance was immediately arranged. He returned to his temporary headquarters at Rosario on March 6 where the electrifying news of the war's end, according to Captain Taunay, caused "delirium to reign among the troops." Many Paraguayan residents among the river ports were stated to have shared in the enthusiasm.[35] Lieutenant Dionísio Cerqueira, however, noted tears on the faces of the returning ragged and gaunt ex-soldiers of Paraguay who had been freed after Cerro Corá.[36]

At Rio de Janeiro Dom Pedro's excitement over the news from Paraguay was tempered by his second thoughts regarding the rather undiplomatic preliminary report of General Câmara referring to the shooting of López instead of his having been taken prisoner. In a letter of April 4 the Barão de Muritiba wrote of these matters to Counsellor Paranhos, and included a note that Dom Pedro had questioned why the death of López had not been authenticated. Muritiba continued in his letter: "The emperor does not wish to consent to the conferring of honors upon Corporal Chico until the matters to which I have referred have been settled. I have not mentioned to him the possibility of a pension for the corporal, but he suggested the convenience of satisfying him with money."[37]

The ranking Paraguayan officers who survived the last action at Cerro Corá were taken to Concepción. They were encouraged to sign a statement highly critical of the policies of their late leader which several of them shortly repudiated. Most were then set at liberty. Several of the more prominent officers, including Resquín, Aveiro, Caballero, and Fidel Maíz, were kept aboard a Brazilian ship because of the threats made against them by the Asunción provisional government. General Resquín was taken to Humaitá where he signed a deposition regarding his wartime role which he, too, later repudiated. Fidel Maíz was taken to Brazil for a short period and was eventually allowed to return to Paraguay.[38]

With the war officially declared ended, a problem arose regarding the return home of the troops. For reasons of possible political flavor Counsellor Paranhos advised the transfer to Brazil of the Voluntários da Pátria battalions in separate and spaced groups.[39] The Conde d'Eu with the support of Liberal party member Pinheiro Guimarães, however, decided that the volunteer units should be returned in as large groups as transport facilities permitted, and within the same period of time so that the men could all share in the justly deserved glory that awaited them. The views of the Conde d'Eu prevailed. He left Paraguay on April 16 with his staff including Alfredo Taunay, and landed at Rio de Janeiro on April 29.[40]

The repatriation of Argentine army units in Paraguay had commenced earlier. In a letter to Mrs. Mann dated February 15, 1870, President Sarmiento reported that he had ordered the return of part of the army, and "with astonishment and public satisfaction," had arranged payment of their back wages—$200 to each soldier.[41]

As was perfectly fitting, one of the first Brazilian army units assigned to return home was placed under the command of Francisco Pinheiro Guimarães. The courageous, sagacious, and versatile doctor was relieved of his position as deputy adjutant general by order of April 15, 1870, and named commander of the 3d Brigade of Voluntários da Pátria. The unit consisted of the 27th, 33d, and 44th Battalions— the 27th included the surviving members of the old 4th Battalion which had been originally recruited in Rio de Janeiro and had been commanded by the doctor himself. The brigade landed at Rio de Janeiro on May 2, 1870, amid a popular demonstration which was classed as unique by the local newspapers.

The men were received at the Arsenal da Marinha by Dom Pedro and the royal family. In its edition of May 3 the *Jornal do Comércio* reported the following speech by the emperor:

Commanders of the brigade and of the volunteers battalions. Accept my embrace for you and your comrades. The rejoicing of the nation attests to the grandeur of your services in the interest of the dignity of our nation; I salute you—Vivam os Voluntários da Pátria! Vivam o Exército Nacional e a Armada Nacional![42]

On May 4 a general review of the brigade by Dom Pedro took place at the Praça Dom Pedro I. The display also included the equally famous 41st Voluntários da Pátria from Bahía. The highlights were a firing exhibition by the veteran soldiers and a mock bayonet charge which created a tremendous sensation among the crowd of applauding spectators.[43]

Dr. Francisco Pinheiro Guimarães was made an honorary brigadier general on May 7, and was later awarded an annual pension for his wartime services. His greatest moment, however, probably occurred on May 18. On the evening of that date he was given a public homage in the Teatro São Luiz. The ceremony was followed by a midnight dinner at the city's famed German restaurant, the Casa Schroeder. Dr. Pinheiro Guimarães definitely proved his mettle as a foremost heroic son of Rio de Janeiro by listening to an incredible program of 41 speeches in his honor which finally terminated at the hour of 5:30 A.M.![44]

Chapter 12

EPILOGUE

FINAL VICTORY in Paraguay was to mean different things for the peoples of La Plata and Brazil. For Paraguay and Brazil, the major contestants, the war had proven to be an immense drain on economic resources. For Argentina, the economic losses of the early war period were balanced to some extent by the heavy commercial activity along the Paraná and at Buenos Aires in the later years. Human losses were severe for all. Estimates of total casualties were set as high as 220,000 for Paraguay and 190,000 for the allies.[1]

The Allies

Argentina and Uruguay.—In Argentina the end of the long war was viewed with mixed impressions. On the one hand the policies of Bartolomé Mitre had been successfully carried to conclusion under his successor, Domingo F. Sarmiento; Buenos Aires had consolidated its position as the undisputed capital city of the united Argentine Republic and had prospered from the heavy wartime commercial movement through its port. On the other hand, old federalist sympathies among the interior provinces, though not extinguished, had perhaps their last great chance for victory in their rivalry with Buenos Aires disappear with the death of Fransisco Solano López and the subsequent assassination in Entre Ríos of Justo José de Urquiza.

In a larger sense, however, the war with Paraguay had definitely advanced the cause of unification among all the provinces. Such terms as "the constitution," "national honor," and "the nation's dignity," had come to hold a new meaning for the troops who had fought through the genuine international struggle with Paraguay. Many of them returned home with a new sense of respect for the *patria grande*, represented by Argentina as a whole, in contrast to former loyalties to the *patria chica*, or an individual province.[2]

The war had never been a completely popular one except perhaps in Buenos Aires, and Argentines were never to view it with the same patriotic pride and fervor which were generated among Paraguayans and many Brazilians. Dating from 1870 the massive tide of European immigration and the advent of large-scale agriculture were to supersede the Paraguayan War among the major episodes in the nation's history. Not until 50 years later did a popular author, Manuel Gálvez, produce a bestselling trilogy which utilized as its central plot the war and Argentina's role.[3]

In a material sense, the end of the war saw the achievement of several Argentine policy objectives. The Paraná River became permanently free to international commerce, and the claims to the old Misiones region were eventually adjusted in Argentina's favor. Territorial pretentions in the Chaco, however, fell short of complete satisfaction. Argentina's desire to establish a common Chaco border with Mato Grosso was contested by Brazil, and the Rutherford B. Hayes arbitration decision in November, 1878, fixed the border at the Pilcomayo River across the Paraguay River from Asunción. Like the other allied nations, Argentina later renounced its claim to financial indemnity by Paraguay. It also eventually returned its share of war trophies in a gesture of friendship with the new Paraguay.

Uruguayan histories, like those of Argentina, have accorded the war a relatively secondary position in the record of national development. The bitter internal political strife between Colorados and Blancos which helped to spawn the war, the wartime assassination of President Venancio Flores, the disappearance of Uruguayan forces as a major component of the allied army, and the lack of strong national enthusiasm for the war were factors which tended to reduce its significance in Uruguay's history. The Paraguayan War, nevertheless, was of importance to South America's smallest republic—its independent status as a buffer state between Argentina and Brazil was permanently confirmed, and the allied support given to Venancio Flores before and after Paysandú established the predominance of the Colorado Party in the nation's developing political democracy. Uruguay, like Argentina, canceled its claims to indemnity from Paraguay and also returned its share of war trophies.

Brazil

As the major contributor to the allied war effort as well as the nation to whose tenacity the final victory was due, Imperial Brazil experienced the heaviest and most varied impact of the conflict. The more than five years of war with Paraguay resulted in repercussions in nearly every sector of the empire's social, political, and economic institutions. An appraisal of these circumstances suggests that the war may have represented the empire's high-water mark.

From the standpoint of its international policy objectives, the empire had achieved the maximum of success. Navigation of the Paraná and Paraguay rivers to Mato Grosso was now completely freed of any possible restrictions by Paraguay, Brazilian claims to the frontier zone between the Apa and Blanco Rivers had been officially recognized, astute diplomacy in the Argentine-Paraguayan Chaco dispute had both assured that Paraguay would remain a buffer state and that its relationships with the empire would be closer, and finally, the threat of a strong and ambitious Paraguay under the leadership of López had been eliminated.

The cost of the achievement of these objectives had been severe. Financially, the war involved expenditures estimated at $300 million. This enormous burden had been met by loans and increased taxes—measures which had not been popular. The nation's banking system, largely in the hands of Mauá, who over extended himself in his wartime Uruguayan operations, reflected signs of the near collapse which was shortly to occur.[4] The price in human lives had also been heavy. Combat losses were set by the government at 24,000. General Dionísio Cerqueira, in his reminiscences of the war, however, estimated that 100,000 Brazilian soldiers had died in the Paraguayan campaigns. As in the case of Union and Confederate losses in the American Civil War, disease had taken a far greater toll than had battles.[5]

In some sectors the war had also acted as a stimulant to economic activity. Its demands had speeded the construction of roads, railways, and river navigation facilities; the naval arsenal at Rio de Janeiro had become a large and efficient establishment capable of building modern ironclads, other government plants and arsenals had been built to produce munitions, and sizable cotton textile factories had been inaugurated at São Paulo.[6] Other developments of equally far-reaching importance included the decision in late 1866 to open the Amazon to international navigation, and the general interest in the extreme western provinces which was awakened both in Brazil and abroad by the reports of returning soldiers and by the literary works of Alfredo d'Escragnolle Taunay. The early phases of industrialization and the new interest in western colonization after 1870 represented new elements in an economy which had previously been wholly dominated by the large, slave-operated sugar and coffee fazendas.

Perhaps the most impressive repercussions of the war were those which occurred in the fields of social and political organization. By 1871 about 30,000 soldiers had been returned to civilian life. Many of these men had been former slaves who had been granted their freedom through army service, or "poor whites" and *caboclos* who had previously lived on meager subsistence standards. Unwilling to return to their former status, these veterans preferred to settle in the workers *bairros* being formed in the suburbs of the larger cities, or to avail themselves of the rewards of some provinces like São Paulo, which had decreed land grants to war veterans. Still others, notably in Northeast Brazil, utilized their army service earnings to buy small strips of land in order to secure a new economic independence.[7]

EFFECT UPON SLAVERY

Although the continued retention by Brazil of slavery as an institution was under severe challenge at the outbreak of the war, it was the war itself that provided a strong stimulus to the forces which eventually caused its abolition. This stimulus may be divided into three aspects: (1) the effects upon the empire's peoples of recruitment and war service, (2) the effects upon the soldiers of duty in foreign territory, and (3) the war's impact upon the empire's leaders.

The systems of recruitment utilized by the Imperial Government and the several inducements which tended to make military service more palatable were forces which struck at the very core of slavery as an institution. For the first time, men from all quarters and all social classes in Brazil were drawn together and given such basic incentives as the possibilities for emancipation, for land ownership, for a transformation in class status, and for social improvement. In addition to these aspects of a social mobility nature, some 100,000 Brazilians soldiers who had never traveled away from the confines of the empire, found themselves during the war in close cooperation with Uruguayan and Argentine soldiers, from countries which had earlier abolished slavery as an institution. Moreover, Brazil's soldiers, as the representatives of a state which still held 1.7 million people in bondage, found themselves in a bitter war with Paraguay, a nation which like Argentina and Uruguay, had also decreed the abolition of slavery. That these circumstances had an impact upon the empire's soldiers was to be pointed out by the Visconde do Rio Branco. In a postwar statement before the Senate, Rio Branco emphasized that the moral pressure exerted by the other nations regarding the slavery issue had been deeply felt not only by him but by all of the empire's soldiers as well.[8]

The developing reaction against slavery generated during the war could also be observed in the highest levels of the government. Dom Pedro, himself, is reported to have returned from his sole visit to the war's theater—the surrender of the Estigarribia invasion force at Uruguaiana in 1865—deeply impressed by the adverse impact upon the empire's reputation which, in the opinion of the other allies, the retention of slavery was producing.[9] Such feeling, clearly discerned and ably capitalized upon by Counsellor Silva Paranhos, encouraged the passage on September 28, 1871, of Brazil's *Lei do Ventre Livre*, the "Rio Branco Law," which, as a forerunner of complete emancipation, provided that children of slaves were henceforth to be free.

THE POSTWAR ARMY

The reception accorded to Brazil's returning veterans showed contrasts. In some instances, like the welcome given to Dr. Francisco Pinheiro Guimarães and his brigade, popular enthusiasm was high. In others, however, the work of pacificists was reported to have generated ill will toward the veterans to the point that one source suggested they were received as if they had been participants in the commission of a crime.[10] Efforts to minimize the service of the volunteer units were so persistent that at one stage the Conde d'Eu was alleged to have threatened his resignation.[11]

The war had produced notable changes within the army. Prior to 1865, it had been a small organization which, though possessing its own military traditions, had reflected the vagaries of political manipulation. More often than not at the mercy of rival politicians who controlled the budget, the army's officers had no effective voice in its management and were subject to political whims for their promotions. Political considerations superseded those of a purely military nature. Dom Pedro, more interested in the arts and sciences, tended to relegate the army to a secondary position of importance.

At the close of the war the army, though again reduced to peacetime size, found itself with a new tradition of achievement and with new forces at its command. Through common war experiences, the men of the ranks, from all sections of Brazil, had developed a bond of unity which had previously not existed. Within the officer class there now figured men of humble origin who had previously held little hope for improvement in social status and who could now count upon the army as a career. In addition to the advantages of social mobility now available to such men, there were generals in command whose stature as wartime heroes could not be ignored or belittled by the empire's political parties. These several factors had combined to develop a new element in Brazil's institutional structure—an element which, though composed of men representing both the Liberal and Conservative parties, had become an autonomous unit. The army's members ceased to speak like representatives of one or the other of the political parties and began to speak as men of the army—determined to further the interests of their own developing organization rather than purely political interests. In brief, a new militant, independent social and political force had arisen within the empire which in a few years became the direct instrument of the empire's downfall.

THE RISE OF REPUBLICANISM.

No less than in the cases of slavery and the army, the Paraguayan War had an impact upon the form of government in Brazil. It might be said that its several effects upon Brazil's peoples and institutions—changes in class structure and social organization, impact upon land settlement, effect upon slavery, rise of the army as a new autonomous force—all combined to operate against the continued retention of a monarchical system of government and its dependence upon the rural latifundia class. These social and institutional changes, together with the impact upon Brazil's veterans of having participated with republican nations in a major conflict, generated a trend toward republicanism which could no longer be curbed. Although many of the older officers were personally loyal to Dom Pedro and appreciated his support for the army during the war, they came gradually to believe that peacetime spelled a possible reversion of the army to its prewar secondary position, and furthermore, that a change in form of government was essential. This feeling was communicated to the younger officers who had sprung from anonymity to fame through war service, and who likewise held the empire's political mechanism in low esteem.[12]

It is indeed of interest to the student of Brazil's institutional development that the Paraguayan War not only gave rise to this trend but was itself the scene for the early career progress of the three men most responsible for the movement which in 1889 made Brazil a republic: Benjamin Constant—"O Fundador da República," and an engineer major at Humaitá in 1867; Manoel Deodoro da Fonseca— "O Proclamador da República," who was promoted three times for bravery and saw active service through the entire war; and Floriano Vieira Peixoto—"O Consolidador da República" and an Iron Marshal in his own right, who participated in all major battles and was a lieutenant colonel at the war's close.

Paraguay

Few defeated nations in the world's military history exhibited such a degree of devastation as the Paraguay of 1870. Its population, now estimated at only 221,000, had suffered war casualties of at least 220,000 people.[13] Among the survivors there were only 28,000 men; women over fifteen were said to outnumber men at a ratio of more than four to one.[14]

The country itself was in a shambles. Battles and armies had wrecked the economy—farms lay unattended for the lack of men, the former large herds of cattle and horses had disappeared, whole families had been extinguished, territorial borders had been shortened by the satisfaction of allied claims, the state treasury and archives were gone, and finally, a violent change had occurred in the system of government. Gone was the totalitarian era of El Supremo, El Ciudadano, and the Iron Marshal. In its place a more democratic form of government had been established by the new constitution of November, 1870. Though later to be canceled, the indemnity owed by the nation was a staggering one, and a Brazilian occupation force was to remain in Paraguay until 1874. As there were similarities between the Paraguayan and American Civil Wars, so the postwar era could be likened in several aspects to the "carpetbag" period of the vanished Confederacy.

The struggle of Paraguay to recover from the bloodiest and most destructive war in Latin American history was to require many years. As a result of the decimation of the population and the property losses suffered, and of the animosities, hatreds, and bitter memories which lingered on, any semblance of a national spirit was necessarily slow in its regeneration. At the end of the century, however, the war's memories had commenced to dim and a new Paraguay slowly made its appearance. Though it could not have been said to have erased the deep imprint of its earlier history, Paraguay had salvaged at least one remarkable tradition—the unconquerable spirit of national pride which had marked its epic defense against the Triple Alliance.[15]

By the mid-twentieth century this tradition had become a national characteristic. It had even transcended the rivalries among Paraguay's several political parties. In 1936, for example, Colonel Rafael Franco, founder of the Febrerista party, was reported to have stated:

> The people of Paraguay can be assured that the immortal spirit and genius of our race has returned to the palace of Solano López, and that in the future Paraguay shall follow the path which carried it in the past to prosperity, greatness, and to its grandest destinies.[16]

Cerro Corá, after March, 1870, reverted to its original quiet, virgin state of natural beauty. While it is still difficult to reach because of the lack of direct transport facilities from Asunción, it has become a Paraguayan national shrine. Francisco Solano López has likewise become the foremost national hero.[17] His remains are entombed in Asunción's Pantheon of the Heroes; at the outskirts of the capital a less formal though equally impressive tribute to the courage and stamina of Paraguay's soldiers exists in the form of a replica of the shell-blasted towers of the Humaitá church, symbol of the grim defense of 1866-68.

Elsewhere in Paraguay reminders of the 1864-70 war are few in number. Aside from the practice of naming streets, avenues, and parks after the war's heroes and major actions— a practice also observed widely in Brazil—and an occasional monument such as at Cerro Corá and Ytororó, no effort has yet been made to erect battle markers or to reserve historic sites as national parks. There are also no cemeteries serving as a final resting place for the countless unknown dead of Paraguay, Brazil, Argentina, and Uruguay. On national holidays, however, public applause at parades in Asunción is heaviest when Paraguay's crack cavalry appears dressed in uniforms of the 1860's, and when the womens' army units and the boys' cadet battalions take the salute.

Piribebuy

The small interior village of Piribebuy exhibits little change today from its aspect in August, 1869. The population of 4,000 is about the same, the houses are still built in late colonial style, the old church still stands in the center of the large central square, streets are still paved with rough cobblestones, and the people have changed but little in their dress and habits. Somewhat to one side of the new international highway connecting Asunción with the Brazilian border at the Iguazú Falls, the village lies unmolested by tourists and secure in its memories of the past. Except for an occasional foreign technician or official interested in sociological or nutrition studies, or perhaps attracted by the history which was made there, visitors are few and Piribebuy is but another of Paraguay's charming colonial-style towns.[18]

At its outskirts, however, the people point with pride to the still visible remains of the "Trench of '69." A small museum has also been opened in the municipal building which houses an absorbing collection of the relics and jetsam of war, and the inquiring visitor may still observe the site and crumbling foundations of the residence once occupied by Martin T. MacMahon. On August 12, 1959, a new feature was added to Piribebuy. It is a bust of a stern-faced man placed on a base located at the point where the Caacupé road enters the town. The inscription reads simply, "El Mariscal López."

Notes

INTRODUCTION

1. Pelham Horton Box, *The Origins of the Paraguayan War* also Box, *Los orígenes de la guerra del Paraguay contra la Triple Alianza*, trans. Pablo M. Ynsfrán. References in subsequent footnotes to this work are to the Ynsfrán translation, particularly in view of the illuminating annotations which it contains.

CHAPTER 1

1. Details regarding the Battle of Piribebuy were selected from the following primary sources: Alfredo d'Escragnolle Taunay, *Memórias do Visconde de Taunay*; Dionísio Cerqueira, *Reminiscências da Campanha do Paraguai*. Paraguayan sources included Fidel Maíz, *Etapas de mi vida*; and Francisco Isidoro Resquín, *Datos históricos de la guerra del Paraguay con la Triple Alianza*.
2. Taunay, *Memórias*, p. 508.
3. *Ibid.*, p. 506.
4. Cerqueira, *passim*; Walter Spalding, *A invasão paraguaia no Brasil*, pp. 544-46.

CHAPTER 2

1. Francisco Pinheiro Guimarães, *Um Voluntário da Pátria*, pp. 124-25. The series of letters from Dr. Pinheiro Guimarães to his father, describing the Paraná and Paraguay river ports in 1857, comprises one of the most interesting contemporary sources.
2. Richard F. Burton, *Letters from the Battlefields of Paraguay*, p. 9; Box, pp. 311-17. In confidential dispatch No. 76 of October 6, 1864, British diplomat Edward Thornton estimated Paraguay's population at 400,000 on the basis of a ratio of eight people for every soldier in a 50,000-man army.
3. George Thompson, *The War in Paraguay*, p. 9.
4. Pinheiro Guimarães, p. 127.
5. The most reliable contemporary accounts of the characteristics of Paraguay's armed forces at the outbreak of the war are found in Thompson, *The War in Paraguay*; and George F. Masterman, *Seven Eventful Years in Paraguay*. Documentary references to the projects of equipping and expanding the army, and of completing the railway and telegraph lines, are found in Arturo Rebaudi, *La declaración de guerra de la República del Paraguay a la República Argentina*.
6. Charles A. Washburn, *The History of Paraguay*, I, 522.
7. Rebaudi, *La declaración*, p. 75; Box, pp. 94-95; Augusto Tasso Fragoso, *História da guerra entre a Tríplice Aliança e o Paraguai*, I, 100-106.
8. Gustavo Barroso, *História militar do Brasil*, p. 205; Washburn, I, 520; Box, pp. 115-33; Tasso Fragoso, I, 107-10.

CHAPTER 3

1. Arturo Bray, *Solano López*, p. 84. Bray's study includes perhaps the most convincing discussion of López' origins and early life. Other details are contained in Washburn, *History*; Box, *Los orígenes*. According to a note by translator Ynsfrán on p. 190 of the latter work, the exact birthplace of López is not known.

2. Box, p. 191.
3. Peter Schmitt, "Las relaciones diplomáticas entre el Paraguay y las potencias europeas, 1840-1870," in *Historia Paraguaya,* III (1958), 70-71.
4. Henri Pitaud, *Madama Lynch,* pp. 231-46. Details regarding Mrs. Lynch's life after the death of López are also contained in the following works: María Concepción de L. Chaves, *Madame Lynch;* and William E. Barrett, *Woman on Horseback.*
5. *Elisa Lynch,* pp. 233, 241.
6. *Letters,* p. 73.
7. Bray, p. 358, quoting testimony of Martin T. MacMahon in House of Representatives Report No. 65, 41st Congress, Second Session.
8. *Ibid.,* p. 132.
9. *Ibid.,* p. 133.
10. *Ibid.,* p. 134; Pitaud, p. 84.
11. Bray, p. 131.
12. *Ibid.,* p. 135.
13. *Ibid.,* p. 136.
14. Washburn, I, 524-25; Box, pp. 210-11.
15. Burton, *Letters,* p. 75.
16. Carlos Pereyra, *Francisco Solano López e la guerra del Paraguay,* p. 203; María Concepción de L. Chaves, pp. 121-22.
17. Varela, p. 264.
18. The composite portrait of Francisco Solano López is based on details selected from the following primary sources: Washburn, I, 566-67; II, 47; Thompson, pp. 326-30; Masterman, p. 57; Burton, *Letters,* pp. 69-72.
19. Varela, pp. 249, 256.
20. Thompson, pp. 326-30; Burton, *Letters,* pp. 69-72.
21. Pinheiro Guimarães, p. 138.
22. *Ibid.,* p. 140.
23. Alcindo Sodré, *Abrindo um cofre,* pp. 1-23.
24. *Ibid.,* pp. 13-42.
25. *Ibid.,* p. 29.
26. *Ibid.,* pp. 28, 42.
27. *Ibid.,* p. 28.
28. Pitaud, p. 230; *Exposición y protesta,* a pamphlet written by Mrs. Lynch in both French and Spanish, was published at Buenos Aires in 1875.
29. Antônio da Rocha Almeida, *Vultos da Pátria,* p. 111.
30. Pinheiro Guimarães, p. 148.
31. *Ibid.,* p. 132.
32. Alcindo Sodré, p. 100.
33. William H. Jeffrey, *Mitre and Argentina, passim.*
34. Burton, *Letters,* p. 167.
35. Thomas J. Hutchinson, *The Paraná, with Incidents of the Paraguayan War,* p. 147.
36. Rebaudi, *La declaración,* p. 75.
37. Manuel Gálvez, *Humaitá,* p. 59.
38. Interview on June 13, 1962, with the Honorable Elbio Arturo Geymonat, member of the Chamber of Deputies of the Republic of Uruguay.
39. Washburn, I, 491.
40. Burton, *Letters,* p. 116.
41. Jeffrey, p. 8.
42. Hutchinson, p. 403.

CHAPTER 4

1. The opinion of this group is perhaps best exemplified in W. H. Koebel, *Paraguay*, pp. 193-94.
2. The small and more recent school of those who have based their evaluations upon the factual evidence of such contemporary observers as Thompson and von Versen is largely exemplified by Arturo Bray in his *Solano López*.
3. *Letters on Paraguay* by the brothers J. P. and W. P. Robertson provides an excellent account of life in Paraguay under Dr. Francia.
4. Rocha Almeida, p. 183.
5. Max von Versen, "História da Guerra do Paraguai" in *Revista do Instituto Histórico e Geográfico Brasileiro*, LXXVI, Part II (Rio de Janeiro, 1913), 64.
6. *Ibid.*
7. *Letters*, p. 321.
8. Thompson, *passim*.
9. Masterman, p. 139.
10. *Ibid.*, p. 33.
11. Pitaud, p. 211; María Concepción de L. Chaves, *passim*.
12. Hutchinson, pp. 306, 316, 342; Burton, *Letters passim*.
13. Masterman, p. 100.
14. María Concepción de L. Chaves, p. 341; Burton, on pages 15-16, also describes the high level of education in Paraguay in 1864. He was perhaps too enthusiastic, however, when he wrote that no Paraguayan was allowed to be analphabetic.
15. Pereyra, p. 55; Rebaudi, *La declaración*, p. 238; Rebaudi's study includes the text of a letter on p. 238 from Foreign Minister Berges to Chargé Bareiro in Paris, dated March 15, 1865, placing the size of the army at 50,000; Burton, *Letters*, p. 9.
16. Thompson, pp. 55-57, 201-9.
17. *Ibid.*, p. 68.
18. Burton, *Letters*, pp. 9-16.
19. Thompson, p. 119.
20. *Ibid.*, pp. 52-56; Von Versen, p. 131.
21. Thompson, p. 18.
22. *Ibid.*, p. 57; Rebaudi, *La declaración*, p. 267.
23. Thompson, p. 52; G. d'Orleans (Conde d'Eu), *Viagem militar ao Rio Grande do Sul*, p. 160.
24. Von Versen, p. 64.
25. Thompson, p. 52.
26. *Ibid.*
27. Burton, *Letters*, p. 321; Conde d'Eu, p. 160.
28. Thompson, p. 56; María Concepción de L. Chaves, p. 148.
29. Thompson, p. 71.
30. Masterman, p. 133.
31. Rebaudi, *La declaración*, p. 209.
32. *Ibid.*, p. 46; Resquín, pp. 40-41.
33. Masterman, p. 108; Thompson, pp. 18, 207.
34. Thompson, p. 68.
35. Gustavo Barroso, *A guerra do López*, p. 231.
36. Burton, *Letters*, p. 15; Thompson, p. 167.
37. Burton, *Letters*, pp. 69-72; Tobias Monteiro, *Pesquisas e depoimentos para a história* p. 118; quoted in Pinheiro Guimarães, p. 40.

204 NOTES (PAGES 46-61)

38. Thompson, *passim*; also Julio César Chaves, *El General Díaz*.
39. Julio César Chaves, *El General Díaz*, passim; maíz, p. 17.
40. Barroso, *História militar*, p. 12.
41. Rocha Almeida, pp. 21-24; Spalding, *passim*.
42. Rocha Almeida, p. 175.
43. José de Lima Figueiredo, *Brasil militar*, p. 42.
44. Rocha Alemida, pp. 143-47; Spalding, *passim*.
45. Rocha Almeida, p. 177.
46. Barroso, *História militar*, p. 73.
47. Lima Figueiredo, *Brasil militar*, p. 64.
48. Barroso, *História militar*, pp. 59-75.
49. Pinheiro Guimarães, p. 202.
50. Lima Figueiredo, *Brasil militar*, p. 50.
51. *Ibid.*, p. 33.
52. *Ibid.*, p. 50.
53. *Ibid.*, p. 79.
54. *Ibid.*, pp. 57-60.
55. *Ibid.*, p. 59.
56. *Ibid.*, p. 61.
57. *Ibid.*, p. 43.
58. *Ibid.*, p. 53.
59. *Ibid.*, p. 56.
60. *Ibid.*, pp. 60-62.
61. Barroso, *História militar*, p. 57.
62. Lima Figueiredo, *Brasil militar*, pp. 62-68; Tasso Fragoso, *História da guerra*, V, 275-76.
63. Barroso, *História militar*, pp. 110-11; Cerqueira, p. 261.
64. *Ibid.*
65. Alcindo Sodré, p. 110.
66. Lima Figueiredo, *Brasil militar*, p. 69.
67. Burton, *Letters*, p. 323; Von Versen, p. 237.
68. Barroso, *História militar*, p. 110.
69. Lima Figueiredo, *Brasil militar*, pp. 53-69.
70. Barroso, *História militar*, pp. 227, 299.
71. João Pandiá Calógeras, trans. Percy Alvin Martin, *A History of Brazil*, p. 215.
72. Lima Figueiredo, *Brasil militar*, p. 75.
73. Magnus Mörner, "El mapa del Mariscal," in *Inter-American Review of Bibliography*, pp. 147-50.
74. Spalding, p. xxvii.
75. *Ibid.*, p. xviii.
76. *Ibid.*
77. *Ibid.*
78. Rocha Almeida, pp. 148-53.
79. Calógeras, p. 211.
80. The portraits of these generals have been prepared from information in Rocha Almeida; Spalding; and José de Lima Figueiredo, *Grandes soldados do Brasil*.
81. Burton, *Letters*, pp. 376-77.
82. *Ibid.*, pp. 384-85.
83. Spalding, p. 437.
84. *Ibid., passim*.

85. See Rocha Almeida, Lima Figueiredo, and Spalding.
86. Burton, *Letters*, p. 350.
87. Taunay, *Memórias*, p. 555.
88. *Ibid.*
89. *Ibid.*, p. 101.
90. Burton, *Letters*, pp. x, 15, 69-72; Hutchinson, pp. 308, 336-37.
91. Spalding, pp. xviii-xix.
92. After the Battle of Pavón, HBM consul Sir Edward Thornton reported that Mitre's army was equipped with Minié rifles, and that the artillery was excellent and manned principally by Italians. Quoted in A. J. Walford, "General Urquiza and the Battle of Pavón," in *Hispanic American Historical Review*, XIX, 4 (November, 1939), 464-93.
93. Von Versen, pp. 56, 98; Burton, *Letters*, p. 325.
94. Pereyra, p. 58.
95. *Ibid.*, p. 118; Box, pp. 291-93.
96. Burton, *Letters*, p. 325.
97. Spalding, p. xix.
98. Burton, *Letters*, p. 202.
99. *Ibid.*, p. 464.
100. *Ibid.*, p. 308.
101. Manuel Gálvez, *Jornadas de agonía* p. 99; María Concepción de L. Chaves, p. 39; Joseph T. Criscenti, commenting on *Mitre and Argentina*, by W. H. Jeffrey, in *Hispanic American Historical Review*, XXXIII, 2 (May, 1953), 282-83.
102. R. B. Cunninghame-Graham, *Portrait of a Dictator*, p. 124.
103. Gálvez, *Humaitá*, pp. 9-11.
104. Cerqueira, p. 155.
105. Gálvez, *Humaitá*, p. 87.
106. Burton, *Letters*, p. 326.

CHAPTER 5

1. *Letters*, p. xii.
2. Rebaudi, *La declaración*, p. 288.
3. Box, *passim*.
4. *Ibid.*
5. *Ibid.*; Rebaudi, *La declaración*, p. 278.
6. Rebaudi, *La declaración*, p. 108.
7. *Ibid.*; Box, pp. 226-27.
8. Box, pp. 226-27; Rebaudi, *La declaración*, p. 278.
9. Thompson, p. 20.
10. Rebaudi, *La declaración*, p. 278.
11. Box, pp. 227-28.
12. Rebaudi, *La declaración*, pp. 15, 109; Box, pp. 227-28.
13. Rebaudi, *La declaración*, pp. 109-10.
14. *Ibid.*, p. 15; Rocha Almeida, p. 90.
15. Thompson, p. 25.
16. *Ibid.*
17. Barroso, *Guerra do López*, pp. 39-47.
18. *Ibid.*
19. Washburn, I, 529.
20. *Ibid.*, pp. 566-70.

21. Rebaudi, *La declaración*, p. 33.
22. Von Versen, p. 36.
23. Pinheiro Guimarães, p. 168.
24. Juan Beverina, *La Guerra del Paraguay*, II, 149.
25. *Ibid.*, p. 150.
26. Alcindo Sodré, p. 85.
27. Pinheiro Guimarães, p. 195.
28. Nelson Werneck Sodré, *Formação da sociedade brasileira*, p. 308.
29. T. Lynn Smith, *Brazil: People and Institutions*, p. 396, quoting J. McF. Gaston, *Hunting a Home in Brazil*, p. 78.
30. Richard F. Burton, *Explorations of the Highlands of the Brazil*, I, 411.
31. *Ibid.*, I, 377.
32. Burton, *Highlands of the Brazil*, II, 267.
33. Taunay, *Memórias*, p. 179.
34. *Ibid.*
35. Smith, p. 484.
36. Beverina, p. 150.
37. Calógeras, p. 225.
38. Lima Figueiredo, *Brasil militar*, p. 65.
39. Werneck Sodré, p. 310.
40. Lima Figueiredo, *Grandes soldados*, p. 72.

CHAPTER 6

1. Pinheiro Guimarães, p. 128.
2. Spalding, *passim*.
3. *Ibid.*, p. xx.
4. Thompson, pp. 31-38.
5. Lima Figueiredo, *Grandes soldados*, p. 227; Tasso Fragoso, I, 228.
6. Spalding, p. xxiv.
7. *Ibid.*, p. xxiii.
8. Thompson, p. 39; see also Martin T. MacMahon, "Paraguay and Her Enemies," in *Harper's New Monthly Magazine*, XL, 237 (February, 1870), 425.
9. Masterman, p. 99.
10. Taunay, *Memórias*, p. 264.
11. Thompson, p. 39.
12. *Ibid.*, p. 38.
13. Rocha Almeida, p. 163.
14. Spalding, pp. 1-2.
15. *Ibid.*, pp. 31-32.
16. Rocha Almeida, p. 178.
17. *Ibid.*; The Military Question, which arose in the early 1880's, became a prime factor in the downfall of the empire. Army officers Cunha Mattos and Senna Madureira were both involved in disputes with civilian authorities concerning alleged reflections on their honor as officers, which were given prominent coverage in the press. The endorsement of the army's position by Manoel Deodoro da Fonseca assured him of support from the armed forces when the republican movement reached a climax in November, 1889.
18. *Ibid.*, p. 101; *passim*.
19. Spalding, pp. 1-2.
20. Rebaudi, *La declaración*, p. 3.
21. Thompson, p. 31.

22. Box, pp. 236-37, 266; Pereyra, pp. 39-52; Von Versen, p. 94.
23. Rebaudi, *La declaración, passim.*
24. *Ibid.,* p. 249.
25. *Ibid.,* p. 39.
26. *Ibid.,* p. 4.
27. *Ibid.,* p. 29.
28. *Ibid.,* p. 33.
29. *Ibid.,* pp. 27-63.
30. *Ibid.,* p. 65; Box, pp. 283-84.
31. Rebaudi, *La declaración,* p. 64.
32. *Ibid.,* pp. 65-66.
33. *Ibid.,* p. 66.
34. *Ibid.,* p. 10; Thompson, *passim.*
35. Washburn, II, 160.
36. An excellent, fascinating, and thorough description of Buenos Aires on the outbreak of war is found in Manuel Gálvez, *Los caminos de la muerte,* pp. 1-117.
37. *Ibid.,* p. 57.
38. Rebaudi, *La declaración,* p. 19.
39. *Ibid.,* p. 15.
40. *Ibid.,* p. 235.
41. *Ibid.,* p. 86.
42. *Ibid.,* p. 50.
43. María Concepción de L. Chaves, p. 353.
44. Box, p. 287.
45. *Ibid.,* p. 289.
46. Pereyra, p. 95.
47. Thompson, p. 167.
48. Rebaudi, *La declaración,* p. 10.
49. Thompson, p. 67.

CHAPTER 7

1. Thompson, p. 71.
2. Washburn, II, 65-66.
3. Thompson, pp. 71-81.
4. Barroso, *Guerra do López,* p. 65.
5. Thompson, pp. 71-81.
6. *Ibid.*
7. *Ibid.*
8. Barroso, *História militar,* p. 241.
9. Spalding, pp. 320-21.
10. Thompson, p. 81.
11. Masterman, p. 262.
12. Hutchinson, p. 308.
13. Alcindo Sodré, p. 88.
14. Barroso, *Guerra do López,* p. 67.
15. Resquín, *passim.*
16. Thompson, p. 83.
17. Spalding, pp. 35-62; Conde d'Eu, *passim.*
18. Spalding, p. 62.
19. *Ibid.,* pp. 92, 164-65.

20. *Ibid.*, p. xli.
21. *Ibid.*, pp. 104-07.
22. *Ibid.*, pp. 146-47.
23. *Ibid.*, pp. 168-70.
24. *Ibid.*, p. 231.
25. *Ibid.*, p. 328.
26. *Ibid.*, p. 469.
27. Alcindo Sodré, p. 88.
28. *Ibid.*, p. 89.
29. Burton, *Highlands of the Brazil*, I, 411.
30. Spalding, pp. 328-69; Thompson, p. 85.
31. Spalding, p. xxviii; Conde d'Eu, p. 135.
32. Spalding, *passim*; Pinheiro Guimarães, *passim*; Cerqueira, *passim*.
33. Spalding, pp. 328-69.
34. *Ibid.*, p. 369.
35. *Ibid.*; Thompson, p. 85.
36. Gálvez, *Los caminos*, p. 216.
37. Alcindo Sodré, p. 94.
38. Spalding, p. 490.
39. *Ibid.*, pp. 502-3.
40. *Ibid.*
41. Barroso, *Guerra do López*, p. 54.
42. *Ibid.*, p. 55; Conde d'Eu, pp. 152-56.
43. Barroso, *Guerra do López*, p. 95.
44. *Ibid.*, pp. 23-27.
45. *Ibid.*, p. 53.
46. Von Versen, p. 34.
47. Spalding, p. 453.
48. *Ibid.*, p. xlviii.
49. *Ibid.*, pp. 282-83.
50. Thompson, p. 92; Conde d'Eu, p. 154.
51. Thompson, p. 95.
52. *Ibid.*, pp. 95-97; Masterman, p. 131.
53. Thompson, pp. 95-97.
54. *Ibid.*, p. 97; Washburn, II, 92.
55. Spalding, *passim*; Cerqueira, *passim*; Pinheiro Guimarães, *passim*.
56. Pinheiro Guimarães, p. 206.
57. Spalding, p. 98.
58. Hutchinson, p. 311.
59. Burton, *Letters*, p. 202.
60. Alcindo Sodré, p. 98.
61. Hutchinson, *passim*; Burton, *Letters*, *passim*; Cerqueira, *passim*.
62. Gálvez, *Los caminos*, p. 251. These terms may be translated as follows: Fish a la Humaitá, Kidneys Mitre, Brains Tamandaré, Tongue Flores, and Brazilian Broad-beans.
63. Alfredo d'Escragnolle Taunay, *A Retirada da Laguna*, p. 31.
64. *Ibid.*, p. 32.
65. Taunay, *Memórias*, pp. 119-20.
66. *Ibid.*, pp. 136-67.
67. Taunay, *Retirada*, pp. 32-33.
68. *Ibid.*, pp. 38-39.
69. *Ibid.*, pp. 39-46.

70. *Ibid.*, p. 60.
71. *Ibid.*, p. 62.
72. Taunay, *Memórias*, p. 341.
73. Taunay, *Retirada*, pp. 86-135.
74. *Ibid.*, pp. 8, 137.
75. Taunay, *Memórias*, p. 417.

CHAPTER 8

1. Masterman, p. 125.
2. Gálvez, *Los caminos*, p. 289.
3. Julio César Chaves, *El General Díaz, passim*; Thompson, *passim*.
4. Thompson, p. 124.
5. Barroso, *Guerra do López*, p. 69.
6. Alcindo Sodré, p. 104.
7. A detailed and absorbing description of this action is contained in Pinheiro Guimarães, pp. 267-89.
8. Rocha Almeida, pp. 184-85.
9. Barroso, *História militar*, p. 271.
10. *Ibid.*; Lima Figueiredo, *Grandes soldados*, p. 184.
11. Alcindo Sodré, p. 104.
12. Thompson, *passim*.; An excellent participant's description of the early Humaitá actions is contained in Cerqueira.
13. Thompson, *passim*; Julio César Chaves, *passim*.
14. Lima Figueiredo, *Grandes soldados*, pp. 50-58; Barroso, *Guerra do López*, pp. 102-3.
15. Donald Barr Chidsey, *The Battle of New Orleans*, pp. 140-41.
16. Cerqueira, p. 183.
17. Barroso, *Guerra do López*, pp. 102-3.
18. Rocha Almeida, p. 180.
19. *Ibid.*, p. 163.
20. *Ibid.*, *passim*; Barroso, *Guerra do López*, *passim*; Pinheiro Guimarães, pp. 210-14.
21. Barroso, *Guerra do López*, p. 77.
22. Pinheiro Guimarães, pp. 216-17.
23. Thompson, p. 149; Barroso, *Guerra do López*, p. 105.
24. Thompson, p. 149; Barroso, *Guerra do López*, p. 106; Juan E. O'Leary, *El libro de los héroes*, pp. 321-22.
25. Thompson, pp. 138-39.
26. Masterman, p. 114; Thompson, p. 165.
27. Masterman, p. 114.
28. Barroso, *História militar*, p. 288.
29. Thompson, *passim*.
30. Thompson, pp. 165-70; Julio César Chaves, *El General Diáz*, p. 100.
31. Perhaps the most informative account in English of this meeting is that contained in Thompson's memoirs. A representative account from the allied point of view is contained in Barroso, *Guerra do López*, pp. 111-26.
32. Pereyra, p. 96.
33. Gálvez, *Humaitá*, pp. 15-16.
34. Provincial attitudes toward the war are described in Félix Luna, *La última montonera*.
35. Alcindo Sodré, p. 111.
36. *Ibid.*, p. 113; Ernesto Senna, *Deodoro, subsídios para a história*, p. 170.

37. Thompson, p. 174.
38. *Ibid.*
39. A surprisingly impartial evaluation of Yataity-Corá and its aftermath is contained in Gálvez, *Humaitá*, pp. 35-56.
40. Rebaudi, pp. 233-34.
41. Thompson, p. 173; Burton, *Letters*, p. 305.
42. Thompson, pp. 168, 177.
43. Barroso, *Guerra do López*, pp. 130-31.
44. Gálvez, *Humaitá*, p. 62.
45. Thompson, pp. 177-81. A vivid account of this major action is also contained in Gálvez, *Humaitá*, pp. 62-76.
46. Thompson, pp. 177-81.
47. Gálvez, *Humaitá*, pp. 70-82.
48. *Ibid.*; Burton, *Letters*, p. 362.
49. Burton, *Letters*, p. 305; Letter to Mrs. Horace Mann from Bienvenida Sarmiento and Faustina S. V. de Belin, dated October 21, 1866, in *Hispanic American Historical Review*, XXXII, 2 (May, 1952), 187-211.
50. Thompson, pp. 181-82.
51. *Ibid.*
52. *Ibid.*, p. 182; Gálvez, *Humaitá*, p. 79.
53. Quoted in Masterman, pp. 121-22.
54. Thompson, p. 155.
55. Von Versen, p. 129.
56. Gálvez, *Humaitá*, p. 100.
57. Maíz, p. 17.
58. Thompson, p. 241.
59. *Ibid.*, p. 185.
60. *Ibid.*
61. Hutchinson, p. 306.
62. Thompson, p. 155.
63. Burton, *Letters*, p. 310.
64. Thompson, p. 99.
65. Von Versen, p. 131; *Thompson*, p. 201.
66. Thompson, p. 69.
67. *Ibid.*, pp. 106, 326-30; Gálvez, *Humaitá*, p. 118.
68. Gálvez, *Humaitá*, p. 121; Thompson, p. 207; Cerqueira, p. 143; Maíz, *passim*.
69. Thompson, p. 207.
70. Masterman, pp. 123-24.
71. Harold F. Peterson, "Efforts of the United States to Mediate in the Paraguayan War," in *Hispanic American Historical Review*, XII, 1 (February, 1932), 2-16.
72. Alcindo Sodré, p. 123.
73. *Ibid.*, p. 128.
74. Peterson, p. 2.
75. Alcindo Sodré, p. 136.
76. Washburn, *passim*.
77. *Ibid.*, II, 221.
78. Masterman, pp. 137-38.
79. Von Versen, *passim*.
80. Pinheiro Guimarães, pp. 185-86.
81. Thompson, p. 151.

82. Burton, *Letters*, pp. 274-75.
83. Cerqueira, pp. 168, 213; *Illustrated London News*, XLIX, 1392, 1393 (October 6, 1866), 336.
84. Burton, *Letters*, pp. 388-89.
85. Barroso, *Guerra do López*, p. 132.
86. Burton, *Letters*, p. 337.
87. *Ibid.*, pp. 388-89, 450.
88. *Ibid.*, p. 386.
89. Barroso, *Guerra do López*, pp. 148-49; Taunay, in his *Retirada da Laguna*, p. 102, reported incidents which were somewhat similar.
90. Cerqueira, pp. 105-9.
91. Gálvez, *Jornadas*, p. 11.
92. Pinheiro Guimarães, pp. 85-86.
93. *Ibid.*, pp. 240-42.
94. Burton, *Letters*, p. 327.
95. Pinheiro Guimarães, p. 217; Cerqueira, p. 280.
96. Pinheiro Guimarães, p. 222.
97. An excellent discussion of the differences between Buenos Aires and the provinces is contained in Alfredo Gargaro, "La Batalla de Pozo de Vargas," in *Boletín de la Academia Nacional de Historia*, XX and XXI, 47 and 48, Buenos Aires, 128-63.
98. Hutchinson, pp. 362-63.
99. Von Versen, p. 69; Gargaro, pp. 131-33; Thompson, p. 187.
100. Gargaro, p. 145.
101. *Ibid.*, pp. 133-34.
102. *Ibid.*, pp. 137-59.
103. *Ibid.*, p. 142.
104. *Ibid.*, p. 145.
105. Thompson, pp. 187, 220.
106. *Ibid.*, p. 190.
107. F. Stansbury Haydon, "Documents Relating to the First Military Balloon Corps Organized in South America," in *Hispanic American Historical Review*, XIX, 4 (November, 1939), 504-16.
108. *Ibid.*, pp. 506-7.
109. *Ibid.*, pp. 512-13.
110. *Ibid.*, p. 515.
111. Pinheiro Guimarães, p. 335.
112. Haydon, p. 505.
113. Thompson, p. 209.
114. Burton, *Letters*, pp. 381-82.
115. Cerqueira, p. 350.

CHAPTER 9

1. Von Versen, pp. 127-29.
2. Barroso, *Guerra do López*, pp. 143-44.
3. Cerqueira, p. 310.
4. Thompson, pp. 228-29.
5. *Ibid.*, p. 230.
6. *Ibid.*, p. 232.
7. Rocha Almeida, p. 119.
8. Thompson, pp. 232-34.
9. *Ibid.*; Hutchinson, p. 337.

10. Thompson, p. 235.
11. *Ibid.*, p. 299; Cerqueira, p. 337.
12. Thompson, p. 242.
13. Alcindo Sodré, p. 141.
14. Calógeras, p. 216.
15. Pinheiro Guimarães, pp. 227-39.
16. Barroso, *Guerra do López*, p. 187.
17. Maíz, pp. 151-54.
18. Thompson, p. 253.
19. *Ibid.*, pp. 261-63.
20. *Ibid.*
21. *Ibid.*, pp. 268-72.
22. Masterman, p. 193.
23. Thompson, p. 272.
24. *Ibid.*, p. 274.
25. *Ibid.*, p. 276.
26. Gálvez, *Jornadas*, p. 5.
27. Alcindo Sodré, p. 242.
28. *Ibid.*, p. 315.
29. Thompson, p. 283.
30. Resquín, pp. 55-57.
31. *Ibid.*
32. Bray, pp. 352-53.
33. Resquín, p. 67.
34. *Ibid.*, p. 100.
35. Maíz, pp. 151-54.
36. *Ibid.*, p. 40; Resquín, p. 101.
37. Masterman, *passim*; von Versen, *passim*.
38. Masterman, *passim*; von Versen, *passim*.
39. Masterman, p. 308.
40. Maíz, p. 170.
41. Masterman, p. 275.
42. E. A. da Cunha Mattos, in von Versen, p. 263.
43. Resquín, p. 101.
44. Maíz, pp. 177-78.
45. Thompson, p. 263.
46. *Ibid.*, p. 267.
47. Maíz, pp. 180-84.
48. *Ibid.*, p. 64; Resquín, *passim*.
49. Cerqueira, p. 309.
50. Burton, *Letters*, pp. 404-5.
51. Barroso, *Guerra do López*, pp. 210-11, quoting Masterman.
52. MacMahon, "Paraguay and Her Enemies," p. 636.
53. *Ibid.*
54. Cerqueira, p. 326; Barroso, *História militar*, pp. 320-34.
55. Rocha Almeida, p. 172.
56. Calógeras, p. 229; Barroso, *História militar*, pp. 320-34.
57. Taunay, *Memórias*, p. 434.
58. Lima Figueiredo, *Grandes soldados*, p. 140.
59. Rocha Almeida, pp. 186-89.
60. Gálvez, *Jornadas*, p. 80; Cerqueira, *passim*; Barroso, *História militar*, *passim*.

NOTES (PAGES 166-179)   213

61. Thompson, pp. 290-98; O'Leary, *El libro de los héroes*, pp. 119-24.
62. Lima Figueiredo, *Grandes soldados*, pp. 152-54.
63. *Ibid.*, p. 185.
64. Rocha Almeida, p. 172.
65. Barroso, *Guerra do López*, p. 194.
66. Thompson, pp. 308-15.
67. Barroso, *Guerra do López*, p. 199; Cequeira, pp. 336-37.
68. Thompson, *passim*; Resquín, *passim*.
69. Martin T. MacMahon, "The War in Paraguay," in *Harper's New Monthly Magazine*, XL, 239 (April, 1870).
70. Cerqueira, p. 341; Gálvez, *Jornadas*, p. 93.
71. Lima Figueiredo, *Grandes soldados*, p. 77.
72. Maíz, p. 197.
73. Thompson, pp. 301-3.
74. Thompson, *passim*; MacMahon, "The War in Paraguay," *passim*.
75. Burton, *Letters*, p. 420; Thompson, p. 308.
76. Burton, *Letters*, p. 464.
77. Barroso, *Guerra do López*, p. 34.
78. O'Leary, *El libro des los héroes*, p. 51.

CHAPTER 10

1. Gálvez, *Jornadas*, p. 100; Barroso, *História militar*, p. 334.
2. Masterman, p. 293; Resquín, p. 117.
3. Barroso, *Guerra do López*, p. 219.
4. Barroso, *História militar*, pp. 334-35.
5. Pinheiro Guimarães, pp. 193-94.
6. Rocha Almeida, pp. 143-47.
7. Cerqueira, p. 367; Gálvez, *Jornadas*, p. 100.
8. Taunay, *Memórias*, p. 447.
9. *Ibid.*; also Barroso, *Guerra do López*, p. 223.
10. Taunay, *Memórias* p. 448.
11. *Ibid.*, p. 447.
12. *Ibid.*, *passim*.
13. Pinheiro Guimarães, p. 172; Taunay, *Memórias*, p. 451.
14. Taunay, *Memórias*, p. 458.
15. Pinheiro Guimarães, pp. 248-49; Taunay, *Memórias*, pp. 462-70.
16. Pinheiro Guimarães, p. 66.
17. Taunay, *Memórias*, p. 463.
18. *Ibid.*, pp. 479-80.
19. Gálvez, *Jornadas*, p. 113.
20. *Ibid.*
21. Resquín, pp. 130-31.
22. *Ibid.*, p. 121; Gálvez, *Jornadas*, p. 116.
23. Taunay, *Memórias*, pp. 481-82; Gálvez, *Jornadas*, p. 126.
24. *Ibid.*
25. MacMahon, "The War in Paraguay," p. 645.
26. Resquín, p. 117; Masterman, p. 293.
27. Masterman, p. 292; Burton, *Letters*, p. 449.
28. Taunay, pp. 484-85; Cerqueira, p. 372.
29. Taunay, *Memórias*, p. 508.
30. *Ibid.*, p. 504; Cerqueira, pp. 376-77.
31. Resquín, p. 138.

32. Taunay, *Memórias*, p. 509.
33. *Ibid.*, p. 527. The reported use of false beards by the boys at Campo Grande has become a proud tradition in Paraguay.
34. *Ibid.*
35. *Ibid.*
36. Barroso, *Guerra do López*, p. 231.
37. Gálvez, *Jornadas*, p. 137; Resquín, *passim*.
38. Cerqueira, pp. 390-91.

CHAPTER 11

1. Taunay, *Memórias*, p. 535.
2. Pereyra, p. 121; Gálvez, *Journadas*, pp. 137-38.
3. Barroso, *Guerra do López*, p. 244.
4. *Ibid.*, p. 233; Hutchinson, pp. 336-37.
5. Cerqueira, *passim*.
6. *Ibid.*, p. 395; Taunay, *Memórias*, *passim;* Pinheiro Guimarães, p. 44.
7. Taunay, *Memórias*, p. 535.
8. *Ibid.*, p. 538-46.
9. *Ibid.*, p. 558.
10. Cerqueira, p. 160.
11. Gálvez, *Jornadas*, p. 102; Taunay, *Memórias*, *passim*.
12. Taunay, *Memórias*, *passim*. The subject of the Paraguayan retreat to Cerro Corá is treated at length in Gálvez, *Jornadas*.
13. Resquín, p. 147.
14. The author has observed numerous pits dug along the old forest trails used by Marshal López.
15. "Letters of Sarmiento to Mary Mann," in *Hispanic American Historical Review*, XXXII, 3 (August, 1952), 351-53.
16. The author spent a day at Cerro Corá during an exploratory expedition in October, 1959.
17. Gálvez, *Jornadas*, p. 170.
18. Resquín, p. 170.
19. *Ibid.*, pp. 170-74.
20. Pereyra, pp. 134-54.
21. *Ibid.*
22. *Ibid.*
23. *Ibid.*; Barroso, *Guerra do López*, p. 259.
24. Letter from the Barão de Muritiba to Paranhos dated April 4, 1870, quoted in Pinheiro Guimarães, pp. 156-57; Tasso Fragoso, V, 160-69.
25. Pereyra, pp. 134-54.
26. Lima Figueiredo, *Grandes soldados*, p. 148.
27. *Ibid.*, p. 186; also Mörner.
28. Gálvez, *Jornadas*, p. 176; Pinheiro Guimarães, p. 156.
29. Maíz, p. 69.
30. Justo Pastor Benítez, in Julio César Chaves, *El General Díaz*, p. 13.
31. Maíz, p. 69.
32. E. A. da Cunha Mattos in von Versen, "*História da Guerra do Paraguai*," pp. 263-67.
33. Resquín, p. 186.
34. Pinheiro Guimarães, p. 44.
35. Taunay, *Memórias*, pp. 575-76.

36. Cerqueira, p. 400.
37. Pinheiro Guimarães, pp. 156-58.
38. Maíz, pp. 70-76.
39. Pinheiro Guimarães, pp. 176-82.
40. Taunay, *Memórias*, pp. 576-77.
41. "Letters of Sarmiento to Mary Mann," in *Hispanic American Historical Review*, p. 354.
42. Pinheiro Guimarães, pp. 256-60, 303.
43. *Ibid.*, pp. 260-61.
44. *Ibid.*, pp. 307-8.

CHAPTER 12

1. Von Versen, p. 57.
2. An interesting portrayal of the war's impact upon Argentina's peoples is presented in the series of short stories contained in Luna, *La última montonera*.
3. Gálvez, *Los cáminos, Humaitá*, and *Jornadas*.
4. C. H. Haring, *Empire in Brazil: A New World Experiment with Monarchy*, p. 83.
5. Cerqueira, p. 401.
6. Werneck Sodré, pp. 310-13.
7. Smith, p. 484, quoting Gregorio Gonçalves de Castro Mascarenhas, *Terras devolutas e particulares no Estado de São Paulo*, pp. 20-21; Pedro Calmón, *História da civilização brasileira*, pp. 226-29.
8. Calógeras, pp. 224-25.
9. *Ibid.*
10. Lima Figueiredo, *Brasil militar*, p. 77.
11. Haring, p. 129.
12. Calógeras, pp. 234-44.
13. Von Versen, p. 57.
14. Haring, p. 82.
15. The prevalence of this tradition may be observed today in nearly every urban center in Paraguay in the names of streets, avenues, parks, and monuments.
16. Pinheiro Guimarães, p. 197.
17. Haring, p. 82; Decree No. 66 of March 1, 1936, declared Francisco Solano López to be the national hero "sin ejemplar."
18. The author has had the pleasure of visiting Piribebuy on many occasions, and on August 12, 1959, he had the honor of inaugurating Paraguay's Second Military Museum in the municipal building.

Appendices

APPENDIX I

Chronology of the War

THE FOLLOWING brief chronological record indicates the dates of the major events of the Paraguayan War and their importance.

OCTOBER, 1864: Uruguay was invaded by Brazilian forces.

NOVEMBER 12, 1864: The Brazilian steamer "Marquês de Olinda" was seized by Paraguay following its call at Asunción. The event marked the beginning of the Paraguayan War.

DECEMBER 14, 1864: President López dispatched a column to invade Mato Grosso.

JANUARY 2, 1865: Uruguayan Blanco General Leandro Gómez surrendered at Paysandú after a heroic siege, and was executed by the victorious Brazilian-Uruguayan Colorado forces of Tamandaré-Mena Barreto-Flores.

MARCH, 1865: Upon being refused permission by Argentina to cross Corrientes, President López presented a brief of Paraguay's position to the National Congress which was followed by a declaration of war against Argentina.

APRIL 13, 1865: Paraguayan forces successfully attacked the river port of Corrientes and seized two Argentine vessels, one being the "Gualeguay" of later war fame.

MAY 1, 1865: The Triple Alliance Treaty was signed at Buenos Aires.

JUNE, 1865: Paraguayan forces under Colonel Antonio de la Cruz Estigarribia invaded Rio Grande do Sul at São Borja.

JUNE 11, 1865: The Paraguayan fleet was defeated at Riachuelo and the right army corps under General Robles was forced to retreat.

SEPTEMBER 18, 1865: Estigarribia surrendered the left army corps at Uruguaiana after the annihilation of Major Duarte's force at Yataí.

NOVEMBER, 1865-MARCH, 1866: The Paraguayan right army corps retreated back across the Paraná River to Paraguayan territory and was slowly followed by the allied forces under Bartolomé Mitre.

APRIL, 1866: The allies succeeded in crossing the Upper Paraná River and established themselves on Paraguayan territory.

MAY, 1866: Battles of Estero Bellaco and First Tuyuty—Paraguayan efforts to dislodge invading allied forces.

SEPTEMBER 3, 1866: The allies successfully stormed the advanced fortified Paraguayan position at Curuzú.

SPETEMBER 12, 1866: The famous López-Mitre conference at Yataity-Corá failed to produce an agreement for the termination of the war.

SEPTEMBER 22, 1866: The allies suffered their worst defeat of the war at the Battle of Curupaity.

MAY-JUNE, 1867: A Brazilian expeditionary force in Mato Grosso suffered defeat in the epic Retreat from Laguna.

AUGUST, 1867: The Brazilian naval squadron finally succeeded in passing the Paraguayan shore batteries at Curupaity.

NOVEMBER 3, 1867: The Second Battle of Tuyuty resulted in failure by the Paraguayans to halt the allied flanking movement to surround Humaitá.

JANUARY, 1868: General Mitre retired from the war and was succeeded by Brazil's Marshal Caxias as allied commander-in-chief.

February 18, 1868: The Brazilian naval squadron succeeded in running the Paraguayan batteries at Humaitá.

February 19, 1868: Uruguayan Provisional President General Venancio Flores was assassinated at Montevideo.

March 1, 1868: A Paraguayan canoe fleet failed in a surprise attack on Brazilian ironclads, and Marshal López resolved to retire from the Humaitá area northward to the Tebicuary River line.

July 24, 1868: Humaitá, Paraguay's "Sebastopol," was evacuated, and the survivors were forced to surrender on August 6 after unsuccessful efforts to reach the new Paraguayan positions.

August, 1868: The allies occupied the deserted Tebicuary line, and Marshal López retreated further north to new positions near Villeta.

October, 1868: The Brazilian river squadron forced the Paraguayan batteries at Angostura, below Villeta.

November, 1868: Marshal Caxias decided again to turn the right flank of the Paraguayan positions, and sent General Argolo via a new Chaco military road.

December 5, 1868: The Brazilian army crossed the Paraguay River unopposed at San Antonio, north of Villeta. The movement was followed by the Battles of Ytororó and Avay.

December 21-27, 1868: In the most bitter fighting of the war, and in the face of heavy losses, Marshal Caxias succeeded in annihilating the Paraguayan army at Lomas Valentinas. Marshal López escaped capture, however, and retired to Cerro León with but a handful of survivors.

December 30, 1868: Colonel George Thompson surrendered the last Paraguayan river fortifications at Angostura.

January, 1869: Marshal Caxias entered the city of Asunción in triumph and subsequently declared the war to have ended.

January-August, 1869: Marshal López, in the Paraguayan Cordillera east of Asunción, performed one of the war's most astonishing feats in the organization of a new army of approximately 10,000 men.

August 12, 1869: Reinforced and rested, the Brazilian army now under the command of the Conde d'Eu, stormed and captured the interior city of Piribebuy, Paraguay's provisional capital since the fall of Asunción.

August 16, 1869: The reorganized Paraguayan army was annihilated at the Battle of Acosta Ñú or Campo Grande, the last major action of the war.

September, 1869-March, 1870: Pursued by Brazilian patrols, Marshal López and the remnants of his army slowly retreated northward through the sparsely populated, dense forest area of Paraguay's Alto Paraná and Amambay regions.

March 1, 1870: Marshal López was finally killed by pursuing Brazilian troops at Cerro Corá, in extreme northeastern Paraguay, and the last Paraguayan resistance forces were overcome. The war thereby ended.

APPENDIX II
The Triple Alliance Treaty

THE ENGLISH LANGUAGE translation of the text of the Triple Alliance Treaty is based on the version contained in George Thompson, *The War in Paraguay*. Portuguese language versions are contained in Walter Spalding, *A invasão paraguaia no Brasil*; and Augusto Tasso Fragoso, *História da guerra entre a Tríplice Aliança e o Paraguai*.

TREATY OF ALLIANCE AGAINST PARAGUAY, SIGNED ON MAY 1, 1866, BETWEEN THE PLENIPOTENTIARIES OF URUGUAY, BRAZIL, AND THE ARGENTINE REPUBLIC, TAKEN FROM THE PAPERS LAID BEFORE THE HOUSE OF COMMONS BY ORDER OF HER BRITANNIC MAJESTY, IN COMPLIANCE WITH HER MESSAGE OF MARCH 2, 1866.

The Government of the Oriental Republic of Uruguay, the Government of his Majesty the Emperor of Brazil, the Government of the Argentine Republic:

The two last being actually at war with the Government of Paraguay, it having been declared against them by acts of hostility by that Government, and the first being in a state of hostility, and its internal safety threatened by the said Government, which caluminates the Republic, and abuses solemn treaties and the international customs of civilized nations, and which has committed unjustifiable acts after interrupting the relations with its neighbors by the most abusive and aggressive proceedings:

Being persuaded that the peace, safety, and well-being of their respective nations is impossible while the present Government of Paraguay exists, and that it is imperatively necessary for the greatest interests that that Government should disappear, at the same time respecting the sovereignty, independence, and territorial integrity of the Republic of Paraguay:

Have resolved to conclude a Treaty of Alliance, offensive and defensive, with that object; and have named their Plenipotentiaries, as follows:

His Excellency the Provisional Governor of the Oriental Republic has named his Excellency Dr. Carlos Castro, Minister of Foreign Affairs; His Majesty the Emperor of Brazil, his Excellency Dr. J. Octaviano de Almeida Rosa, Counsellor and deputy to the National Legislative Assembly and officer of the Imperial Order of the Rose; his Excellency the President of the Argentine Republic has named his Excellency Dr. Rufino de Elizalde, Minister of Foreign Affairs—who, having exchanged their respective credentials, which they found in good and due form, agreed to the following:

Art. 1—The Oriental Republic of Uruguay, his Majesty the Emperor of Brazil, and the Argentine Republic, unite themselves in an offensive and defensive Alliance for prosecuting the war provoked by the Republic of Paraguay.

Art. 2—The Allies will contribute with all the means at their disposal, by land and by water, as they may find convenient.

Art. 3—The operations of the war commencing in Argentine territory, or in Paraguay bordering on Argentina, the chief command and direction of the allied arms will be confided to the President of the Argentine Republic and General-in-Chief of its Army, Brigadier-General Bartolomé Mitre.

The maritime forces of the Allies will be under the immediate command of Vice-Admiral Viscount Tamandaré, Commander-in-Chief of the squadron of his Majesty the Emperor of Brazil.

The land forces of the Republic of Uruguay, a division of the Argentine forces, and one of the Brazilian forces, which will be indicated by their respective commanders, will form an army under the immediate orders of the Provisional Governor of the Oriental Republic, Brigadier-General Venancio Flores.

The land forces of His Majesty the Emperor of Brazil will form an army under the immediate orders of its General-in-Chief, Brigadier Manuel Luís Osório.

Although the high contracting Powers have agreed not to change the field of operations, yet, with the object of protecting the sovereign rights of the three nations, they have determined that the chief command shall be reciprocal should any operations have to be carried on in Oriental or Brazilian territory.

Art. 4—The internal military order and economy of the allied troops will depend solely on their respective chiefs.

The victuals, ammunition, arms, clothing, equipment, and means of transport of the allied troops will be supplied by their respective States.

Art. 5—The high contracting Powers will give each other any assistance which they may require, under the forms to be stipulated on that particular.

Art. 6—The Allies bind themselves solemnly not to lay down their arms, unless by mutual consent, until they have abolished the present Government of Paraguay, nor to treat separately with the enemy, nor sign any treaty of peace, truce or armistice, or any convention whatever to put an end to or to suspend the war, unless by the common consent of all.

Art. 7—The war not being against the people of Paraguay, but against the Government, the Allies will admit a Paraguayan Legion, formed of the citizens of that nation, who wish to assist in deposing the said Government, and they will furnish it with all necessaries in the form and under the conditions which shall be established.

Art. 8—The Allies moreover bind themselves to respect the independence, sovereignty, and territorial integrity of the Republic of Paraguay. Consequently, the Paraguayan people may elect their own Government, and give it any institutions they deem fit; none of the Allies incorporating it, nor pretenting to establish any protectorate, as a consequence of this war.

Art. 9—The independence, sovereignty, and territorial integrity of the Republic of Paraguay will be guaranteed by the high contracting Powers collectively, in conformity with the foregoing article, for the term of five years.

Art. 10—It is agreed by the high contracting Powers that the exemptions, privileges, or concessions which may be obtained from the Government of Paraguay, shall be gratuitous and common, and if conditional shall have the same compensation.

Art. 11—When the present Government of Paraguay has disappeared, the Allies will proceed to make the necessary arrangements with the authorities which may be constituted, to insure the free navigation of the Rivers Paraná and Paraguay, so that the rules or laws of that Republic do not obstruct or prevent the transit and direct navigation of the war or merchant vessels of the allied States, on their voyages to their respective territories and dominions which do not belong to Paraguay; and to establish the necessary guarantees for the effectiveness of the arrangements, under the condition that these laws of River Police, although made for the two rivers, and also for the River Uruguay, shall be established by common accord between the Allies and other States on the boundaries, for the term which shall be stipulated by the said Allies, should those States accept the invitation.

Art. 12—The Allies also reserve to themselves to concert the measures most conducive toward the guarantee of peace with the Republic of Paraguay after the fall of the present Government.

Art. 13—The Allies will name Plenipotentiaries, to make arrangements, conventions, or treaties with the Government which may be established.

Art. 14—The Allies will demand from this Government the payment of the expenses of the war which they have been forced to carry on, and also the payment of damages caused to public and private property, and to the persons of their citizens, without an express declaration of war—also of the damages subsequently done in violation of the laws of war. In like manner the Oriental Republic of Uruguay will demand indemnification for the damages caused by the Government of Paraguay, in the war she has been forced to take a part in, in defense of her safety, threatened by that Government.

Art. 15—The manner and form of liquidation and payment, proceeding from the above-mentioned causes, will be determined in a special convention.

Art. 16—With the view of avoiding discussions and wars regarding the question of boundaries, it is agreed that the Allies will demand from the Government of Paraguay, that in its treaties of limits with their respective Governments, the following basis shall be adhered to:

1. The Argentine Republic will be divided from that of Paraguay, by the Rivers Paraná and Paraguay, as far as the boundary of Brazil, which, on the right side of the River Paraguay, is the Bahía Negra.

2. The Empire of Brazil will be divided from the Republic of Paraguay on the side of the Paraná, by the first river below the Seven Falls, which, according to the late map of Mouchez, is the Ygurei, following its course from its mouth to its rise.

3. On the left side of the Paraguay, by the Rio Apa, from its mouth to its rise.

4. In the interior of the tops of the mountains of Maracayú the streams running eastward will belong to Brazil, and those running westward to Paraguay—a straight line, as far as possible, being drawn from the tops of those mountains to the rises of the Apa and Ygurei.

Art. 17—The Allies guarantee to each other, reciprocally, the faithful execution of any arrangements and treaties which may be concluded in Paraguay, in virtue of which, it is agreed that the present Treaty of Alliance shall always remain in full force and vigor, in order that these stipulations be respected and carried out by Paraguay.

1. With the object of obtaining this result, they agree, that in case one of the high contracting parties cannot obtain from the Government of Paraguay the fulfillment of an agreement, or in case that Government should pretend to annul the stipulations agreed upon with the Allies, the other powers will employ means to make them respected.

2. Should these means prove useless, the Allies will concur, with all their power, to obtain the execution of the stipulations.

Art. 18—This treaty will remain secret until the principal object of the Alliance has been obtained.

Art. 19.—Those stipulations of this treaty which do not require legislative authorization for their ratification, will come in force as soon as they are approved by the respective Governments, and the others when the ratifications are exchanged, which will be within the term of forty days from the date of said treaty, or sooner, if possible, and will take place in the city of Buenos Aires.

In faith of which, we, the undersigned Plenipotentiaries of his Excellency the Provisional Governor of the Oriental Republic of Uruguay, of his Majesty the Emperor of Brazil, and of his Excellency the President of the Argentine Republic, in virtue of our full powers, have signed this treaty, placing thereto our seals, in the city of Buenos Aires on the 1st May, in the year of Our Lord 1865.

Signed: Carlos Castro, J. Octaviano de Almeida Rosa, Rufino de Elizalde.

PROTOCOL

Their Excellencies the Plenipotentiaries of the Argentine Republic, of the Oriental Republic, and of his Majesty the Emperor of Brazil, assembled in the Foreign Office, agree:—

1. That in compliance with the Treaty of Alliance of this date, the fortifications of Humaitá shall be demolished, and that no other or others of that kind shall be permitted to be constructed, thereby interfering with the faithful execution of the treaty.

2. That as it is a necessary measure towards guaranteeing peace with the Government which may be established in Paraguay, not to leave it any arms or elements of war, all those found will be equally divided among the Allies.

3. That any trophies or booty which may be taken from the enemy shall be divided between the Allies by the one who makes the capture.

4. That the Generals commanding the allied armies shall concert the means of carrying these stipulations into effect.

And they sign the present in Buenos Aires, on the 1st May, 1865.

Signed: CARLOS CASTRO, RUFINO DE ELIZALDE, J. OCTAVIANO DE ALMEIDA ROSA.

APPENDIX III

The Lomas Valentinas Note

THE FOLLOWING is an informal translation of the major portion of the text of the note sent by Marshal Francisco Solano López to the allied commanders on December 24, 1868, during the Lomas Valentinas campaign. It is based on the texts contained in George Thompson, *The War in Paraguay*, pp. 301-3; and Arturo Bray, *Solano López*, pp. 370-72.

TO THEIR EXCELLENCIES,
  MARSHAL THE MARQUES DE CAXIAS,
  COLONEL-MAJOR D. ENRIQUE CASTRO,
  BRIGADIER GENERAL D. JUAN GELLY Y OBES.

The Marshal President of the Republic of Paraguay ought perhaps to decline sending a written answer to Their Excellencies, the Generals-in-Chief of the Allied Army, in war against the nation over which he presides, on account of the unusual tone and language; incompatible as it is with military honor.

. . . .

These are precisely the sentiments which, more than two years ago, moved me to place myself above all of the official discourtesy with which the elect of my country has been treated during this war. At Yataity-Corá I then sought, in an interview with His Excellency the General-in-Chief of the Allied Army and President of the Argentine Republic, General Bartolomé Mitre, the reconciliation of four sovereign states of South America which had already begun to destroy each other in a remarkable manner; but my initiative met with no answer but the contempt and silence of the allied governments, and new and bloody battles on the part of their armed representatives, as you call yourselves. I then more clearly saw that the tendency of the war of the allies was against the existence of the Republic of Paraguay and, though deploring the blood spilled in so many years of war, I could say nothing, and, placing the fate of my Fatherland and its generous sons in the hands of the God of Nations, I fought its enemies with loyalty and conscience, and I am disposed to continue fighting until that God

and our arms decide the definite fate of the cause.

Your Excellencies have thought fit to inform me of the knowledge you possess of my actual resources, thinking that I have the same knowledge of the numerical forces of the allies, and of their everyday increasing resources. I have not that knowledge, but I have more than four years' experience that numerical force and those resources have never influenced the abnegation and bravery of the Paraguayan soldier, who fights with the resolution of the honorable citizen and of the Christian man, and who opens a wide grave in his country rather than see it even humiliated. Your Excellencies have thought fit to remind me that the blood spilled at Ytororó and at Avay should have determined me to avoid that which was spilled on the 21st instant; but Your Excellencies doubtless forgot that those very actions might have shown you beforehand, how true all is that I say about the abnegation of my compatriots, and that every drop of blood which falls to the ground is a new obligation for those who survive.

After such an example, my poor head will bear the burden of the ungentlemanly threat (if I may be allowed the expression) which Your Excellencies have considered it your duty to notify to me. Your Excellencies have not the right to impeach me before the Republic of Paraguay, my Fatherland, for I have defended it, I am defending it, and I will yet defend it.

My country imposed that duty on me and I take glory in fulfilling it to the last; as for the rest, I shall leave my deeds to history, and I owe an account of them only to my God.

If blood is still to flow, He will lay it to the account of those who are responsible. For my part, I am still disposed to treat for the termination of the war upon bases equally honorable for all the belligerents, but I am not disposed to listen to an intimation that I lay down my arms.

Inviting Your Excellencies, therefore, to treat of peace, I consider that I am, in my turn, fulfilling an imperious duty towards religion, humanity, and civilization, as well as what I owe to the unanimous cry that I have just heard from my generals, chiefs, officers, and troops, to whom I have communicated Your Excellencies' intimation—and also what I owe to my own name.

I ask Your Excellencies' pardon for not citing the date and hour of your notification, as they were not on the document which was received in my lines at a quarter past seven this morning.

God preserve Your Excellencies many years,

        Francisco S. López,
        Marshal President,
        Republic of Paraguay

Bibliography

PRINCIPAL SOURCES

Memoirs, Travelers' Accounts, Official Reports, Documents; and Contemporary Essays, Articles, and Newspaper Reports

ALBERDI, Juan B. *Grandes y pequeños hombres del Plata*. Paris, n.d.
───────. *Los intereses argentinos en la Guerra del Paraguay con el Brasil*. Paris, 1865.
───────. *Las disenciones de las repúblicas del Plata y las maquinaciones del Brasil*. Paris, 1865.
───────. *Las dos guerras del Plata y su filiación*. Paris, 1867.
───────. *El Imperio del Brasil ante la democracia de América. Colección de artículos escritos durante la Guerra del Paraguay*. Asunción, 1919.
AGRIPPO, Menino. *O govêrno e o povo do Brasil na guerra paraguaia*. Campos, 1867.
AMERLAN, Alberto. *Nights on the Rio Paraguay—Scenes of War and Character Sketches*. trans. Henry S. Suksdorf. Buenos Aires, 1902.
AZEVEDO, M. de. *Rio da Prata e Paraguai—Quadros guerreiros*. Rio de Janeiro, 1871.
BARROS, A. J. *Guerra do Paraguai, O Almirante Visconde de Inhaúma*. Rio de Janeiro, 1870.
BENITES, Gregorio. *La Triple Alianza de 1865, escapada de un desastre en la guerra de invasión al Paraguay*. Asunción, 1904.
───────. *Anales diplomático y militar de la guerra del Paraguay*, 2 vols. Asunción, 1906.
───────. *Guerra del Paraguay, las primeras batallas contra la Triple Alianza*. Asunción, 1919.
BURTON, Richard F. *Letters from the Battlefields of Paraguay*. London, 1870.
───────. *Explorations of the Highlands of the Brazil*. 2 vols. London, 1869.
CAMARA LIMA, Patrício A. da. *Manuscripto de 1869 ou resumo histórico das operações militares dirigidas pelo Marechal d'exercito Marquêz de Caxias na campanha do Paraguai*. Rio de Janeiro, 1872.
CENTURION, Juan C. *Memorias de Juan C. Centurión o sea reminiscencias históricas sobre la Guerra del Paraguay*. 3 vols. Buenos Aires, 1894-97.
CERQUEIRA, Dionísio. *Reminiscências da Campanha do Paraguai*. Rio de Janeiro, n.d.
CODMAN, John. *Ten Months in Brazil, with Notes on the Paraguayan War*. New York, 1872.
COSTA, Pereira da. *História da guerra do Brasil contra as repúblicas do Uruguai e Paraguai*. 4 vols. Rio de Janeiro, 1870-71.
DIAZ, César. *Memorias inéditas del general oriental Don César Díaz*. Buenos Aires, 1878.
GARCIA, Manuel. *Paraguay and the Alliance against the Tyrant Francisco Solano López*. New York, 1869.
GARGARO, Alfredo. "La Batalla de Pozo de Vargas," in *Boletín de la Academia Nacional de Historia*, XX and XXI, 47 and 48. Buenos Aires, n.d.
GARMENDIA, José Ignacio. *Recuerdos de la Guerra del Paraguay; Campaña de Pikiciry*. Buenos Aires, 1884.

——————. *Recuerdos de la Guerra del Paraguay; Batalla del Sauce, Combates de Yatayti-Corá y Curupaiti*. Buenos Aires, 1885.
——————. *La cartera de un soldado*. Buenos Aires, 1890.
——————. *Campaña de Humaytá*. Buenos Aires, 1901.
HAYDON, F. Stansbury. "Documents Relating to the First Military Balloon Corps Organized in South America," in *Hispanic American Historical Review*, XIX, 4 (November, 1939).
HOMEN DE MELLO, Francisco I. M. "Viagem ao Paraguai em Fevereiro e Março 1869; Cartas ao Sr. Ten. Cor. Benedicto Marcondes Homen de Mello," in *Revista do Instituto Histórico e Geográfico do Brasil*, XXXVI. Rio de Janeiro, 1873.
HUTCHINSON, Thomas J. *The Paraná, with Incidents of the Paraguayan War*. London, 1868.
Illustrated London News, XLIX, 1392 and 1393 (October 6, 1866).
KENNEDY, A. J. *La Plata, Brazil, and Paraguay during the Present War*. London, 1869.
"Letters of Sarmiento to Mary Mann" in *Hispanic American Historical Review*, XXXII, 2 (May, 1952), and 3 (August, 1952).
LOPEZ, Francisco Solano. *Proclamas y cartas del Mariscal López*. Buenos Aires, 1957.
LYNCH, Alicia. *Exposición y protesta*. Buenos Aires, 1875.
MACMAHON, Martin T. "Paraguay and Her Enemies," in *Harper's New Monthly Magazine*, XL, 237 (February, 1870).
——————. "The War in Paraguay," in *Harper's New Monthly Magazine*, XL, 239 (April, 1870).
MAIZ, Fidel. *Etapas de mi vida*. Asunción, 1919.
MASTERMAN, George F. *Seven Eventful Years in Paraguay*. 2d ed. London, 1870.
MITRE, Bartolomé. *Cartas polémicas sobre la Triple Alianza y la Guerra del Paraguay*. Buenos Aires, 1871.
——————. "Guerra del Paraguay—Memoria militar," in *Revista del Instituto Paraguayo*, Nos. 44-47 (1903-4).
——————. *Archivo del General Mitre*. 25 vols. Buenos Aires, 1911-13.
MONTENEGRO, J. A. *Guerra do Paraguai, Memórias de Mme. Dorothea Duprat de Lasserre, Versão e notas de J. A. Montenegro*. Rio Grande, 1893.
D'ORLEANS, G. (Conde d'Eu). *Viagem militar ao Rio Grande do Sul*. São Paulo, 1936.
Papers Relating to the Foreign Relations of the United States. Washington, 1870.
Paraguayan Investigation. H. R., 41st Congress, 2nd Session. Report No. 65, Vol. II. Washington, 1870.
PAZ, José María. *Memorias póstumas*. 2 vols. Buenos Aires, 1917.
PEREIRA DA SILVA, J. M. *Memórias de meu tempo*. Rio de Janeiro, 1895.
PINHEIRO GUIMARAES, Francisco. *Um Voluntário da Pátria*. 2d ed. Rio de Janeiro, 1958.
REBAUDI, Arturo. *La declaración de guerra de la República del Paraguay a la República Argentina*. Buenos Aires, 1924.
RESQUIN, Francisco Isidoro. *Datos históricos de la guerra del Paraguay con la Triple Alianza*. Buenos Aires, 1896.
ROBERTSON, J. P. and W. P. *Letters on Paraguay: Comprising an Account of a Four Years' Residence in that Republic under the Government of the Dictator Francia*. 2 vols. London, 1838.

Sena Madureira, A. de. *Guerra do Paraguai.* No place, 1870.
Sodre, Alcindo. *Abrindo um cofre.* Rio de Janeiro, 1956.
Spalding, Walter. *A. invasão paraguaia no Brasil.* São Paulo, 1940.
Talavera, Natalicio. *La Guerra del Paraguay.* Buenos Aires, 1958.
Taunay, Alfredo d'Escragnolle. *Diário do Exército,* Rio de Janeiro, 1870.
——————. *Memórias do Visconde de Taunay.* São Paulo, 1948.
——————. *A Retirada da Laguna.* 14th ed. São Paulo, 1957.
Thompson, George. *The War in Paraguay.* London, 1869.
Varela, Hector F. *Elisa Lynch.* Buenos Aires, 1934.
Victorica, J. "Reminiscencias históricas de la Guerra del Paraguay," in *Revista de Derecho, Historia y Letras,* VI. Buenos Aires. 1900.
——————. *Urquiza y Mitre.* Buenos Aires, 1906.
von Versen, Max. "História da Guerra do Paraguai," in *Revista do Instituto Histórico e Geográfico Brasileiro,* LXXVI, Part II. Rio de Janeiro, 1913.
Washburn, Charles A. *The History of Paraguay.* 2 vols. Boston, 1871.
Wisner, Francisco. *El Dictador del Paraguay José Gaspar de Francia.* Notes by Julio C. Chaves. Buenos Aires, 1957.

SECONDARY SOURCES

Postwar Studies, Essays, Monographs, Biographies; Other Literary Works

Almeida, Manoel Antônio de. *Memórias de um sargento de milícias.* Rio de Janeiro, 1944.
Azevedo Pimentel, Joaquim S. de. *Episódios militares.* No place, 1897.
——————. *O Onze de Voluntários da Pátria.* No place, 1909.
Baez, Adolfo J. *Yatayty-Corá; una conferencia histórica.* Buenos Aires, 1929.
Baez, Cecilio. *El Mariscal Francisco Solano López.* Asunción, 1926.
Baltazar da Silveira, Carlos. *A campanha do Paraguai.* No place, 1900.
Barrett, William E. *Woman on Horseback.* New York, 1952.
Barros Lins, Ivan Monteiro de. *Benjamin Constant, 1836-1891.* Rio de Janeiro, 1936.
Barroso, Gustavo. *A guerra do López.* 3d ed. São Paulo, 1929.
——————. *História militar do Brasil.* São Paulo, 1938.
Best, Félix. *Historia de las guerras argentinas.* 2 vols. Buenos Aires, 1960.
Beverina, Juan. *La Guerra del Paraguay.* 5 vols. Buenos Aires, 1921.
Blomberg, Hector Pedro. *La dama del Paraguay.* Buenos Aires, 1942.
Bormann, José B. *O Marechal Duque de Caxias, Fotografia militar.* Rio de Janeiro, 1880.
——————. *História da Guerra do Paraguai.* 3 vols. Buenos Aires, 1901.
Box, Pelham Horton. *The Origins of the Paraguayan War.* 2 vols. Urbana, 1927.
——————. *Los orígenes de la guerra del Paraguay contra la Triple Alianza.* Translated by Pablo M. Ynsfrán. Asunción, 1936.
Bray, Arturo. *Solano López.* Buenos Aires, 1945.
Bunkley, Addison Williams. *The Life of Sarmiento.* Princeton, 1952.
Calmon, Pedro. *História da civilização brasileira.* 4th ed. São Paulo, 1940.
Calogeras, João Pandiá. *A History of Brazil.* Trans. Percy Alvin Martin. Chapel Hill, 1939.
Carcano, Ramon J. *Guerra del Paraguay.* 3 vols. Buenos Aires, 1941.
Carlyle, Thomas. *El dictador Francia.* Trans. L. M. Drago. Buenos Aires, 1937.
Carrasco, Gabriel. *La población del Paraguay antes y después de la guerra.* Asunción, 1905.

228 INDEPENDENCE OR DEATH

Cascudo, Luís da Câmara. *López do Paraguai.* No place, 1927.
——————. *O Conde d'Eu.* São Paulo, 1933.
Centurion, Carlos R. *Historia de las letras paraguayas.* Buenos Aires, 1947-52.
Cesar, Guilhermino. *História da literatura do Rio Grande do Sul, 1737-1902.* Pôrto Alegre, 1956.
Chaves, Julio César. *El General Díaz.* Asunción, 1957.
——————. *La revolución paraguaya de la independencia.* Asunción, 1961.
Chaves, María Concepción de L. *Madame Lynch.* Buenos Aires, 1957.
Chidsey, Donald Barr. *The Battle of New Orleans.* New York, 1961.
Cova, J. A. *Solano López y la epopeya del Paraguay.* 4th ed. Caracas, 1956.
Cunningham e Graham, R. B. *Portrait of a Dictator.* London, 1933.
Decoud, Adolfo. "Solano López," in *Revista de Derecho, Historia y Letras,* VII. Buenos Aires, 1900.
Decoud, Hector F. *Sobre los escombros de la guerra; una década de vida nacional.* Asunción, 1925.
Dominguez, Manual. *El alma de la raza.* Asunción, 1918.
——————. *Causas del heroísmo paraguayo.* Asunción, 1903.
Fernandes de Sousa, Antônio. *A invasão paraguaia em Mata Grosso.* Cuiabá, 1919.
Fitzgibbon, Russell H. *Uruguay: Portrait of a Democracy.* New Brunswick, 1954.
Fonseca Filho, Hermes da. *Dois grandes vultos da República.* Pôrto Alegre, 1935.
Galvez, Manuel. *Los caminos de la muerte.* 2d ed. Buenos Aires, 1928.
——————. *Humaitá.* Buenos Aires, n.d.
——————. *Jornadas de agonía.* Buenos Aires, n.d.
——————. "Por qué occurió la guerra del Paraguay," in *La Nación.* Buenos Aires, October 7, 1928.
Garcia Mellid, Atilio. *Proceso a los falsificadores de la historia del Paraguay.* 2 vols. Buenos Aires, 1964.
Godoi, Juan Silvano. *Monografías históricas.* Buenos Aires, 1893.
——————. *Últimas operaciones de guerra del General Díaz, vencedor de Curupaity.* Buenos Aires, 1897.
Gonzalez, José F. *Corrientes ante la invasión paraguaya.* Corrientes, 1916.
Gonzalez, J. Natalicio. *Solano López, diplomático.* Asunción, n.d.
——————. *Cuentos y parábolas.* Buenos Aires, 1922.
Haring, C. H. *Empire in Brazil: A New World Experiment with Monarchy.* Cambridge, 1958.
Inman, Samuel Guy. "The Heart of South America; Archival Finds in the Tragical History of Paraguay," in *South American,* VI, 6. New York, 1918.
James, Preston E. *Latin America.* 3d ed. New York, 1959.
Jefferson, Mark. *Peopling the Argentine Pampa.* New York, 1926.
Jeffrey, William H. *Mitre and Argentina.* New York, 1952.
Jourdan, Emílio. *História das campanhas do Uruguai, Matto Grosso, e Paraguai.* 3 vols. Rio de Janeiro, 1893.
Koebel, W. H. *Paraguay.* London, 1917.
——————. *British Exploits in South America.* New York, 1917.
Kolinski, Charles J. "The Death of Francisco Solano López," in *The Historian,* November, 1963.
Leite de Castro, João V. *Diccionário geográphico e histórico das campanhas do Uruguai e Paraguai.* Rio de Janeiro, 1892.
Lemos, Britto. *Guerra do Paraguai.* Bahia, 1907.

LEVENE, Ricardo. *A History of Argentina.* Trans. William Spence Robertson. Chapel Hill, 1937.
LICHTBLAU, Myron I. *The Argentine Novel in the Nineteenth Century.* New York, 1959.
LIMA FIGUEIREDO, José de. *Grandes soldados do Brasil.* Rio de Janeiro, 1944.
——————. *Brasil militar.* Rio de Janeiro, 1944.
LIMA, Oliveira. *O Império Brasileiro, 1822-1889.* São Paulo, 1927.
LOBO VIANA, José F. *A epopeia da Laguna.* No place, 1920.
LOURIVAL DE MOURA, Col. A. *As fôrças armadas e o destino histórico do Brasil.* São Paulo, 1937.
LUNA, Félix. *La última montonera: cuentos bárbaros.* Buenos Aires, 1955.
MAGNESCO, Silvio. *Guerra del Paraguay.* Buenos Aires, 1913.
MECHAM, J. Lloyd. *Church and State in Latin America.* Chapel Hill, 1934.
MEIRELES, Teotónio. *O exército brasileiro na campanha do Paraguai.* No place, 1877.
MONTEIRO, Tobias. *Pesquisas e depoimentos para a história.* Rio de Janeiro, 1913.
MONTENEGRO, J. Artur. *Fragmentos históricos, homens e fatos da Guerra do Paraguai.* Rio Grande, 1900.
MORAES, E. Vilhena de. *O Duque de Ferro.* No place, 1933.
MORNER, Magnus. "El mapa del Mariscal," in *Inter-American Review of Bibliography,* No. 10 (June, 1960).
NASH, Roy. *The Conquest of Brazil.* New York, 1926.
O'LEARY, Juan E. *Nuestra epopeya.* Asunción, 1919.
——————. *El libro de los héroes.* Asunción, 1922.
——————. *El Mariscal López.* 2d ed. Madrid, 1925.
——————. *El héroe del Paraguay.* Asunción, 1927.
OSORIO, Joaquim e Fernando Luís. *História do General Osório.* Pelotas, 1915.
OURO PRETO, Visconde de. *A marinha de Outr'ora.* Rio de Janeiro, 1894.
PENDLE, George. *Paraguay, A Riverside Nation.* 2d ed. New York, 1956.
PEREIRA DE SOUSA, Octávio. "História da Guerra do Paraguai," in *Revista do Instituto Histórico e Geográfico Brasileiro,* No. 102. Rio de Janeiro, 1927.
PEREYRA, Carlos. *Francisco Solano López e la guerra del Paraguay.* Buenos Aires, 1945.
PETERSON, Harold F. "Efforts of the United States to Mediate in the Paraguayan War," in *Hispanic American Historical Review,* XII, 1 (February, 1932).
PINTO DE CAMPOS, Joaquim. *Vida de Luís Alves de Lima e Silva, Duque de Caxias.* No place, 1878.
PITAUD, Henri. *Madama Lynch.* Asunción, 1958.
RAINE, Philip. *Paraguay.* New Brunswick, 1956.
REBAUDI, Arturo. *Guerra del Paraguay; La conspiración contra el Mariscal López.* Buenos Aires, 1917.
——————. *Guerra del Paraguay, Vencer o morir.* Buenos Aires, 1920.
——————. *Lomas Valentinas.* Buenos Aires, 1925.
REH, Emma. *Paraguayan Rural Life.* Washington, 1946.
ROCHA ALMEIDA, Antônio da. *Vultos da Pátria.* Rio de Janeiro, 1961.
SANCHEZ QUELL, H. *La diplomacia paraguaya de Mayo a Cerro Corá.* 3d ed. Buenos Aires, 1957.
SARMIENTO, Carlos de. *Estudio crítico sobre la Guerra del Paraguay.* Buenos Aires, 1890.
SARMIENTO, D. F. *Vida de Dominguito.* Buenos Aires, 1938.

SCHMITT, Peter. "Las relaciones diplomáticas entre el Paraguay y las potencias europeas, 1840-1870," in *Historia Paraguaya*, III. Asunción, 1958.
SCHNEIDER, Louis. *A Guerra da Tríplice Aliança*. Trans. M. T. Alves Nogueira with notes by J. M. da Silva Paranhos. 2 vols. Rio de Janeiro, 1875-1876.
SEEBER, Francisco. *Cartas sobre la guerra del Paraguay*. Buenos Aires, 1907.
SENNA, Ernesto. *Deodoro, subsídios para a história*. Rio de Janeiro, 1896.
SERVICE, Elman R. and Helen S. *Tobatí: A Paraguayan Town*. Chicago, 1954.
SHERBININ, Betty de. *The River Plate Republics*. New York, 1947.
SMITH, T. Lynn. *Brazil: People and Institutions*. Rev. ed. Baton Rouge, 1954.
SODRE, Nelson Werneck. *Formação da sociedade brasileira*. Rio de Janeiro, 1944.
SOSA, Julio María. *La defensa de Montevideo y la guerra del Paraguay*. Montevideo, 1907.
SOUSA, Docca. *Causas da guerra com o Paraguai*. Pôrto Algre, 1919.
TASSO FRAGOSO, Augusto. *História da guerra entre a Tríplice Aliança e o Paraguai*. 5 vols. Rio de Janeiro, 1934.
TAVARES, Raúl. *A marinha brasileira na Guerra do Paraguai*. No place, 1926.
TORRES HOMEN, J. S. *Annães das guerras do Brasil com os estados da Prata e Paraguai*. Rio de Janeiro, 1911.
URIÉN, Carlos M. *Curupaity*. Buenos Aires, 1921.
WALFORD, A. J. "General Urquiza and the Battle of Pavón," in *Hispanic American Historical Review*, XIX, 4 (November, 1939).
WARREN, Harris G. *Paraguay: An Informal History*. Norman, 1949.
————. "The Paraguayan Image of the War of the Triple Alliance," in *The Americas*, XIX, 1 (July, 1962).
WHITE, Edward L. *El Supremo, A Romance of the Great Dictator of Paraguay*. New York, 1916.
WILLIAMS, Mary W. *Dom Pedro the Magnanimous, Second Emperor of Brazil*. Chapel Hill, 1937.
ZINNY, Antonio. *Historia de los gobernantes del Paraguay, 1535-1887*. Buenos Aires, 1887.

Index

A Reforma, 174
Acosta, Padre José I, 162
Acosta Nú, battle of, 179-80. *See also* Campo Grande, battle of
Aeronautical service: use of balloons in the Paraguayan War, 145-48
Aguirre, Atanasio, 71
Alberdi, Juan Bautista, xiii
Alén, Colonel Paulino, 156
Allen, James and Ezra, 146-47
Amazon River: Brazilian policy toward, 12, 195
Andrade Neves, General José Joaquim de, 61, 80, 167-69
Angostura: surrender of, 170
Anti-war demonstrations: Argentina and Battle of Pozo de Vargas, 143-45, 154
Antônio João Ribeiro: death at Dourados, 83
Antunes Gurjão, General Hilário Maximiano, 61, 165
Apa River, 12
Aquidaban-Niqüí River, 185, 186
Argentina: characteristics in 1864, 4-6; anti-war demonstrations and revolts, 143-45
Argolo, General Alexandre Gomes de: portrait of, 61
Armed forces: comparison of Paraguay and Brazil, 63
Armored train experiments, 177
"Asociación de Mayo," 6
Asunción: railroad and telegraph innovations, 9; bombardment of, 155; occupation of, 171-72; Pantheon of the Heroes, 199
Avay, battle of, 166-67; viii
Aveiro, Colonel Silvestre, 169, 190
Ayala, Cipriano: mission to Buenos Aires, 89

Bado, Captain José Matías, 122, 162
Banco de Itapirú, action of, 116
Barbacena, Felisberto Caldeira Brant Pontes, Marquês de, 48
Barral, Condessa de: relationship with Dom Pedro II, 26-28
Barrios, Inocencia López de, 189
Barrios, General Vicente: at Second Battle of Tuyuty, 152-53; mentioned, 75, 82, 99, 159-61
Barroso de Silva, Admiral Francisco Manoel: participation in naval Battle of Riachuelo, 97-99; 115
Basualdo, revolt at, 109
Bedoya, José Díaz de, 175
Bedoya, Rafaela López de, 189
Bedoya, Saturnino, 160-61
Berges, José: war ultimatum, 72-73; 159-61
Bermejo River, 11
Blanco Party of Uruguay, 13
Blanco River, 11
Bliss, Porter, xiii; 159-60
Blyth, J. and A. and Company, 18, 38
Bogardo, Dean, 159
Bourbon, Princess Teresa Cristina Maria de, 27
Bowen, George, 90
Bowlin mission, xii, 21
Box, Pelham Horton, xiv
Brazil: characteristics in 1864, 13-16
British technicians: service in Paraguay, 38-40
Bruguez, General José María, 97-99, 116, 159-60
Burton, Richard F.: funeral of Flores, 34; portrait of a Paraguayan soldier, 41; comments regarding Brazilian recruitment, 78; overview of the war, 96; mentioned, xiii, 19, 22, 38, 43, 103, 122, 133, 140, 141, 162-63, 170

Caacupé, 171, 176, 177, 179
Caballero, General Bernardino, 47, 152, 165-66, 179-80, 188, 190
Caballero, Colonel Pablo, 2
Cabichuí, 135
"Caçadores Henriques," 47
Camelotes, 156
Caminos, Luis, 176, 186, 188
Camisão, Colonel Carlos de Morais: on Laguna expedition, 111-13
Campo Grande, battle of, 179-80. *See also* Acosta Nú, battle of

231

232 INDEPENDENCE OR DEATH

Campos, Luis Mará, 129
Canabarro, General David: portrait of, 61; in Uruguaiana campaign, 101, 103, 106-07
Canoe attacks on Brazil's fleet, 155, 156
Canstat affair, 11
Carillo de López, Doña Juana, 161-62, 189
Carlyle, Thomas, xii
Carneiro de Campos, Colonel Frederico, 74-75
Carneiro Monteiro, General Victorino, 179
Castro, General Enrique, 67-68
Caxias, Luís Alves de Lima e Silva, Duque de: portrait of, 58-59; appointment as Field Marshal, 139; balloon experiments, 146-47; at Battle of Ytororó, 165; retirement from the war, 171-72; mentioned, 15, 29, 56, 159, 162, 166-70
Centurión, Juan C., 47, 161
Cepeda, battle of, 6, 21
Cepo uruguayo, 160
Cerqueira, Dionísio, 3, 119, 135, 143, 148, 150, 168, 178, 180, 182, 183, 189, 194
Cerro Corá: description of, 185; final action at, 186-87; mentioned, viii, 162, 199, 200
Cerro León, 9, 40, 166, 167-70 *passim*; 176
Céspedes, Lieutenant, 146, 165
Chaco, 7
"Chatas," naval barges, 96-97
Chiripás, 42, 105
Chodasiewicz, Colonel R. A., 146-48
Cholera epidemic, 143
Christie, William Dougal, 29. See also Questão de Christie
Club del Pueblo, 175
Cochrane, Admiral Lord, 57
"Comité Revolucionario," 87
Colorado Party of Uruguay, 13, 193
Concepción, 183, 189, 190
Conde d'Eu: at Uruguaiana, 100, 105, 107; appointment to field comand, 173-75; mentioned, 1, 43, 177, 178-79, 181-83, 189, 190, 196
Congréve rockets: use of at First Battle of Tuyuty, 119; use of at Battle of Campo Grande, 179

Conspiracy episode, 155, 157-62
Constant, Benjamin, 198
Corrales, action at, 114-15
Corrêa da Câmara, General José Antônio: in last action at Cerro Corá, 186-89; mentioned, 61, 85, 166, 182
Corrientes, port of: in 1864, 5; Paraguayan capture of, 90-95; allied occupation of, 109-10
Costa Lôbo, Dr. Manoel Cardoso da, 187
Cuerpo de Bogabantes, 156
Cunha Mattos, Major Ernesto Augusto da, 85, 152, 161, 170, 188
Curupaity, battle of, viii, xii, 127-30
Curuzú, assault on, 123-24

Deodoro da Fonseca, Colonel Manoel, 62, 116, 125, 165, 198
Destinadas, 183-84
Diário do Exército, 174
Dias, Marcílio, 98
Díaz, Isidora, 188
Díaz, General José: military qualifications, 47; at Corrales, 115; at Battle of Curupaity, 128-30; death of, 132; mentioned, 25, 41, 116
Disciplinary measures in the Brazilian army, 142
Dom Pedro II: prewar problems, 14, 15, 16; contrast with López, 17; portrait of, 25-30; reaction to Riachuelo, 99; at siege of Uruguaiana, 102, 104-06; attitude toward peace negotiations, 125, 136-37; mentioned, 3, 69, 108, 109, 157, 173, 189, 191, 196, 197, 198
Drago, Manoel Pedro, 111
Duarte, Major Pedro, 103-04

Egusquiza, Félix, 72-73, 174
El Peruano: protest against Triple Alliance Treaty, 94
El Semanario: declaration of war against Argentina, 88; 94, 135
Elizalde, Rufino de, 71, 87, 92-93
English Question, 15, 29, 72, 106
Estabelecimento redoubt, 53, 155
Estigarribia, Colonel Antonio de la Cruz: Uruguaiana campaign, 95, 101-07

INDEX 233

Fariña, Lieutenant José María, 170
Farroupo Rebellion, 15, 28-29, 48
Fialho, Major Anfrísio, 172-73
Flores, General Venancio: personal portrait, 33-34; return to Uruguay, 70; mentioned, 13, 67, 103, 104, 106, 121, 154, 193
Fonseca, Major Eduardo Emiliano da, 165
Fonseca, Colonel Hermes da, 171
Fonseca, Dr. João Severiano da, 165-66
Fort Coimbra: capture of, 81-83
Francia, Dr. José Gaspar Rodríguez de, xii, 7, 9, 36-37
Franco, Colonel Rafael, 199

Gálvez, Manuel, 193
Gaston, J. McF., 78
Gelly y Obes, General Juan A., 66-67
Genés, Ignacio, 155
Gente de côr, 50, 79
Gomes Jardim, Paulino, 102
Gômez, Colonel Leandro, 84-86
Gould, G. Z.: description of quadrilátero, 131; peace talks, 136; 145
Grillos, 160
"Gualeguay": use by Paraguay in action on the Upper Paraná, 115
Guaraní Indians, 7
Guarda Nacional, 49, 79, 76-79 *passim*
Guardia Nacional, 65
"Guerra Grande," 15

Harper's New Monthly Magazine, xiii
Hayes, Rutherford B., xiv, 193
Hospital conditions: at Corrientes, 143
Humaitá: location, 12; communications with, 9, 44; passage by Brazilian squadron, 154-55; Paraguayan withdrawal from, 156-57; replica of church, 199; mentioned, 38, 131
Hutchinson, Thomas J.: portrait of Urquiza, 35; description of Argentine recruitment, 144; mentioned, 99, 133

Ibicuí, 182
Ignacio, Admiral José Joaquim, 139
Illustrated London News, xii, 94, 140
Isabel, Princess, 22
Itá-Ibaty, battle of, 162, 164, 167-70, 175

Ituzaingó, battle of, 45, 48

Jornal do Comércio, 174, 191

Kaiser Wilhelm II, 36
Kruger, American naval mine expert, 45, 123

La América, 92, 124
La Estrella, 135, 179
La Nación Argentina, 32, 91, 121
La Tribuna, 91
Lacerda, Corporal José Francisco: "Chico Diabo," 186, 187-88, 189
Laguna, retreat from, 110-13
Land topography: Paraguay's defensive system, 44
Lei do Ventre Livre, 196
Lesica and Lanus: Brazilian army contractors, 182-83
Lettsom, H. G.: terms of the Triple Alliance Treaty, 93
Leyes de Partida, 160
Lima e Silva, Luís Alves de. *See* Caxias, Lima e Silva, Luís Alves de, Duque de
Lisboa, Admiral Joaquim Marques. *See* Tamandaré, Lisbôa, Joaquim Marques, Barão de
Loizaga, Carlos, 175
Lomas Valentinas, campaign of, 40, 162-70
Lopes, José Francisco, 112-13
López, Carlos Antonio: description, 8; foreign policy, 11; mentioned, 18, 37
López, Benigno, 159-62
López, Francisco Solano: origins and early life, 17-23; arbiter at San José de Flores, 6, 19-21; personal portrait of, 23-25; military experience and qualifications, 37-47 *passim*; during the "Marquês de Olinda" incident, 74-76; negotiations with Argentina, 86-90; re naval Battle of Riachuelo, 96-99; effect of Uruguaiana campaign, 107-08; during the Upper Paraná campaign, 114-15; at Yataity-Corá Peace Conference, 124-27; at Battle of Curupaity, 130; at Paso Pucú headquarters, 132-38; at Second Tuyuty, 150-54; during the conspiracy period, 155, 157-62; at the

234 INDEPENDENCE OR DEATH

Battle of Itá-Ibaty, 168-70; reorganization of the Paraguayan Army, 175-77; retreat from Campo Grande, 181-85 *passim*; death at Cerro Corá, 185-89; mentioned, v, xiv, 3, 8, 9, 12, 17, 69, 71, 109, 192, 199, 200
López, Major Juan Francisco, 169
López, Doña Juana Carillo de. *See* Carillo de López, Doña Juana
López, Venancio, 159-62, 184
Lowe, Thaddeus S. C., 146
Lynch, Elisa Alicia: at Piribebuy, 2; *Exposición y protesta*, 28; portrait of, 18-19; mentioned, 9, 161, 169, 185, 186, 188

MacMahon, Martin T.: description of Piribebuy, 176-77; mentioned, xiii, 19, 163-64; 168-69; 181, 184, 200
Maíz, Fidel, 132, 158, 160, 186, 188, 190
Mallet, General Emilio Luís: attack on Piribebuy, 1; action at Siege of Paysandú, 85; at Battle of First Tuyuty, 118-19; mentioned, 48, 49, 54, 61, 178
Manduvirá River: destruction of Paraguay's navy, 182
"Mangrullos," 131-32
Manlove, James, 137-38, 160
Mann, Mrs. Mary, 129, 184, 190
Mariz e Barros, Commander, 115
"Marquês de Olinda," vii, 74-75
Martínez, Colonel Francisco, 125, 157
Martínez, Juliana Ynsfrán de, 157, 160
Masterman, George F.: operation of magic lantern set, 135-36; mentioned, xiii, 39, 159-61
Maté, viii, 100, 148
Mato Grosso: frontier problems of, 11; communications to, 15; Paraguayan invasion of, 81-84; supplies captured in, 83-84; postwar status of, 194; mentioned, 29, 110-13
Memoria Militar, 149
Mena Barreto, General J. L., 167
Mena Barreto, General João Manoel, 1-2, 61, 102, 178
Mena Barreto, General João Propício, 84-85
Mesa, Captain Pedro Ignacio: command of Paraguayan Navy, 44; at naval Battle of Riachuelo, 96-99

Militarism: effect of the war upon Brazil, 196-97
Misiones, 11, 87
Mitre, Bartolomé: personal portrait of, 30-33; military qualifications of, 65-66; war prophecy, 91; at Yataity-Corá Peace Conference, 124-27; Argentine anti-war disturbances, 144-45; *Memoria Militar*, 149; mentioned, 6, 106, 109, 129, 154, 192
Mitre, General Emilio: portrait of, 66; mentioned, 171, 175
Molina, Juan Esteban, 161
Monte Caseros, battle of, 6, 45
Montoneras, 5, 64
Morgenstern, Enrique Wisner von, 131
Muritiba, Barão de, 189

Naval mines and torpedoes, use of, 123
Nuevo Bordeus colony, 11

Octaviano de Almeida Rosa, Francisco, 91, 102, 127
Orléans, Gastão de. *See* Conde d'Eu
Oroño, Nicasio, 65
Osório, General Manoel Luís: personal portrait of, 59-60; at Second Battle of Tuyuty, 149-50; at Battle of Avay, 166-67; mentioned, 48, 116, 120-21, 175, 179

Page, Lieutenant Thomas Jefferson: map of Paraguay, 56; 187
Pakenham, J. J., 153
Palacios, Bishop, 159-60
Palleja, León de, 67
Paraguay: characteristics in 1864, 7-12
Paraguayan War: major phases, 70, Appendix I
Paraná, port of, 5
Paranhos, José Maria da Silva, 76, 172-73, 174, 175, 188, 189, 190. *See also* Rio Branco, Visconde do
Parodi, Dr. Diego Domingo, 179
Paso la Patria: Brazilian camp characteristics, 140-143; 114
Passo de São Borja, action at, 101-02
Passo do Rosário, battle of. *See* Ituzaingó, battle of
Paunero, General Wenceslao, 94-95, 144
Pavón, battle of, 6

Paysandú, siege of, 84-86
Paz, General José María, 18
Paz, Marcos, 103, 154
Peace overtures, 1866-67, 136. *See also* Yataity-Corá
Peixoto, Colonel Floriano, 46, 62, 103, 116, 166, 186, 187, 198
Pilcomayo River, 11
Pinheiro Guimarães, Dr. Francisco: letters regarding Paraguay, 29-30; at Battle of First Tuyuty, 120; homecoming reception, 190-91; mentioned, 58, 108, 142-43, 147, 155, 174, 196
Piratini Republic, 15
Piribebuy: battle of, 1-3, 178-79; description of village, 176-77; mentioned, 169, 171, 200
"Plano de Pirayú," 178
Polidoro da Fonseca Quintanilha Jordão, General, 62, 175, 179
Poncho Verde, Peace of, 15, 48
Porteños, v, 30
Portinho, Colonel José Gomes, 150
Pôrto Alegre, Souza, Manoel Marques de, Barão de: personal portrait of, 60; at Curuzú, 123-24; at Second Tuyuty, 149-53; mentioned, 48-49
Portocarrero, Doña Ludovina, 82
Portocarrero, Colonel Hermenegildo de Albuquerque, 37, 56, 81-82
Pozo de Vargas, battle of, 145. *See also* anti-war demonstrations
Pykysyry River, 162, 164, 167

Quadrilátero: description of, 130-32
Quatrefages, Dr. Jean Louis Armand de, 19
"Questão de Christie," 15, 29, 72, 106.
"Questão Militar," 85, 152

Rawson, Guilhermo, 89
Republicanism, rise of in Brazil, 197-98
Residentas, 183-84
Resquín, General Francisco Isidoro, 47, 82-83, 100, 108, 158-61, 177, 179, 186, 188, 190
Rhode Island Company, xii, 11
Riachuelo, naval battle of, 55, 96-100
Rio Branco, Visconde do; private archives, 2; anti-slavery legislation, 196.

See also Paranhos, José Maria da Silva
Rio de Janeiro, in 1864, 14
Rivarola, Cirilo, 175
Rivarola, Colonel Valois, 166
Rivas, Antonio, 104
Robles, General Wenceslao, 89, 94-95
Romero, Captain José, 165
Rosario, port of, 183, 189
Rosas, Juan Manuel de, 6, 8, 15

Saldanha da Gama, Luís Felipe de, 85
Sampaio, General Antônio, 61, 119-20
Sánchez, Francisco, 159, 186, 188
San Fernando, 156, 158, 160, 162
San José de Flores, agreement of, 6, 19-21
San Nicolás de Arroyo, pact of, 6
Saraiva, José Antônio, 13, 71
Sarmiento, Domingo F., xiii, 129, 184, 190, 192
Sarmiento, Dominguito, 129
Semana Ilustrada, 120
Sertanejos, 13
Seward, William H., xiii
Slavery, volunteers in Brazil, 78-79, 195-96
Soares, Joáo, 187
Souza, Manoel Marques de. *See* Pôrto Alegre, Souza, Manoel Marques de, Barão de
Sousa Netto, General Antônio de, 15, 71
Stewart, Dr. William, 39

Tacuari, battle of, 37
Talavera, Natalicio, 135
Tamandaré, Lisbôa, Joaquim Marques, Barão de, 13, 58, 106, 128, 139
Taunay, Captain Alfredo d'Escragnolle: at Piribebuy, 2; at Escola Militar, 62; Brazilian recruitment, 78; participation in Laguna campaign, 110-13; mentioned, 174, 178-79, 182, 183, 189, 190, 195
Tayí, action at, 150
Taylor, Alonzo, 39, 160-61
Tebicuary River, retreat to, 150, 156
Tejedor, Carlos, 20
Telegraph, use of, 133
Terços, 47
The Buenos Aires Standard, 32

Thompson, Colonel George E.: re Paraguayan army characteristics, 41-43; at Battle of Curupaity, 128; at Second Tuyuty, 152-53; surrender at Angostura, 170; mentioned, xiii, 39, 46, 107, 122, 156, 157, 161, 167
Thornton, Sir Edward, 71, 72, 106
"Trench of '69," 200
Trés Bocas, 114
Triple Alliance Treaty: negotiation, terms, and effect, 91-94
Truenfeldt, Fischer von, 45, 133, 135, 160
"Turututús," 133
Tuyuty: first battle of, viii, 117-22; second battle of, 149-54

Unitarios, 6
Urbieta, Major Martín, 83, 113
Urquiza, Justo José de: sword of Cepeda, 21; personal portrait of, 34-35; mentioned, 6, 66, 109, 192
Urquiza, Waldino, 86
Uruguaiana, siege of, 100-08
Uruguay: characteristics in 1864, 12-13

Varela, Felipe, 145
Varela, Hector F., 19, 22-23
Vargas, Manoel do Nascimento, 3
Vedía, Agustín de, 124
Velasco, Governor Bernardo, 87
Versen, Max von, 38, 43, 137-38, 159-61, 170
Via dolorosa: Paraguayan retreat to Cerro Corá, 184-85; *frontispiece*
Vianna de Lima, César Sauvan, 71-76
Victorica, Benjamin: mission to Paraguay, 88
Vilagran Cabrita, João Carlos de, 37-38, 56, 109, 116
"Villa del Salto," incident of, 72-73
Villa de Unión, peace agreement of, 33, 86
"Voluntários da Pátria:" organization and recruitment, 76-77; return from the war zone, 190-91; mentioned, v, 101, 108

Wagener, Wilhelm, 45, 179
Wanderley, Captain Teodoro, 189
Washburn, Charles Ames: role in the "Marquês de Olinda" incident, 75; role in the conspiracy episode, 159-63 *passim*; mentioned, xiii, 13, 137
"Water Witch" incident, 11, 115
Watts, John, 39, 96, 99, 137, 160
Whytehead, William, 39

Xavier de Souza, Field Marshal Guilherme, 172, 174

Yataí, battle of, 104
Yataity-Corá, peace conference of, 124-27, 169
Ynsfrán, Captain Julio, 182
Ynsfrán, Pablo M., xiv
Ytororó, battle of, viii, 164-66, 200

Zamba de Vargas, 145

Gran Chaco

River Paraguay

Riacho Quiá

Curuzú

Carrisal

Carrisal

Laguna Chichi

Laguna Lopez

Curupayty

Chichi Marshes

Thick Jungle

Paso Pucú

Head Quarters

Laguna Piris

Piris

Paso Gomez

Espini

Tuyuti

Allied Camp

Yatai y Corá

Anale

Estero Bella

Estero Bellaco S.

Palm Forest